Federal-Metropolitan Politics and the Commuter Crisis

NUMBER TWO: METROPOLITAN POLITICS SERIES

Federal-Metropolitan Politics and the Commuter Crisis

By Michael N. Danielson

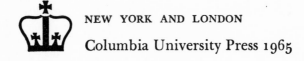

NEW YORK AND LONDON

Columbia University Press 1965

Michael N. Danielson is Assistant Professor of Politics and Public Affairs at Princeton University.

For my wife, Patti

Preface

Any light this study sheds on federal-metropolitan politics is due in considerable measure to the assistance I have received from many friends and institutions. My debt is especially large to three people: Richard T. Frost, formerly at Princeton University and now Vice-President of Reed College, under whose guidance the study took shape; Jameson W. Doig, a Princeton colleague and author of a companion study in this series; and Wallace S. Sayre, Eaton Professor of Public Administration at Columbia University and guiding hand of the Metropolitan Region Program, who helped in many ways to make this book possible. Duane Lockard of Princeton University and Howard N. Mantel, Lyle C. Fitch, and Sumner Myers, all of the Institute of Public Administration in New York City, read the manuscript at various stages of its development and offered constructive criticism. In addition, Marver H. Bernstein and H. H. Wilson of Princeton University, David B. Truman of Columbia University, William N. Cassella of the National Municipal League, and Wilfred Owen and George A. Graham of The Brookings Institution provided assistance and encouragement of one kind or another.

A special word of thanks is due the many public and private officials in many metropolitan areas and in Washington. The study rests in large part on the information and insights which these busy men provided.

Work on the study began in 1960 while I held a Princeton National Fellowship. The bulk of the research and writing was undertaken with the aid of a grant from the Metropolitan Regional Program at Columbia University. My research in Washington was aided by The Brookings Institution, which made its facilities available during the 1960–61 academic year. Some of the work on the final chapters was completed while I was on the staff of the Institute of Public Administration. In addition, the study profited from my six months' service as a consultant to the Institute during its 1961 study of urban transportation for the Department of Commerce and the Housing and Home Finance Agency. The final manuscript was prepared with the assistance of a grant from the Princeton University Research Fund.

The typing skill and good spirits of Florence Kaplan, Violet Lewis, Eleanor Wentworth, Joan Martin, Evelyn Datz, and Doris Lake have been appreciated, as has been the assistance of Katherine M. Purcell of the Columbia University Press, who helped prepare the manuscript for publication.

Somehow my wife has found time to help with problems far afield from her native ground of microbiology.

My indebtedness to all these people, of course, does not alter my full responsibility for what has or has not found its way between these covers.

MICHAEL N. DANIELSON

Princeton, N.J.
September, 1964

Contents

Metropolitan Politics Series

This is the second in the series of books resulting from the metropolitan study program begun at Columbia University in 1957 and supported by a grant from the Ford Foundation.

The faculty committee supervising this program and serving as editors of the series are Wallace S. Sayre, Chairman, Richard E. Neustadt and David B. Truman of the Department of Public Law and Government of Columbia University, and William N. Cassella, Jr., of the National Municipal League.

Abbreviations of Agencies and Organizations

AAR	Association of American Railroads
AMA	American Municipal Association
BPR	Bureau of Public Roads
HHFA	Housing and Home Finance Agency
ICC	Interstate Commerce Commission
IMGBRS	Inter-Municipal Group for Better Rail Service
IPA	Institute of Public Administration
MRC	Metropolitan Regional Council
MRTC	Metropolitan Rapid Transit Commission
NACO	National Association of County Officials
NARUC	National Association of Railroad and Utility Commissioners
NJBPUC	New Jersey Board of Public Utility Commissioners
NY-NJTA	New York–New Jersey Transportation Agency
NYPSC	New York Public Service Commission
PNYA	Port of New York Authority
RLEA	Railroad Labor Executives Association
RPA	Regional Plan Association
UTTB	Urban Traffic and Transportation Board (Philadelphia)

Introduction

The two natural elements in our system are now [1886]
the Community and the Nation. The former is the point
of real local self-government; the latter that of general
self-government; and in the adjustments of the future
these are the forces which will carry with them the determining power.

JOHN W. BURGESS

Metropolitan development poses challenges for political institutions at all levels of the American federal system. Sweeping
changes in urban living patterns coupled with rapid population
increases have spread people, commerce, and industry far beyond
the political boundaries of the city. By 1960, two out of three
Americans lived in metropolitan areas, half of them outside the
central cities. Since the city seldom extends its jurisdiction to
encompass the newer areas and campaigns for regional government usually fail, the metropolis functions without a central political system. In these politically fragmented areas, the complexity,
magnitude, and scope of contemporary urban problems often
place solutions beyond the fiscal and jurisdictional capabilities
of the local governments. Seeking help, the metropolitan areas
have found the state and national governments increasingly responsive to the political pressures of growing urban majorities.
As a result, urban problems rarely remain the exclusive concern
of the localities, and relations between the metropolitan areas
and the higher levels of government have proliferated.

With the growth of metropolitan areas has come a revival of
interest in urban politics. In the past decade, a number of studies
have examined metropolitan political systems, usually focusing on

political behavior within the metropolis.[1] Despite mounting state and federal involvement in the affairs of city and suburb, however, considerably less attention has been paid to external metropolitan politics, to the relations of the various components of the metropolis with the higher levels of government.[2]

+   This is a study of federal-metropolitan politics. Its primary purposes are the analysis of political interaction in federal-urban relations and the examination of political behavior within the metropolis in the light of these relations. To these ends, the study is concerned with the determinants of metropolitan and federal attitudes relative to national roles in regional problems, the channels of information and influence between the metropolis and the national government, and the impact of federal-urban interaction on the political process at the metropolitan and national levels. The focus of the study is the relationships between the national government and the major metropolitan areas during the formative years of the rail commutation and mass transportation issues. Because participants from the New York region played a key role in the politics of mass transportation between 1958 and 1961, particular attention is given to interaction between Washington and the nation's largest metropolis.

Analysis of metropolitan politics from the point of view of federal-urban relations on the mass transportation issue tends to support the propositions set forth in recent studies of political behavior within the metropolis. Whether one examines the metropolis from within or from without, fragmentation of governmental responsibilities among a multiplicity of territorial jurisdictions is the cardinal fact of political life in the larger metropolitan areas; it shapes both political behavior within the metropolis and relationships with state and federal governments. In the absence of central instrumentalities, public policies affecting the metropolitan area are made either by its components acting unilaterally or by regional surrogates—special districts, the states, or the national government. Within such unstructured systems, regional values win few adherents. The submetropolitan or supermetropolitan institutional base of the various participants fosters conflicting interests, a diversity of conditions and concerns, and differing perceptions of shared problems. For some metropolitan actors,[3] particularly the business and civic interests of the central city, the institutional base is conducive to viewpoints which value political reorganization, regional planning, or area-wide transport arrangements. But less cosmopolitan values usually predominate in the politically and psychologically fragmented metropolis.

As for relationships between the metropolis and the national government, here too political fragmentation has a pervasive influence. Political activity on the mass transportation issue indicates that the patterns of federal-metropolitan politics are determined largely by the particularist perceptions and interests of the various components of the metropolis. In dealing with Washington, as in their internal relations, most participants in metropolitan politics do not define their interests in a regional frame of reference. Instead, they tackle shared problems from the limited point of view of their particular institutional base, be it central or satellite city, suburb, congressional district, or state. Contributing to this lack of common goals, in external as in internal metropolitan politics, are the different impacts of metropolitan growth and change on various sectors of the metropolis and the partisan cleavages that divide the Democratic cities from the Republican suburbs. Both these factors make federal financial assistance more attractive and more politically palatable to the older urban centers than to the outlying areas. As a consequence, metropolitan actors bring to their relations with Washington differing perceptions of the federal role in regional problems, a variety of strategies to be pursued at the national level, and goals ranging from federal inaction or withdrawal to massive assistance.

Equally important, the patterns of federal-metropolitan politics are shaped by the federal political process. The diffusion of responsibilities for urban affairs in the national executive and in Congress multiplies the points of access for metropolitan actors in Washington, encourages a variety of approaches to a particular problem, and enhances the possibilities of stalemate. Congressional personnel, procedures, and perceptions also play an important role in conditioning relations with the local units. Of special consequence for federal-metropolitan politics is the anti-urban bias of the House of Representatives and the greater effectiveness of senators as spokesmen for metropolitan interests. And finally, when metropolitan issues of any consequence are contested in the federal arena, the outcome is affected by a broad range of national considerations that differ significantly from the determining factors at the regional or local level.

The Transportation Act of 1958 and the Housing Act of 1961 are the benchmarks of this study. The 1958 legislation, by making it easier for the railroads to discontinue commuter trains, precipitated a mass transportation crisis in the New York region, heightened concern over the future of commutation in a handful of other metropolitan centers, and made the federal government a visible if negative participant in the commuter politics of the large metropolitan areas. By recognizing a positive federal responsibility for mass transportation, the 1961 omnibus housing act marked the initial victory of a metropolitan coalition whose formation was sparked by the 1958 commuter crisis. The study examines in detail the response of metropolitan interests to the Transportation Act of 1958, the forging of the federal aid coalition, and the political activity in Washington and the urban centers that produced the 1961 mass transportation legislation.

Prior to the Transportation Act of 1958, few metropolitan actors perceived the commuter rail problem, much less the larger mass transportation question, in federal terms. Aside from the routine regulation of commuter trains by the Interstate Commerce Commission, the federal government's metropolitan transportation functions were limited to urban highways. Following the 1958 commuter crisis in New York, however, a number of proposals for federal action on rail commutation received attention. In addition, interest was revived in federal aid schemes that had attracted little notice prior to the passage of the Transportation Act. The resulting variety of the proposals afforded metropolitan interests an opportunity to pursue courses of action in Washington that reflected particular goals and strategies on the transportation issue. Since 1961, however, attention has been focused on efforts to expand the mass transit assistance program initiated that year, efforts which culminated in the passage of the Urban Mass Transportation Act of 1964. Regional actors unsympathetic to financial assistance faded from the federal-metropolitan picture, while the patterns of action of those involved in the post-1961 efforts to secure federal aid have been substantially the same as those analyzed in the study.

The study concentrates on the relations between the national government and the New York area for two reasons. First, inhabitants of the region played a dominant role in the commuter issue throughout the period under study. Since New York's rapid transit and commuter rail systems are the largest in the nation, this predominance of New Yorkers in the federal-metropolitan politics of mass transportation is not surprising. Second, concentration on a single metropolitan area affords an oportunity to examine in depth the activities of a wide range of metropolitan interests and to analyze closely the interplay between internal developments and external politics.

Although the New York region admittedly is unique in a quantitative sense, focusing on its relations with Washington does not pose serious obstacles to generalization about federal-metropolitan politics. Despite its size and complexity, the region's political processes are hardly singular. The actions, perceptions, and attitudes of the various metropolitan actors examined here fall into similar patterns in other areas. The problems faced by the region's leaders in dealing with areawide concerns—fragmented responsibilities, inadequate jurisdictions, limited budgets, the inability to tap regional resources, the absence of consensus on areal goals, and the lack of regional consciousness—are the common facts of political life in all large metropolitan areas. Moreover, the channels of information and influence utilized and the federal setting encountered by regional actors from New York on the transportation issue will not vary significantly for actors from other areas or for interaction on other issues.

PART ONE

The Background

CHAPTER I

The Setting

Rapid transit is indeed the fundamental reality of the so-called metropolitan community, the thing in common.

ROBERT C. WOOD

Transportation made the modern metropolis possible; almost everywhere it is the preeminent metropolitan concern. No other urban problem causes such widespread public frustration, irritation, and preoccupation with inadequacies. Moreover, transportation creates situations and poses issues unique to the metropolis: commutation, transit, and traffic congestion are synonomous with metropolitan living. Most important, transportation decisions have a crucial impact on the shape and the future of the metropolis, involve vast public outlays, and require difficult political choices. As a consequence, debates over the transportation system ultimately affect the totality of interests in a metropolitan area.

Metropolitan transportation issues normally arise from two closely related developments: the expansion of highway facilities to serve an increasingly affluent, mobile urban population particularly in the suburbs, and the decline of public transportation, especially the rapid transit and commuter rail systems of the great metropolitan centers.[1] This chapter examines the implications of these developments for urban transportation policy and politics in the postwar years before the passage of the Transportation Act of 1958. Special attention is given to the plight of the commuter railroads and to the transportation situation in the New York region, since these two aspects of the metropolitan transportation problem provide the backdrop for much of the federal-metropolitan politics of mass transportation between 1958 and 1961.

Transportation and the Metropolis

For centuries the city has been a product and a prisoner of transportation technology. Not until the advent of the horsedrawn omnibus in 1832 were most men able to work at a place beyond walking distance from their residences. The city in the early nineteenth century was circular, only a few miles in diameter. Advances in rail transport development rapidly changed its face. Large numbers of workers could be concentrated in the central business district during the day and quickly dispersed in the evening to the far corners of the urban hinterland. In the age of mass transportation, which lasted from the Civil War to World War I, cities became star-shaped as fingers of development sprang up along the transit and suburban rail lines. All this was changed by the revolution in personal transportation wrought by the automobile. The internal combustion engine, the pneumatic tire, the Model T, and the public highway produced the modern rubber-dominant metropolis. The individual was released from his dependence on common carriers, while urban development was liberated from the restrictions imposed by fixed transportation facilities. Once again urban areas tended toward a circular shape, but their diameter had increased tenfold. In the transit era the city was a political unit; the metropolis of the automobile age is an agglomeration of governmental jurisdictions.

Since only the automobile satisfied most of the travel needs of the vast majority of the residents of the dispersed metropolis, automobile ownership spiraled and public highway investments mounted. Between 1930 and 1960, the number of automobiles on the nation's highways almost tripled, from 26.8 to 73.8 million, while annual local, state, and federal outlays for highways increased more than fivefold ($1.8 to $9.6 billion) during roughly the same period (1932–60). Because of high costs and the rural bias of most state highway departments, however, highway building in metropolitan areas usually trailed far behind needs. The results were monumental traffic jams and strong pressures for massive construction programs. A new era for urban motorists dawned with the passage of the Federal-Aid Highway Act of 1956. Designed to implement the long-projected 41,000-mile National System of Interstate and Defense Highways, the program proposed to spend approximately 45 percent of the planned $41-billion federal outlay in urban areas.

A generation of highway building has left an indelible stamp on urban transportation politics. Where private transit companies once ruled supreme, highway agencies now dominate the scene, their central role assured by public preferences, user charges, profitable toll facilities, state and federal aid, and well-organized political pressures. Equally important, in the Automobile Age the localities lost control over the key decisions affecting the metropolitan transportation system. Except for the larger central cities, fragmentation denies most jurisdictions sufficient resources and territorial scope to tackle highway matters beyond local streets, traffic, and parking. User financing through state and federal automobile excise taxes has led to state development and, increasingly, federal financing of the major urban highways. In return for the loss of control over their roads, the metropolitan areas have reaped the benefits of highway networks developed on a regional basis without disruption of the fragmented institutional system of the metropolis.

The growth and strength of the highway complex has been paralleled by the decline and weakness of public transportation. While motor vehicle registrations doubled during the first postwar decade, transit ridership was halved. Saddled with an unprofitable concentration of traffic in the rush hours, self-sufficiency requirements, burdensome debt structures, and a lack of access to state and federal funds, public transportation has been far less effective than the highway agencies in the competition for the favor and support of a public which in increasing numbers never uses transit.

Buses, using the new highways and providing a service easily adjusted to changing land-use patterns, have adapted better to contemporary urban development than the inflexible, high-fixed-cost rail systems which a generation ago moved most people in urban areas. Today rapid transit and commuter rail service appeals primarily to travelers journeying to work in the great business districts of the largest metropolitan areas. Since this traffic is concentrated in the rush hour, it necessitates uneconomical investments in equipment and labor, which lie idle most of the time.[2] By 1958, falling patronage and mounting losses had resulted in public ownership for all the nation's remaining rapid transit systems. And almost every railroad still operating commuter trains was threatening to terminate service unless the public provided help through fare increases, tax relief, or subsidies.

Of all the urban carriers, the fifteen privately owned commuter railroads operating in five metropolitan areas—New York, Chicago, Philadelphia, Boston, and San Francisco (see Table 1)—

TABLE 1
Principal Commuter Railroads

Railroad*	Metropolitan Area	Commutation Revenue, 1956
Long Island	New York	$27,313,491
New York, New Haven & Hartford	Boston–New York	12,694,968
New York Central	New York	11,874,050
Pennsylvania	New York–Philadelphia	10,706,971
Illinois Central	Chicago	8,032,105
Chicago & North Western	Chicago	7,272,309
Lackawanna	New York	5,199,039
Jersey Central	New York	3,692,719
Southern Pacific	San Francisco	3,026,331
Boston & Maine	Boston	2,865,275
Reading	Philadelphia	2,831,205
Erie	New York	2,815,644
Burlington	Chicago	2,208,879
Rock Island	Chicago	2,048,851
Milwaukee Road	Chicago	1,474,073

*These 15 carriers represented 97 percent of the aggregate 1956 commutation revenue.

SOURCE: *Railroad Passenger Train Deficit* (1959), 306 ICC 466.

have faced the most serious problems. In 1958, with the exception of the Long Island Railroad, they received no assistance from local, state, or federal agencies. Their prime contacts with government were the tax collector and the regulatory commissions which controlled service and fares. While the public rapid transit systems were commonly restricted to the central city, most commuter lines carried the bulk of their riders across the political boundaries of the fragmented metropolis, making the initiation of local public support dependent on the forging of intergovernmental arrangements. High wage rates, archaic work rules, and full-crew laws resulted in considerably higher labor costs on the commuter lines. In addition, utilization of equipment and operating personnel was less efficient than on the central-city rapid transit systems because the concentration of traffic in the peak hours was much heavier on the suburban lines.

Commuter railroads responded to this gloomy situation with a variety of policies. In an attempt to win back the profitable nonrush-hour business, some sought to improve service, particularly with new equipment. Although Chicago's rail lines were initially successful with this approach, experiments elsewhere failed to reverse the basic trends. More common were efforts to raise historically low commutation rates.[3] Higher fares were rarely secured without expensive proceedings before regulatory agencies, and they usually depressed off-peak ridership without producing sufficient revenues to make significant dents in deficits. Another tactic was reduction or elimination of service, a policy hindered by the reluctance of state regulatory agencies to permit the termination of services deemed essential by local interests. Other approaches failing, the commuter railroads retrenched, refusing to invest capital in suburban services which rendered no return. Since labor costs were rigid, savings were realized through deferring equipment maintenance. Starving commuter service in this way inevitably produced an invidious cycle of deteriorating plant and service with declining patronage, particularly on the off-peak and weekend trains.

Concern over the troubles of public transportation was not widespread in postwar America. Dependence upon transit for the journey to work tends to vary with the age and size of metropolitan areas. The lesser regions accommodated to the automobile with relatively little difficulty. In the newer urban areas, particularly of the West and Southwest, public transportation's role had never been very significant, since development had been influenced strongly by the highway from the beginning. As a result, in most metropolitan areas few business interests were dependent upon public transportation, and transit riders were a small and uninfluential minority—composed largely of those too young, too old, or too poor, to own an automobile.

Only in the great central cities and their commuting suburbs did the growing weakness of mass transportation spur public concern. The number of areas involved was not large, although their influence was considerable: twenty cities with more than half a million inhabitants each accounted for two-thirds of the nation's transit riders, while almost three-fourths of all rail commuters used facilities in New York, Chicago, or Philadelphia. Products of the transit age, these cities could neither afford nor accommodate transportation systems based exclusively on the automobile. Regardless of who paid for their construction, urban highways removed sizable blocks of valuable property from the tax rolls and required increased city outlays for maintenance, police, parking, and traffic control. Without adequate public transportation, particularly for the journey to work, urban leaders could foresee only more automobiles, bigger traffic jams, larger transportation budgets, and continued erosion of the downtown areas.

Although apprehensive of complete dependence on the automobile, the cities were neither against highway development in general nor interested in Draconian choices between public and private transportation. Spurred by the slighting of urban highway needs by state roads agencies controlled by rural interests, city leaders had been in the forefront of the fight for the vast federal aid program commenced in 1956. The inherent advantages of the highway and the automobile for recreation, local shopping, and the journey to work outside the metropolitan core was unchallenged. Urban leaders did, however, criticize exclusive reliance on the automobile as well as the availability of outside assistance

solely for highways while public transportation remained dependent upon hard-pressed local governments or pessimistic private operators.

To a growing number of the larger cities, rail systems appeared
essential if the metropolitan core was to retain its economic pre-
eminence. Despite their rigidity and high fixed cost, steel wheels
on steel rails offer unsurpassed passenger-carrying capacity and
exclusive rights of way, which assure freedom from slowdowns
due to congestion.[4] As a consequence, those urban centers with
public rail systems were seeking capital for improvements in the
1950s. At the same time, the great cities dependent upon rail commutation and their bedroom suburbs were exploring methods of
preserving essential services. Other major metropolitan areas—
including San Francisco, Los Angeles, Washington, and Atlanta—
began to investigate the possibilities of developing urban rail
systems. Support for these efforts came from the many planners
and transportation specialists who preached the virtues of "balanced rail-rubber" programs, by which they usually meant a
heightened emphasis on rails. To achieve this goal, the experts
advocated comprehensive metropolitan transportation and land-
use planning and the replacement of the typical anarchy of transportation agencies in the politically fragmented metropolis with
comprehensive and coordinated transportation policy-making and
implementation on a regional basis.

These efforts to preserve, improve, and develop urban rail systems faced formidable political barriers. The large cities were
struggling to meet existing transportation obigations. Unilateral
action on their part to support commuter rail lines which served
suburbanites was not feasible economically or politically. Subsidization of rapid transit or commuter rail lines on a regional
basis would run afoul of all the obstacles to joint enterprises in
metropolitan areas, including the mutual distrust of the suburbs
and the central city, the unwillingness to venture into the un-
charted waters of unequal costs and benefits, and the suburban
fear of losing control over local affairs. Another hurdle for public
transportation was the dedication of the powerful public and
private highway groups to the preservation of a bountiful status

quo. To preclude any shift in the allocation of urban transport resources away from highways, the rubber alliance disparaged the
utility of public transportation. Proposals for the employment of
highway or automobile-user funds for mass transportation purposes were opposed bitterly. Equally distasteful were schemes
which would restrict the freedom of the roads agencies to plan
and build highways or proposals which would burden highway
bodies with unwanted responsibilities for the undercapitalized
and economically marginal urban rail systems. The experience
of the New York region (Figure 1) in the pre-Transportation Act
period is illustrative of the conditioning role of these political
factors on efforts to resolve mass transportation problems.

Transportation Politics in the New York Region

No other metropolitan area rivals the New York area's population, employment, number of governmental units, or wealth.[5]
Over 500 local governments, twenty-two counties, half a dozen
major transport authorities, three states, and uncounted private
operators, ranging from giant corporations like the New York
Central Railroad to one-man taxicab companies, make the transportation planning and policy structure of the New York region
inordinately complex. Yet the region has not been immune to the
general population and transportation trends which are changing
the urban landscape. Over the past thirty years, New York City's
population has increased 14 percent; outside the city the growth
has been 77 percent. Moreover, while the region as a whole added
2.2 million residents in the decade ending in 1960, New York
City lost 100,000 inhabitants. The dispersion of people and jobs
and the development of a vast highway network have produced a
relative decline in the importance of rapid transit and commuter
rail lines. Highway agencies receive the lion's share of public
funds and dominate transportation planning and policy-making.
Premier among the highway agencies are the bi-state Port of New
York Authority (PNYA) and Robert Moses' Triborough Bridge
and Tunnel Authority, whose combined efforts often seemed to

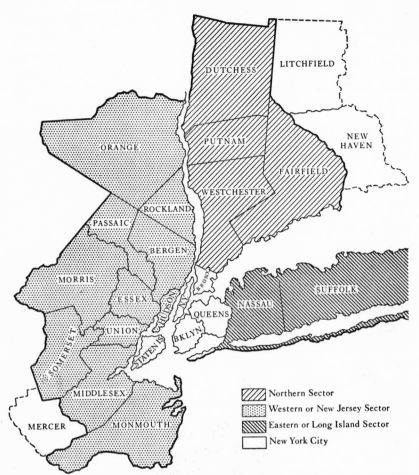

Figure 1. The tri-state metropolitan region. Source: Institute of Public
Administration

be of "awe-inspiring magnitudes." [6] With a monopoly of the
lucrative toll facilities which traverse the region's waterways, these
wealthy, powerful, and autonomous agencies and their allies in
the state roads departments, turnpike authorities, and highway-
user groups have wanted to have nothing to do with the region's
rail systems, which in 1959 reported capital needs of almost a billion dollars.[7] As Wood has pointed out, the "wide disparities
between the rail and auto agencies with respect to financial re-

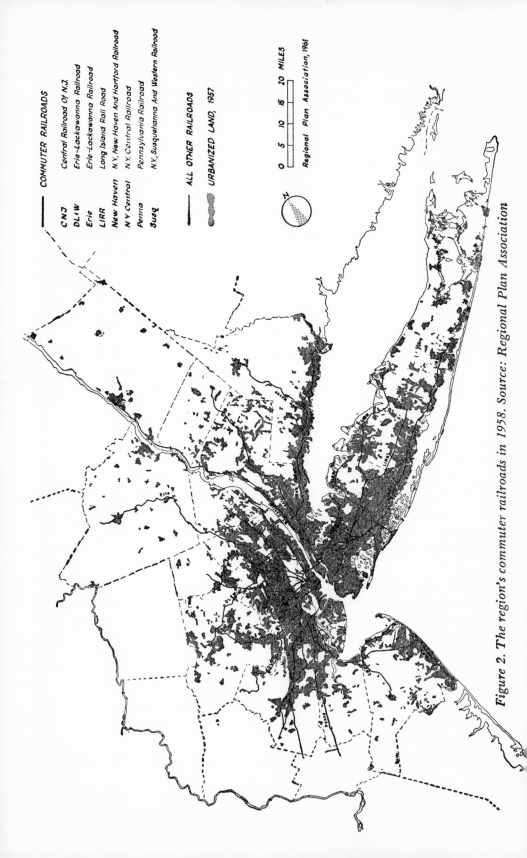

COMMUTER RAILROADS

CNJ	Central Railroad Of N.J.
DL&W	Erie-Lackawanna Railroad
Erie	Erie-Lackawanna Railroad
LIRR	Long Island Rail Road
New Haven	N.Y, New Haven And Hartford Railroad
N Y Central	N.Y. Central Railroad
Penna	Pennsylvania Railroad
Susq	N.Y, Susquehanna And Western Railroad

ALL OTHER RAILROADS

URBANIZED LAND, 1957

0 5 10 15 20 MILES

Regional Plan Association, 1961

Figure 2. The region's commuter railroads in 1958. Source: Regional Plan Association

sources, organizational arrangements, legal responsibility, and attitudes" underlie the transportation politics of the New York region.[8]

In one important respect, however, New York's transportation problems and politics are unique. Nowhere else does mass transportation play so vital a role. The region's size, geographic configuration, and, most significant, its massive central business district combine to produce traffic volumes that can be handled only by rail. The economic vitality of the 9 square miles of Manhattan south of Central Park—the nation's corporate headquarters, financial heart, and communications center—required in 1958 the daily concentration of over 2½ millon people. Moving 80 percent of them during the rush hours was the task of the most extensive urban rail system in the United States. Over 200 miles of subways haul 3½ million passengers each day, 64 percent of all the nation's rapid transit rides. The suburban rail networks (see Figure 2), spreading a 1,200-mile web into all but one of the region's twenty-two counties, carried in 1958 over 250,000 commuters, 42 percent of the national total. Approximately 190,000 of them commuted during the rush hours. Of the latter, 73,000 came from New Jersey, 59,000 from Westchester and Fairfield Counties to the north, and 58,000 from Long Island to the east.[9]

For decades, commuter railroads have been the most neglected link in the region's mass transportation system. They suffer from all the normal woes associated with the provision of suburban services—fixed routes, changing travel habits, the five-day work week, technological obsolescence, inept management, and excessive labor costs. A special problem was the Hudson River barrier, which necessitated a ferry trip to reach Manhattan on all but two of New Jersey's suburban lines. This inconvenience was a major factor in the 60 percent decline of trans-Hudson commuter rail trips between 1930 and 1958.[10] While the situation was most perilous in New Jersey, nowhere was it promising: commuter deficits for the region's railroads approached $30 million in 1958.[11]

Public policy had done little to protect the regional interest in adequate commuter service. State and local policies imposed a heavy burden on the railroads. New Jersey's rail taxes were the highest in the nation, and New York was in second place.[12] Most of these revenues went to local governments, which opposed tax relief, particularly since there was little correlation between rail tax receipts and the benefits derived from continued commuter service. Hudson County, for example, obtained three-fourths of all the local rail taxes collected in New Jersey, but contributed a far smaller percentage of the state's commuters to Manhattan. Only after bankruptcy threatened to put the region's largest commuter line, the Long Island Railroad, out of business did New York State, New York City, and communities in Nassau and Suffolk Counties extend tax relief on a special basis in 1954. When a crisis arose on the Staten Island Rapid Transit two years later, New York City leased the line at the rental equivalent of all local taxes and fees.

Aside from the Long Island case, the three states' involvement with commuter rail matters had been confined to the regulation of fares and service in the period before 1958. Regulating by the traditional case-by-case method, the commissions were not guided by overall policies for either the preservation or the termination of suburban services. In arbitrating the perennial struggle between the railroads and the local groups, however, the commissions were more responsive to community pressures than to railroad briefs and statistics. Carrier complaints over the state commissions in the New York region—one executive claimed his railroad had "about 98 per cent uncooperation in the State of New Jersey" [13]—became a major factor in inducing Congress to augment the Interstate Commerce Commission's regulatory authority in the Transportation Act of 1958.

Neither the difficulties of the commuter railroads nor the lack of public help were new problems in the late 1950s. For more than thirty years plans had been prepared by a variety of organizations to save, improve, expand, and finance the region's suburban rail network. Almost without exception, these studies concluded that the commuter system was an uncoordinated, inefficient, unprofitable public necessity requiring governmental intervention on some comprehensive basis. Although specific prescriptions often generated controversy, there was little disagreement with the general diagnosis. Yet by mid-1958 public involvement beyond regulation had been limited to sporadic responses to crises on particular lines. As one railroad president put it, "I get the impression that a lot of people would like to see something done . . . so long as they would not become involved in paying for it." [14]

The most ambitious effort to overhaul rail commutation began in 1954, when New York and New Jersey created the Metropolitan Rapid Transit Commission (MRTC) to study the trans-Hudson mass transport problem and to recommend solutions. Early in 1958, the MRTC proposed that a regional transit district—composed of New York City, Orange and Rockland Counties, and the northern New Jersey counties—be established to subsidize existing commuter services and build additional facilities, possibly including a $400-million transit loop under the Hudson River. Annual deficits were projected at $12 million. By the time Congress was considering the Transportation Act of 1958, however, the plan's prospects were not promising, since widespread opposition developed in New Jersey.

Regional transportation schemes such as that proposed by the MRTC had failed in the past because of a lack of a perceived common interest in the New York area in solving a costly and complex problem. Faced with growing demands on limited resources and competing with one another for jobs and residents, the region's governments have been wary of programs dealing "with the allocation of scarce physical resources under circumstances which do not promise equal benefits or equal costs for the jurisdictions involved." [15] Furthermore, particularism and the lack of shared goals deriving from the fragmented institutional base are compounded by the region's size, structure, and interstate character. Unlike smaller areas, which have a single focus, the New York region, with six other cities over 100,000,[16] contains many components which do not recognize New York City as the area's natural leader. The region's scope and the fragmented institutional base have shaped private as well as public activity. Unlike Pittsburgh, St. Louis, and Atlanta, where the business community has provided regional leadership, an areawide economic elite has not emerged in New York because "there is too much business

and . . . too many leaders" in a region "100 miles wide and
15 million people strong." [17]

Of the region's many units, New York City's interest in areal
approaches to the commuter problem was most evident in the
pre-Transportation Act period. Since the city was served by rail
lines which fanned out in all directions, central business district
interests, including the great metropolitan newspapers, naturally
viewed the problem in a regional frame of reference. The city government's desire to promote cooperation within the region had
led Mayor Robert Wagner to organize in mid-1956 the Metropolitan Regional Conference (MRC), a voluntary association of
the area's top elected officials.[18] Following the lead of the city,
which provided staff and underwrote its $50,000 annual budget,
the MRC supported a tri-state approach to the commuter rail
problem.

Despite the strong interest of the central business district in
preserving commuter service and the Mayor's support for regionalism, City Hall provided little leadership on the commutation
issue in the pre-Transportation Act period. Transit was the traditional rail transport concern of the city's political leaders, since
subway fares affected almost every resident, while few of New
York City's voters used the suburban rail system. Also dampening
Mayor Wagner's enthusiasm for active involvement in the commuter issue were the costs involved. As the suburban rail situation deteriorated and demands for public action mounted, the
Mayor insisted that the city—which provided over $100 million
in annual subsidies to the Transit Authority and had granted
substantial tax relief to the Long Island Railroad and the Staten
Island Rapid Transit—was bearing its fair share of the regional
mass transportation burden.

Outside New York City, there was little support for approaches
to the rail question involving the entire region. Fairfield County
commuters recognized that the New Haven Railroad's problems
required cooperative action between New York and Connecticut, but they had little sense of sharing a common concern with
New Jersey. These perceptions were reciprocated across the Hud-

son. Furthermore, with only 9 percent of northern New Jersey's work force employed in New York, many Jerseyites were not convinced that the interstate commutation problem deserved either a high priority or subsidization by the 91 percent that worked within the state. In Westchester County and elsewhere in the New York suburbs, intrastate arrangements, perhaps following the Long Island prototype, seemed a more realistic approach than grandiose regional schemes.

A good many people in the New York area, particularly in New Jersey, could see no point in creating another agency, whether bi-state or tri-state, as long as the Port of New York Authority apparently possessed both the jurisdiction and financial capacity to tackle the regional rail problem. Time and again, the Port Authority fended off these forays, emphasizing that there was an "absolute incompatability between railroad deficits and the PNYA's contractual limitations with its bondholders . . . to confine itself to self-supporting projects." [19] Early in 1955, the PNYA had covered its flank, providing the MRTC with $800,000 for its rapid transit studies in exchange for a "Memorandum of Understanding," which foreclosed a Port Authority role in any deficit-incurring transportation system the commission might propose. Political support for the PNYA mass transportation position came from both governors, a majority of the two legislatures, and most of the region's larger newspapers, as well as its select and influential constituency in New York banking and investment circles.

As a result of these policies and developments, the New York region was ill-prepared in mid-1958 to deal with the commuter railroad problem. Except in emergencies, public policy had done little to protect the regional interest in adequate suburban service. Regulatory, taxation, and investment policies had been detrimental to the preservation of rail commutation. Numerous studies and repeated warnings, pointing to further deterioration and ultimate collapse, had been ignored. Crisis again would be necessary to produce action; only this time the emergency was far more serious than in the past and involved a new element, the federal government.

The Federal Government and Urban Transportation

During the quarter-century that ended in 1958, the national government's activities in metropolitan areas steadily expanded. Beginning with aid to private housing in the early 1930s, the list of federal urban programs grew to include public housing (1937), urban highways (1944), airports (1946), water pollution (1948), urban renewal (1949), metropolitan planning (1954), air pollution (1955), and sewage treatment (1956). Underlying this expansion of responsibilities was urban growth and the inevitable, if sometimes delayed, translation of numbers into political influence in a democracy. By 1960 half the states had more than 50 percent of their population within metropolitan areas, and only four were without a metropolitan area. As a result, fewer and fewer congressmen, particularly senators, with their statewide constituencies, were immune from the claims of cities and suburbs. Equally sensitive to metropolitan needs was the presidency, with its dependence in the Electoral College on the large urban states.

Despite the proliferation of federal activities in metropolitan areas, by 1958, urban political influence had yet to involve the national government in the mass transportation problem. Outside the District of Columbia, federal interest in urban public transportation was limited to the regulation of suburban rail service by the Interstate Commerce Commission. The venerable ICC regulated commutation in typical fashion, employing a case-by-case adjudicatory approach, failing to develop plans or policies to guide its suburban rail determinations, and usually supporting the railroads' position. According to one commissioner, the ICC's commuter goal was to "get the fare as high as . . . was reasonable and make up the deficit off other traffic." [20] The result was a system in which "periodic increases in commutation rates [were] a seemingly endless process since the causes that make for deterioration remain unchecked." [21]

The ICC's limited jurisdiction, passive regulatory role, and railroad orientation made it an unlikely source of help for the metropolitan areas with mass transportation problems. Elsewhere in the federal exectutive and in Congress, the prospects for enlisting support were dimmed by the Eisenhower Administration's opposition to new federal urban ventures, the dominant role of highways in federal urban-transportation thinking, the dispersion of transportation responsibilities in Washington, the lack of widespread interest in involving the national government in mass transportation, and the obstacles to urban innovation in the Congress.

Although new federal-metropolitan programs were commenced after 1953, the Eisenhower Administration was never enthusiastic about extending the national government's responsibilities for "local" matters. The President agreed with the Commission on Intergovernmental Relations' conclusion that it was "clearly the responsibility of the States to assume leadership in seeking solutions for the problems of metropolitan government." [22] In 1957, Eisenhower's Joint Federal-State Action Committee minimized the federal role in urban affairs and recommended returning functions and revenues to the states.[23]

Moreover, the Administration viewed the $41-billion interstate highway program as its contribution to the solution of metropolitan transportation needs.[24] Spokesmen were fond of pointing out that the highway program would allocate to city and suburb twenty times the billion dollars previously spent by the national government for all its urban projects. Rumblings of discontent over the impact of the interstate highways on the urban landscape —one commentator wrote acidly of the "new roads and urban chaos," while another complained that "we are in the process of spending billions of dollars for expressways in metropolitan areas with almost no effective effort to decide on the basic outlines of a community blueprint to help guide this investment" [25]— changed few minds in Washington. The Bureau of Public Roads (BPR) continued to oppose diversion of highway funds for public transportation purposes. Standing behind the BPR was a group of national interests which have been described as the "most unique and massive coalition of single-minded pressures ever to hit the American scene." [26] Automobile users, truckers, manufacturers and suppliers, highway builders, and state and local road officials

were united in their devotion to the inviolability of federal highway trust funds and their depreciation of what they called "inefficient, inflexible, and uneconomical" mass transportation.

Federal involvement in urban public transportation was also
hindered by Washington's lack of a "mechanism even for ex-
amining such problems comprehensively and making intelligent
national decisions." [27] Responsibilities for transportation regulation and promotion in the national government traditionally have
been divided among numerous executive and independent agencies, producing a system in which "each form of transportation
has its champion and no agency is by law in a position to offer an
over-all viewpoint." [28] The Department of Commerce's Under
Secretary for Transportation was the top federal executive with
transportation responsibilities. But this official was not an effective policy center because he lacked control over transportation decisions made in other departments, agencies, and commissions, as well as over programs developed within the Department
of Commerce in the semi-autonomous BPR. As for urban transportation policy, one critic found "no evidence that federal and
state [highway] agencies, or Congress and state legislatures, have
sought to develop a transport policy at all, much less one related
to the other factors involved in making metropolitan communities
more livable and economically efficient." [29] The federal government's chief urban instrumentality, the Housing and Home
Finance Agency (HHFA), played no role in urban transportation
planning or development. In 1957, the Administrator of HHFA,
while emphasizing that urban highways were "a common problem" of his agency and BPR, complained that "The housing
agencies . . . have no direct responsibility for the highway program—none at all." [30]

Congress too had ignored the public transport aspects of the
urban transportation problem. Prior to 1958 no congressional
committee had looked into the mass transportation question.
Sporadic efforts by a few urban congressmen to interest their colleagues in the commuter rail and rapid transit problems had been
fruitless in the period before the enactment of the Transportation
Act of 1958. Serious obstacles stood in the way of changing this

situation. Compared with ubiquitous urban problems such as highways or sewage treatment, mass transportation, because of its importance in only a few large metropolitan areas, had limited political appeal in Congress. Moreover, its economic significance was far less than that of the highway-automobile complex, which supported a sixth of the economy and whose influence reached into every congressional district. Institutional factors also posed formidable roadblocks. In a Congress dominated by rural and small-town conservatives, particularly in the House, the urban areas were less influential than their numerical strength would indicate. In addition, the committee system, the appropriations process, and other congressional procedures facilitate delay and obstruction rather than action.

These several factors combined to make unpromising the prospects of federal involvement in the mass transportation problem or even its rail commutation aspect. At this juncture, however, Congress and the Eisenhower Administration unexpectedly brought the federal government directly into the suburban rail picture and indirectly into the entire mass transportation question through a general railroad relief-and-aid measure.

CHAPTER II

The Transportation Act of 1958

There is little question but that today our railroads are in
a serious condition. A mighty industry has come upon sick
and precarious times.   SENATOR GEORGE SMATHERS

Railroad passenger deficits quintupled during the first dozen
postwar years, from $140 million in 1946 to $724 million in
1957.[1] Over the same period the railroads' share of intercity freight
traffic dropped 31 percent. For a decade, the mounting troubles of
the railroads sparked a good deal of talk but little action in
Washington. Then, late in 1957, recession, plummeting rail earnings, and the specter of bankruptcy welded Democrats and Republicans, liberals and conservatives, Congress and the Administration into a broad coalition in support of the Transportation
Act of 1958. The prime objective of the Transportation Act's
authors was to alleviate the railroads' financial difficulties by improving their competitive position, broadening federal regulatory
powers over passenger service, and providing federal loan guarantees. Beyond a desire to remove the burden placed on rail earnings by unprofitable suburban services, the bill's architects had
little interest in metropolitan transportation.

None the less, the Transportation Act's passenger-train provisions had an immediate impact on urban transportation politics
and federal-metropolitan relations. One effect, not unintended,
was the enhancement of the bargaining position of the commuter
railroads, a development which precipitated a severe commuter

crisis in the New York region and intensified public concern in other metropolitan areas served by suburban rail systems. Another, though unplanned, long-run consequence of the Transportation Act was the increase in the number of metropolitan actors looking toward Washington for help with their mass transportation problems. In addition, the politics of passenger-train regulatory reform shaped attitudes on the rail commutation issue in Washington, particularly in the "commerce cluster"—the House and Senate Commerce Committees, the Department of Commerce, and the ICC—which had a significant effect on federal-metropolitan relations in the months after the passage of the bill. Finally, the behavior of urban participants in the politics of the Transportation Act illustrates the impact of the metropolis' political fragmentation on federal-metropolitan relations.

The Campaign for Passenger Service Reform

By the mid-1950s, elimination of unprofitable trains had become the railroads' principal weapon in the fight to reduce suburban losses. Almost every carrier in the New York area sought to cut service. In 1955, the Lackawanna Railroad petitioned the New Jersey Board of Public Utility Commissioners (NJBPUC) for permission to end service on its Boonton branch. The following year the New York, Susquehanna, and Western Railroad commenced efforts to drop all its passenger trains. All lines operating trans-Hudson ferries sought ICC approval for the discontinuance of these exceedingly unprofitable services, which accounted for $3.7 million of the New Jersey railroads' $16.7-million 1956 suburban deficit.[2] Early in 1958, the New York Central's petition to abandon passenger service on its Putnam division was granted by the New York Public Service Commission (NYPSC). These efforts in the New York region were part of an overall postwar attempt by the railroads to eliminate unprofitable suburban and intercity trains, an effort which reduced the nation's passenger-miles by a third in a decade.

As passenger deficits increased in the early 1950s, railroad dissatisfaction with the delays, expensive proceedings, and occasional rejections encountered in their dealings with state regulatory agencies mounted. To overcome these hurdles, the railroads wanted the ICC, normally sympathetic to their needs, to be given power to authorize the discontinuance of interstate passenger service "where it constitutes a burden on interstate commerce," as well as "similar power to authorize the removal of other unprofitable local services which effect a burden on interstate commerce." [3] Under the Transportation Act of 1920, ICC jurisdiction over train service was limited to the authorization of complete abandonment of a rail line. Discontinuance of service short of abandonment was the responsibility of the state regulatory commissions. Late in 1957, the ICC's passenger-service role, at least in the New York region, was restricted further by a federal court ruling that the New York Central's Weehawken ferries were an integral part of its West Shore division and could not be abandoned under the 1920 act unless all services on the line were terminated.[4] This meant permission to discontinue the highly unprofitable trans-Hudson ferries would have to be secured from the NJBPUC, which had successfully fought the ICC in the courts on the ferry issue and which the carriers found to be among the most unreasonable of the state regulatory commissions. As a consequence, railroads operating in New Jersey, particularly the New York Central, were especially anxious in 1958 to secure ICC jurisdiction over passenger trains.

Opposition to federal control over passenger service came from the state commissions, the railway labor unions, and local groups dependent upon continued passenger service. The National Association of Railroad and Utility Commissioners (NARUC) contended that the carriers were magnifying the problem out of proportion, since "reasonable" demands with respect to train service were rarely refused by its members.[5] An interest in maintaining jobs on passenger trains made the railroad brotherhoods allies of the state commissions. Local user and civic groups joined the NARUC and the Railway Labor Executives Association (RLEA), defending state regulation as more sensitive to local needs. In 1958, Joseph Harrison, a former counsel for the NJBPUC, candidly expressed this sentiment to a group of Essex County officials:

The Interstate Commerce Commission is concerned with a national transportation policy. It does not take into consideration primarily the concern of the residents or the economic necessities of a given area such as the North Jersey area. . . . [We] are not going to get . . . the sympathetic and the complete understanding that we will say the New Jersey Public Utilities Commission has and can have as compared to what the Interstate Commerce Commission is going to do.[6]

During the 1950s legislation was introduced in each session of Congress authorizing the ICC to permit discontinuance of passenger trains when the Commission found an unreasonable burden on interstate commerce, but the railroads were unable to win sufficient adherents to overcome the opposition inspired by the state commissions and the unions. In 1955, the carriers' lagging cause received a boost from President Eisenhower's Advisory Committee on Transportation Policy and Organization, headed by Secretary of Commerce Sinclair Weeks. Underscoring the burden of unprofitable passenger service on interstate commerce, the Weeks Committee endorsed the railroads' proposal, recommending that the ICC be empowered to override state bodies when the continuance of a particular service would result in "a net revenue loss or otherwise unduly burden interstate and foreign commerce provided reasonably adequate serviec in lieu thereof is available."[7] Legislation designed to implement these recommendations died in Congress, however, and interest in railroad problems flagged until a business slump brought a precipitous decline in rail carloadings and earnings in late 1957, particularly in the East.

On January 13, 1958, in response to this darkening situation, Senator George Smathers' Subcommittee on Surface Transportation commenced a 3½-month inquiry that would hear 103 witnesses and accumulate 2,355 pages of testimony on the "Problems of the Railroads." A co-sponsor of the 1955 Weeks legislation and no antagonist of the rail carriers, Smathers, a Florida Democrat, emphasized his concern over the railroads' woes at the outset:

These first hearings will inquire only into the conditions of the railroads, for the railroads still remain as the bedrock of the transportation [system], vital to a vigorous and healthy industrial economy. . . . It is clear that a study must be quickly undertaken, and solutions proposed to the problems presented if we are to keep the railroads alive, and a part of an effective transportation system in these United States, and if we are to keep them completely out of Government ownership.[8]

Before the hearings opened, one of the most articulate spokesmen for urban interests in Congress, Senator Joseph Clark of Pennsylvania, a former mayor of Philadelphia, suggested that the subcommittee look into the mass transportation problem. Smathers, emphasizing that his prime concern was the future of the railroads rather than the fate of suburban rail service, told Clark that metropolitan transportation was beyond the scope of his inquiry.[9]

A phalanx of railroad executives opened the hearings. Presidents of twenty-one major lines painted a gloomy picture of their future if existing conditions persisted. All agreed that Congress must do something about irrational and unfair regulation, the railroads' lack of freedom to fix competitive freight rates, motor carriers who were exempt from ICC regulation, outmoded and costly labor arrangements, excessive state and local taxation of rail properties, government subsidies to competing forms of transportation, and the mounting burden of passenger deficits.

Federal control over passenger-train discontinuance was pressed with new vigor. The Association of American Railroads (AAR) argued that the ICC should be given authority to permit discontinuance and consolidation of trains and facilities when it found the decisions of a state regulatory body to constitute an undue burden on interstate commerce.[10] New York Central president Alfred Perlman, bitter over the adverse federal court ruling in the West Shore ferry case, contended that state regulation had to be replaced either by federal jurisdiction or unfettered passenger pricing according to the "laws of economics" rather than the "dictates of local pressures." [11] Backing for the railroads' position on passenger service came from both the ICC and the Department of Commerce. Pointing to the lack of evidence of undue delay on the part of the state commissions, the ICC had taken a noncommittal stand on the Weeks Committee's 1955 recommendation. But the deteriorating railroad situation in 1958 led the ICC to stress the federal interest in the elimination of unprofitable passenger services.[12] Secretary Weeks restated the Administration's position that the ICC should be "given original jurisdiction over the discontinuance or curtailment of services and facilities." [13] Railway labor again opposed increasing the ICC's power over passenger service. Some dissent also came from the state commissioners, but the apparent futility of opposition in the light of the widespread sympathy for the railroads in Washington made them less vociferous than in the past.

Few witnesses at the hearings expressed concern about the future of rail commutation under discontinuance controlled by the ICC. Since the subcommittee's interest in suburban rail service was limited to its impact on rail earnings, no effort was made to solicit the appearance of metropolitan interests. Of the large cities dependent upon commutation, only Philadelphia recorded its views with the subcommittee. After Smathers' rebuff of Clark, however, Mayor Richardson Dilworth confined his activity to the insertion of a statement which stressed the importance of preserving existing commuter lines, the need to recognize that rail commutation was a public service requiring financial support, and the requirement for Congress to foster intergovernmental approaches to the problem. Appended to Dilworth's letter was a policy statement adopted by the American Municipal Association (AMA) the previous December, which called for federal loans for mass transportation capital improvements.[14] Only one commuter made an appearance at the hearings. Nathan Klein, an attorney and founder of a small commuter group on the Long Island Railroad did little to enhance the metropolitan cause. By indiscriminately indicting the railroad industry and the regulatory agencies for conspiracy, malfeasance, cupidity, and incompetence, Klein's testimony served only to antagonize Smathers and his colleagues.[15]

In the absence of other urban spokesmen, concern for the fate of suburban services under a broadened federal mandate in train discontinuance was voiced by Eastern rail officials. President George Alpert of the New York, New Haven & Hartford Railroad emphasized the need to maintain commuter services and the impossibility of a private corporation providing such services without public help. He asked Congress to earmark 1 percent of the entire federal highway appropriation for the support of mass transportation, including commuter railroads. Pennsylvania Railroad president James Symes concurred with Alpert on the essentiality of suburban service and the need for public funds to preserve it. He, too, wanted consideration to be given to "providing Federal funds, similar to Federal aid highway funds, for mass transportation facilities in metropolitan areas—in the direct interest of avoiding excessive highway expenditures and costly parking facilities." [16] Symes and Alpert received no support for these proposals from other rail executives or from the members of the Surface Transportation Subcommittee.

The Smathers Bill Becomes a Law

On April 30, less than a month after the close of the hearings, the subcommittee submitted a report and a draft bill to the parent Interstate and Foreign Commerce Committee.[17] The report attributed the railroads' decline to a number of factors, including the development of other forms of transportation offering intense competition to the rail carriers, large amounts of government aid to competing modes of transport, "ancient and outmoded . . . overregulation," and old-fashioned attitudes on the part of railroad management. The $724-million passenger deficit was assigned a major share of the blame for the railroads' depressed financial condition. State and local governments were held responsible for two of the railroads' prime burdens: commutation services operated at "enormous losses" and excessive taxation of rail properties.

To alleviate the burden of passenger deficits, the subcommittee recommended ICC jurisdiction over discontinuance and a clarification of the Commission's powers to set intrastate commuter rates.[18] As for the future of suburban services, Smathers and his colleagues expressed confidence that the enhanced regulatory position of the carriers would "lead to the prompt finding of appropriate solutions by local authorities."

The passenger-train provisions of the Smathers bill went beyond the public recommendations of the railroads. Not only was the ICC given jurisdiction over all passenger-train service, but the bill permitted discontinuance without formal commission action. This was accomplished by amending the Interstate Commerce Act to permit a carrier to discontinue any train, ferry, station, or depot used in interstate or intrastate commerce within 30 days of posting notice unless the ICC entered upon an investigation into the proposed discontinuance. The ICC was not required to intervene, and if the Commission failed to investigate, the service would be terminated without further public action. Even if the ICC became involved, however, discontinuance was quite likely since the bill provided that service could be continued for up to one year only if the ICC found it was "required by public convenience and necessity," was not an undue burden on interstate commerce, and would "not result in a net loss" to the carrier. The last provision was crucial, since most passenger and practically all suburban trains ran at a net loss under the ICC's method of allocating costs to passenger traffic.

Because of the threat it posed to suburban rail service, the net-loss provision sparked some belated interest from the New York region in the Smathers bill. Within the Surface Transportation Subcommittee, Senator William Purtell of Connecticut sought unsuccessfully to secure the deletion of the net-loss section because of its possible effect on commuter service in Fairfield County.[19] As the bill moved to the Senate floor in early June, the chairman of the NYPSC, Benjamin Feinberg, aired the issue by condemning the provisions of the Smathers bill which weakened state control over passenger rates and service. Feinberg underscored the net-loss clause as especially onerous and predicted that passage of the bill would result in the abandonment of all passenger service in the East.[20] Picking up Feinberg's argument, Senator Jacob Javits of New York told the Senate that the bill as written "must be opposed by Senators who come from large cities as I do, because we cannot tie around the necks of our people this kind of noose whereby at one fell swoop service may be discontinued." Javits then offered an amendment which eliminated the net-loss section. But Smathers had the votes to defeat the proposal, which drew support from only a handful of metropolitan senators, mostly from the New York region.[21] However, an important change was made in the passenger-service section in the Senate. Led by Senator Richard Russell of Georgia, Southerners opposed to federal incursions on states' rights secured the elimination of the provision of the Smathers bill which gave the ICC jurisdiction in intrastate discontinuance.[22]

By the time the proposed Transportation Act of 1958 reached the House floor, Southern Democrats already had eliminated the intrastate passenger-service proposal in committee.[23] And during the debate, the states'-rights advocates, joined by a few suburban congressmen from the New York region, prevailed upon Commerce Committee chairman Oren Harris to drop the net-loss proviso. Harris agreed because he felt that the remaining criteria of undue burden on interstate commerce and of public convenience and necessity were sufficient to achieve the basic objectives of railroad financial relief. However, this important change did not satisfy a few diehard Southerners, who offered an amendment to kill the entire train-service provision. They were joined by Frank Osmers, a New Jersey Republican fearful of the consequences of the Smathers bill for his Bergen County constituents' commuter trains, net loss or no net loss. Outlining the efforts of the MRTC to provide a local solution (without mentioning his own opposition to the MRTC's loop proposal),[24] Osmers pleaded for time until these endeavors bore fruit. The anti-train-service amendment failed, 30–118, and the House then passed the bill, 348–2. One of the two holdouts was Osmers, whose "Nay" later won him a modicum of fame back home as a minor prophet.[25]

As the bill moved to conference committee for adjustment of

the differences between the House and Senate versions, concern over the probable impact of the net-loss criterion on suburban service in the New York region generated another flurry of activity. Senator Clifford Case of New Jersey urged the Senate conferees to preserve vital rail services in the nation's largest metropolitan area by accepting the House version. Taking up the cudgels again, Feinberg warned the conference committee that failure to eliminate the net-loss clause would cause the cessation of commuter services and, in turn, the strangulation of economic life in the major Eastern metropolitan centers. At Feinberg's request, New York's Governor Averell Harriman wired the conferees, imploring them to eliminate the net-loss provision. Although troubled by the Senate's retention of the net-loss provision, at this juncture Feinberg was even more distressed by Smathers' attempt to restore in conference the intrastate discontinuance provisions previously rejected in both houses. ICC jurisdiction over intrastate passenger service in New York would endanger the future of the state's two most important commuter lines, the Long Island and the New York Central. Feinberg rallied other state utility commissions to dissuade the conference committee from accepting Smathers' proposal. Bitter resentment over these moves was voiced by Perlman of the New York Central, who had just threatened to close Grand Central Terminal and to halt all commuter service if state tax relief were denied. Perlman protested the "Johnny-come-lately" tactics of Feinberg and Harriman, neither of whom had appeared at the hearings or, according to the outspoken rail executive, had ever done anything to help the commuter railroads.[26]

While these protests helped eliminate the net-loss provision, they did not forestall Smathers' resurrection of ICC jurisdiction over intrastate discontinuance. No longer convinced that the net-loss section was essential to the elimination of unprofitable trains, Smathers persuaded the other Senate conferees to retain the provision until the House delegation agreed to reinstate a federal role in intrastate passenger service. Once this compromise was accepted by the conference committee, the protests of Southern congressmen and state utility commissioners over the restoration of intrastate ICC jurisdiction were to no avail. As almost always happens, the conference committee's compromise bill breezed through both houses.

On August 12, President Eisenhower signed the Transportation Act of 1958. The passenger-service provisions, which became section 13a of the Interstate Commerce Act, consisted of two parts. The first covered interstate trains and ferries, and followed the original Smathers bill except for the deletion of the net-loss proviso. Section 13a(1) provided that a carrier might discontinue 30 days after posting notice unless the ICC intervened, regardless of state constitutional provisions, laws, or court orders. Service could be ordered continued by the Commission for four months pending investigation, hearing, and decision. If the ICC found the service to be required by public convenience and necessity and not an undue burden on interstate commerce, it could require its continuation for one year, at the end of which the carrier might reinstitute the proceeding. As in the version prepared by the Surface Transportation Subcommittee and unlike the abandonment procedures in the 1920 Transportation Act, which required an ICC investigation and hearing, the new section placed the ICC under no mandate to intervene or grant a hearing when a carrier sought to terminate an interstate train or ferry.

The second part dealt with intrastate trains and provided that in the event a state constitution prohibited discontinuance or a state commission had denied a petition or not acted within 120 days of presentation, a carrier might petition the ICC for permission to cut an intrastate train or ferry. The Commission could grant this authority only after full hearings and findings that present and future public necessity and convenience permitted it and that continued operation constituted "an unjust and undue burden upon the interstate operations of such carrier . . . or upon interstate commerce." [27]

First Impressions on the Commuter Issue

Official Washington took its first look at the commuter problem in 1958; it came away strongly convinced that the federal government's prime concern in the matter should be the railroads rather than the metropolitan areas. Given the rail-crisis context of the Senate investigation and the "railroad-commerce" frame of reference of the principal parties, these findings probably were foreordained. From the beginning, Smathers left no doubt as to where his sympathies lay. Clark's request for an inquiry into the mass transportation problem, the proposals for federal aid from Alpert and Symes, and a query from New Jersey's senators about the possibilities of the subcommittee recommending federal commuter rail assistance all produced negative responses.

In its report, the Surface Transportation Subcommittee cleverly coupled increased federal power to eliminate commuter service with local responsibility for its preservation. "Basically," Smathers and his colleagues concluded, "the commuter service problem is a local one." Therefore, it was judged "desirable to leave to the local government agencies involved the job of seeking specifically tailored solutions to their particular problems." The federal government's responsibility for interstate commerce, however, would not permit it to stand by idly awaiting local action. Thus, ICC facilitation of discontinuance would eliminate the drain of commutation on the financial health of the railroads while spurring the local communities to action.[28] If the metropolitan areas could not find a way to support suburban service, then they would have to do without it. As Smathers argued in the Senate, Washington must not tell a suburban railroad:

You will have to operate your business whether you can make a profit or not. You will have to run the business whether you take all the stockholders' money or whether you have to take up your tracks or cars and sell them for scrap. Nevertheless, you must run the business.[29]

The Smathers report was influential in shaping attitudes on commutation within Congress, the Administration, and the ICC. The House Commerce Committee agreed that suburban services were a great drain on the earning capacity of the carriers and that it was "unreasonable" to expect freight shippers to subsidize these losses. Local communities were assigned the responsibility of underwriting the service if they wanted it preserved.[30] The Commerce Department's commitment to the Smathers' viewpoint on commutation was evident in a report released in early 1960, which termed mass transportation "primarily a local problem" and echoed the subcommittee in its concern for the deleterious effect of suburban losses on the overall health of the railroads.[31] For the ICC, consideration of the commuter problem in a railroad frame of reference came naturally. In both its annual report for 1958 and the passenger-deficit investigation of 1959, the ICC indicated its concurrence with the Smathers findings on the need to unburden interstate commerce and local responsibility for preserving suburban service.[32]

Thus, examination of the commutation problem in 1958 in terms of the general railroad situation produced consensus in the commerce complex of legislative, executive, and regulatory agencies that suburban rail service was a local problem, that the federal government's concern was to foster the termination of this burden on a vital element of the national transportation system, and that there was no federal responsibility for mass transportation as such. Support from outside the government for this general position came in 1959, when, in an authoritative study on railroad policies for the influential Brookings Institution, James Nelson concluded that support of commutation services was a local matter.[33] Before any effective action could be taken at the federal level on behalf of metropolitan mass transportation, either the attitudes that took shape during the consideration of the Transportation Act of 1958 would have to be altered or the commerce agencies would have to be bypassed.

Metropolitan Interests and the Transportation Act

Largely unrepresented at the Smathers hearings and relatively impotent in the cloakrooms and committee chambers, the cities and suburbs dependent upon rail commutation were not very influential in shaping the Transportation Act of 1958. To be sure, urban efforts bore fruit in the elimination of the net-loss provision. This was a significant victory, since retention of the clause would have resulted in the speedy decimation of interstate suburban service. But the procedure whereby interstate trains could be discontinued without ICC intervention, which became a major issue immediately after the Transportation Act went into effect, escaped urban notice. Moreover, the metropolitan areas were unable to alter the almost universal perception of the issue in railroad rather than in urban terms. However, given the railroad crisis context of the Transportation Act and the lack of interest on the part of the commerce committees and agencies in the metropolitan side of the story, it is unlikely that a far more extensive mobilization of urban pressures would have affected substantially either the general climate of opinion in Washington or the legislative outcome.

The railroad context of the 1958 proceedings also played a major role in muting the response of the metropolitan areas. Most parties in the commuting areas were unaware of the possible effect of the Smathers proposals on the future of commutation. State, county, city, and local officials, to say nothing of local groups, possess neither the staff nor the resources to analyze the torrent of federal legislative proposals for possible impact within their jurisdiction. Normally, they depend on the press, pressure groups, and contacts with congressmen and other officials in Washington. But the suburban rail aspects of the Senate investigation received relatively little attention in the metropolitan news media, which concentrated on Smathers' main theme of the need to help the railroads. Except for the state utility commissioners, the governmental lobbies, such as the Council of State Governments, the AMA,[34] the U.S. Conference of Mayors, and the National Association of County Officers (NACO), were inactive. Urban congressional involvement was belated, and few constituents were alerted to the threat to their commuter trains. As a result, interest in this "railroad" legislation was meager among those with a stake in suburban rail service.

Because few perceived a threat to essential rail services, the interest generated by the Smathers investigation in urban areas was largely favorable. For example, the New Jersey State Chamber of Commerce, hardly oblivious to the state's mass transportation needs, applauded the Senate proposals because they promised to help the New Jersey railroads (who were, of course, members of the Chamber of Commerce) and bolster its economy but ignored the suburban train issue.[35] Congressmen from the metropolitan areas received a fairly heavy volume of mail from rail security holders, railroad labor, and business groups favoring the bill and very little registering disapproval; practically none of the latter mentioned the threat to suburban service. Representative William Widnall of New Jersey spoke for most persons both inside and outside Congress when he explained that "Many of us who voted for the Railroad Act of 1958 . . . did so with the idea of improving the general financial lot of the railroads and certainly did not feel it should be an opening wedge for decreasing commuter service." [36]

Metropolitan activity was also inhibited by the rudimentary state of thinking on the question of federal involvement in mass transportation. Almost everywhere, commuter politics were dominated by local efforts. In New York, the MRTC's proposals, the controversy over the Port Authority's responsibility for mass transportation, and the perennial struggle over service and fares preoccupied most of the active participants in the region's commuter politics. Absorption in the immediate was particularly characteristic of suburban behavior. In New Jersey, a commuter spokesman complained after the passage of the Transportation Act that the investigation was headed by "a senator from a state that does not have a single commuter train operating within its borders" and that "No one thought to ask a single commuter what he felt about that phase of the problem that concerned him the most—his ability to get to and from work without undue hardship." [37] Yet while the legislation was under consideration, this suburbanite's only contact with Washington was a request to Senator Case and Representative Osmers that they intervene to remedy "a travesty of justice in the exclusion of [a] commuter's testimony" in a ferry-fare case before the ICC.[38]

As a result of the railroad context of the Transportation Act and of the local focus of commuter politics, the passenger-train service issue was a poor competitor for urban attention in 1958. Public officials, who rarely enter a particular political arena without good cause, perceived few compelling reasons to embroil themselves in the Smathers investigation or legislation. For most it was an extraneous matter, superfluous to their more pressing concerns. Even in New York, the metropolitan area with the greatest latent interest in the question because of the size of its commuter system and the large amount of interstate service, involvement was spotty and belated. Except for Purtell's ineffectual attempt to dissuade his Surface Transportation Subcommittee colleagues from endangering commuter service in southwestern Connecticut, no one from the region sought to influence the Transportation Act's passenger provisions during the crucial stages of legislative formulation. Not until the floor debate did Feinberg's impetus prod a number of regional congressmen into the fray. Except for Feinberg, Harriman, and the handful of congressmen, public officials from the New York region eschewed the question entirely. After the New Jersey senators reported Smathers' lack of interest in federal aid for commutation, Trenton ignored the Transportation Act. Unlike Philadelphia's Dilworth, Mayor Wagner was too preoccupied with other problems even to bother registering his views with the Surface Transportation Subcommittee. Ironically, in view of later events, George Alpert of the New Haven presented the region's case for preserving rail commutation in 1958.

Although urban activity on the Transportation Act was low key, in one important respect it was characteristic of federal-metropolitan politics: particularist rather than regional considerations motivated involvement and shaped goals. In almost every instance, responses reflected the fragmented institutional base of the metropolis. Senator Purtell and Representative Albert Morano of Fairfield County limited their concern to the effect of the net-loss clause on New Haven commuter trains running between the Connecticut suburbs and New York, while Osmers worried about Bergen County's links with Manhattan. State forays, too, were a product of subregional vantage points. New Jersey was interested in federal aid for its commuter lines. Feinberg's prime concern was suburban service in New York, particularly the intrastate operations of the New York Central and the Long Island. Only Senator Javits, whose roots were in New York City, consistently discussed the problem in a regional frame of reference.

To conclude, the Transportation Act of 1958 was passed without much concern for the future of rail commutation or much interest on the part of the great majority of officials responsible for mass transportation in the metropolitan regions or the groups interested in preserving commuter service. Through default, metropolitan viewpoints were ignored in this initial encounter with the federal government on the commuter problem. The pattern of federal-metropolitan interaction was quite rudimentary because of the general lack of interest and information. Finally, it should be noted that the federal arena is one in which national groupings, such as that interested in helping the railroads, have considerable advantages over latent local interests. Lacking internal cohesion, mobilization, allies, effective lobbying, influential congressional support, and sympathetic executive agencies, the metropolitan areas dependent upon rail commutation faced insuperable obstacles in securing a hearing for their case in 1958. And since no one tried very hard to present the metropolitan brief, it was quite simple for all concerned to ignore urban and suburban views.

PART TWO

Crisis and Response

CHAPTER III

The Commuter Crisis

It was perfectly clear to me that the passage of that bill in the form it was signed was the end of commuter service in the United States. REPRESENTATIVE FRANK OSMERS

The train-service provisions of the Transportation Act of 1958 provided the nation's commuter railroads with a potent weapon. In the wake of the new law, tremors shook each of the major commuting centers. The new section on interstate discontinuance was, however, far more formidable than the intrastate proviso. Since few rail commuters in Chicago, Philadelphia, Boston, and San Francisco were served by the now extremely vulnerable interstate suburban lines, the Transportation Act's immediate impact was concentrated in the New York region, where almost half of all rail commuters crossed state boundaries. And because three-quarters of the area's interstate commuters lived west of the Hudson, its consequences were most severe in the New Jersey sector of the area.

Hardly had the ink dried on President Eisenhower's signature when the New York region's interstate carriers seized the initiative. Employing the new procedure, they eliminated ferries and commuter trains and threatened the complete termination of suburban service. Coupled with the imminent demise of the MRTC, these unexpected railroad moves that were made possible by the new federal law precipitated a prolonged crisis in the autumn of 1958. This emergency brought the commuter rail issue to the forefront of public attention and turned most participants in New York's commuter politics to Washington for help in resolving the problem.

The Meaning of the Transportation Act

A test of the new train-service provisions came quickly in the New York region. On August 12, the day the law was signed, the New York Central posted notices announcing the discontinuance of service on its West Shore ferry line. The following day, the Erie took similar action on its trans-Hudson ferries. For the New York Central victory now seemed near after half a decade of frustrated efforts to drop the ferries. Typical of the regional reaction was an editorial in the New York *Herald Tribune* entitled, "First Ferries Go—Then Railroads Too?" which concluded that it was "certainly high time to begin working out policy that will keep the commuter roads in business." [1]

Since the ICC had sanctioned termination of the ferries the previous year, only to be reversed in the courts, favorable action was expected on the Central's move to discontinue under the new federal rules. However, the ICC's manner of granting the request touched off a sharp controversy. Much to the surprise and consternation of the interested parties in New Jersey, the ICC exercised its clear option under the interstate discontinuance section of the Transportation Act and did not investigate the railroad's proposal. For this omission, the ICC, the law, and the railroads came under heavy fire. New Jersey officials contended that the Transportation Act denied due process by permitting the ICC to supersede state regulation without the safeguards of a hearing against arbitrary action. The ICC, on the other hand, claimed that its decision not to investigate was fully justified on the basis of the special circumstances in the case:

Technically, we did permit it to be discontinued without a hearing under the 1958 act, but we had just finished three years of hearings before the 1958 act was involved. All that would have been done would duplicate the record and go through the same thing again.[2]

New Jersey's Attorney General, the NJBPUC, communities along the West Shore in New Jersey and New York, and the Citizens United Transit Committee, the group which had led the long fight to preserve suburban rail service in Bergen and Rockland Counties, attempted in vain to halt the proposed discontinuance. In mid-September, a federal district court in Newark heard an ICC attorney echo the Smathers subcommittee in arguing that the interest of the nation in preserving the freight-hauling role of the railroads was paramount and that Congress had "complete power to determine to what extent and in what manner interstate commerce is to be protected against local interests."[3] By a two-to-one decision, the court accepted the ICC's views and rejected the plaintiffs' contention that public convenience and necessity mandated continued ferry service on the West Shore. Nor did the court find convincing the argument that ICC approval of the New York Central's action without a hearing was a violation of the Fifth Amendment. The Transportation Act of 1958 was held to be constitutional and the ICC to have acted within its prerogatives. Refusing to review the substance of the case or to order the Commission to hold further hearings, the court justified its position on the grounds that the failure of a regulatory commission to act was not reviewable.[4] The ruling was appealed, and the discontinuance stayed pending review by the U.S. Supreme Court.

The Crisis Commences

The New York metropolitan region's long-simmering commuter crisis rapidly came to a boil during the last four months of 1958. The Transportation Act, the ferry actions, and the ICC's refusal to permit hearings were followed in mid-September by a gloomy ICC examiner's report on the future of passenger service, which predicted that the continuation of present trends would result in the elimination of all passenger trains in the United States by 1970. The only consolation that commuters and public officials in the large metropolitan areas could derive from examiner Howard Hosmers' findings was the conclusion that "Commutation traffic . . . probably will be the last form [of passenger service] to disappear." [5]

After years of drift, the commuter railroads took the offensive. Their attorneys burned the midnight oil preparing requests for fare hikes and notifications of service cuts. Early in September, Alfred Perlman, the New York Central's outspoken president, brandished his new weapon at a press conference. Declaring ferry and passenger service on the West Shore doomed and the Westchester operation imperiled by excessive taxation, he lashed out at the "super politicians" of New York and New Jersey, who were "flogging" the commuter railroads.[6] The New York *Times* saw Perlman's blunt warning as handwriting on the wall:

As a sort of last angry man of the railroad presidents he is really doing the public a service in trying to warn of an inevitable situation before it is too late for remedy. The choice as to whether railroads are to go on supplying commuter service lies not with the railroads but with the public.[7]

As the railroad pressures intensified, regional interest in the commuter issue grew. Government officials, the press, and a host of private parties rushed to get into the act. For the beleaguered MRTC and its supporters, the emergency afforded a last opportunity to bolster a lagging cause. Crisis also invigorated the forces seeking to assign commuter responsibilities to the Port Authority, a turn of events which the Authority continued to oppose with its formidable resources. The MRTC's dismal political prospects in New Jersey and the manifold difficulties involved in securing a PNYA role revived interest in a tri-state approach to the region's mass transportation problems. As the crisis worsened, Mayor Wagner, the MRC, the major New York City newspapers, the Regional Plan Association (RPA), and a number of central-city civic and business groups endorsed the tri-state principle. Of the many suggestions put forward, the one that aroused the most interest was the Fifth Avenue Association's proposal for a conference of the three governors and the Mayor to lay the basis for regional action.

No meeting, however, was possible, pending the outcome of New York's gubernatorial election. Further delay became inevitable when Governor-elect Nelson Rockefeller declined to meet with Governors Robert Meyner and Abraham Ribicoff and Mayor Wagner prior to his inauguration in January. Meanwhile the crisis deepened. In mid-November, the New Jersey railroads announced a $30-million deficit for the first nine months of 1958. They threatened to cease all service unless the state terminated its "discriminatory tax pattern and regulatory harassment." [8] A week later, Alpert called upon New York City, Westchester County, and Connecticut to grant the New Haven $1 million in tax relief and cash subsidies. On December 1 the Lehigh Valley Railroad, which served only a handful of commuters, caused a minor stir by announcing that it would seek to eliminate all passenger service. Four days later, Perry Shoemaker, president of the Delaware, Lackawanna, & Western Railroad, declared that his railroad, New Jersey's largest commuter carrier, would abandon all passenger service unless immediate relief from all property taxes was granted. At the same time, the Pennsylvania Railroad announced that it would discontinue most of its nonrush-hour service to Manhattan.[9]

Although these threats were concentrated in New Jersey, where almost all commuter service was interstate and appeared on the verge of extinction, they were insufficient to save the MRTC's district proposal, which expired in the lower house of the legislature early in December. After four years of effort and months of controversy, the climax for the MRTC came during the peak of the crisis at public hearings before an Assembly committee in Trenton on November 24 and December 3, 1958. Far outweighing supporters, opponents led by representatives of the Jersey City Merchants Council, the Inter-Municipal Group for Better Rail Service (IMGBRS), the MRC, the Morris and Hudson County Freeholders, the State League of Municipalities, and the New Jersey Motor Bus Association, reiterated their complaints— the high price tag, the fear of unequal costs and benefits, the plan's Manhattan focus, the lack of a role for the Port Authority, and the district's alleged inadequate jurisdiction.[10] On the scene to dash the hopes of those who sought a PNYA solution was its executive director, Austin Tobin. Pointing to the PNYA's $800,000 contribution to the MRTC studies, Tobin slammed the door on a transit role for the Port Authority with the declaration that "we have nothing more to contribute to this problem." [11] On that note, after the failure of last-minute efforts in the New Jersey legislature to produce an acceptable compromise, the MRTC proposals passed into limbo.

The Search for Solutions

The commuter crisis of the winter of 1958–59 did not produce a uniform reaction in the New York region. From the outset, differing perceptions of the problem, and the varied capabilities for action rooted in the fragmented institutional base, prompted responses designed to serve the interests of particular jurisdictions and groups rather than the area as a whole. Consequently, no single plan emerged from the crisis. Instead, a number of efforts were launched in the hope of resolving the suburban rail issue with the maximum benefit and minimum cost to the sponsoring party. Among these diverse endeavors, most important in terms of their impact on the pattern of federal-metropolitan politics were the state programs designed to preserve essential commuter service, the suburban-inspired congressional attempts to modify the new federal train-service provisions, and the central-city campaign for federal mass transportation assistance. Although only the first of these efforts was instrumental in easing the crisis itself, each played an important role in shaping the relationship between metropolitan and federal actors on the rail transport issue.

As the crisis moved into 1959 unabated, attention focused on the long-awaited meeting of the region's major political figures. The prospect of tax relief, subsidies, or some other form of public assistance led the railroads to shelve their threats pending the outcome of the conference. Commuters implored their political leaders for assurances that their links between home and office would not be broken. For the advocates of a regional approach, the lengthening crisis buoyed hopes that Mayor Wagner and the governors could achieve the cooperative breakthrough on the suburban rail front that had eluded the area for a generation. But these latter expectations were dashed when the political leaders finally sat down together on February 10. Differences rooted in the region's fragmented political system—of constituency, of fiscal and jurisdictional capacity, and of viewpoint—prevailed over the pleas for unity.

The problem at the conference was basic: each of the major participants perceived the problem in a different light. Wagner came to the meeting committed to a minimal financial role for the region's local governments (particularly New York City), a tri-state approach, and federal aid. The latter position, as will be seen in Chapter VI, was a product of his enlistment in a campaign for federal help organized by Philadelphia's Mayor Dilworth. Although federal mass transportation assistance was too new an idea to elicit much support from the private groups represented at the conference, spokesmen for the Fifth Avenue Association and the Regional Plan Association backed the Mayor's plea for a regional undertaking.

Despite the worsening situation in New Jersey, Governor Meyner journeyed to New York City on February 10 with no proposals of his own. However, he was determined to see his way through the crisis without jeopardizing a precariously balanced budget. During the early stages of the emergency, he had sought to wish away the problem by assigning responsibility for a solution to the carriers, arguing that "The railroads cannot continue to take the stand that they should operate passenger services at a profit." [12] Since this position had obvious limitations, Meyner and his aides had begun to explore more realistic means of preserving commuter service. However, nothing definite had been formulated by the time of the conference. Because federal involvement and a tri-state approach seemed least likely to make financial demands on New Jersey, Meyner found himself in the camp of fellow-Democrat Wagner.

A different perspective shaped the perceptions of Connecticut's Governor Abraham Ribicoff. It was clear to Ribicoff that his state's vital interests were limited to Fairfield County and its rail link with Manhattan. "In all fairness to the people of Connecticut," Ribicoff told his colleagues at the conference, "I couldn't get involved in New Jersey's problems. They are more complicated and heavier sums of money are involved." [13] Connecticut's interest, he made clear, was limited to proposals which would keep the New Haven in business.

New York's Governor, Nelson Rockefeller, was the key figure at the February 10 session. During his campaign Rockefeller termed the elimination of commuter rail service "an intolerable prospect." He promised that New York would "insure adequate, efficient, convenient commuter services for the residents of our great metropolitan area." [14] But the Governor was interested in neither grandiose regional schemes nor federal aid. Except for approximately 11,000 Westchester residents who rode the New Haven and a handful of reverse commuters to New Jersey, New Yorkers were not threatened by the new vulnerability of interstate suburban service. Moreover, since almost none of his constituents had to cross state lines to get to work, regional approaches were unnecessary and unilateral state action was feasible from Rockefeller's point of view. This situation led the Governor to insist that the problem be met with "each state taking action itself on a coordinated basis." [15]

Closely paralleling Rockefeller's position was that of the Port Authority. With the collapse of the MRTC proposals and the prolongation of the crisis, pressures on the PNYA to assume commuter responsibilities mounted. New Jersey's League of Municipalities, the MRC, and Wagner joined the chorus of northern New Jersey leaders calling for PNYA action. At the conference, Tobin attempted to counter these thrusts, urging a "modest" approach in line with Rockefeller's call for suggestions limited to "immediate steps." Tri-state and other regional schemes, in the PNYA view, were unnecessary, since each commuter rail line's troubles were "separate and individual problems physically, financially and politically." [16] Since areawide action was impossible without New York State's participation and a willingness on the part of all parties to make financial contributions, the views of Rockefeller and Tobin carried the day.

Press reaction was mixed. Applauding Rockefeller for "being practical about railroads" and for his "emphasis on action by the states and localities," the Republican *Herald Tribune* rebuked Democrats Wagner and Meyner for favoring "reliance on Washington." Although unhappy because the tri-state approach had foundered, the *World-Telegram & Sun* was pleased that there was agreement that commutation "boils down to a local problem." The *Journal-American*, however, warned that letting "the three States and the various municipalities and the railroads all deal with the problem separately . . . is what has been going on for decades and the plight of the commuter lines has become progressively worse." [17]

Governor Rockefeller followed the February 10 meeting with swift action to end the crisis by preserving and improving vital suburban service within New York. Within six weeks, the legislature had approved a program built around state and local tax abatement and a state-financed car-purchase plan to be administered by the Port Authority. Since Rockefeller's program promised local tax relief and new cars for the New Haven, the emergency also subsided in Fairfield County.

In New Jersey, however, crisis conditions persisted throughout the spring. The failure of the conference was a serious blow: State Senator Walter Jones of Bergen County spoke for suburbanites throughout the northern portion of the state when he called February 10 a "black day for rapid transit and regional cooperation." [18] Less than a month later the faint possibility of judicial relief faded when the U.S. Supreme Court refused to review the Weehawken ferry case.[19] On March 24, 1959, the New York Central closed the ferries. Commuters were encouraged by the management to abandon the West Shore trains (which were still in service but would end their runs at the deserted ferry terminal) for through bus service to Manhattan.[20] Now only state or local action or a change in the federal law could save commuter rail service in northern New Jersey. In response to mounting constituency pressures from the suburbs, New Jersey congressmen chose the latter course. As will be seen in the next chapter, they introduced legislation designed to mitigate the impact of the Transportation Act on the Jersey suburbs until solutions were hammered out by state and local authorities.

While members of the New Jersey congressional delegation were trying to persuade Senator Smathers to hold hearings on their proposals, the commuter lines west of the Hudson intensified their pressures. On April 9, the Lackawanna Railroad announced that all service would terminate in two months unless it were granted a $700,000 fare increase, a $400,000 tax reduction, $900,000 in financial assistance from the Port Authority, and a guarantee against operating losses. A few days before, Erie president Henry von Willer had told reporters that "In the absence of any government assistance in New Jersey for what is obviously a public service, our only recourse is through the medium of service curtailment and fare increases." A month later, in announcing a $2-million commuter loss in 1958, the Jersey Central threatened to discontinue its entire passenger operation if the NJBPUC failed to allow a 40 percent fare hike.[21] At the same time the Lackawanna posted notices on stations and trains announcing that, under the provisions of the Transportation Act of 1958, service would end on June 9, 1959.

Not until June 3, 1959, the day before the hearings on the proposals for changes in the Transportation Act opened in Washington and six days before the scheduled end of service on the Lackawanna, was there a break in the tension in New Jersey. On that day, the Lackawanna indicated that the rapid tempo of study by the state's newly created Division of Railroad Transportation of the State Highway Department had persuaded it to delay for "a reasonable length of time before taking this drastic action." [22] Two weeks later Governor Meyner made public the proposal of Highway Commissioner Dwight Palmer which ended, at least temporarily, the commuter crisis. In a sharp break with highway tradition in the region, Palmer recommended that New Jersey Turnpike Authority surpluses be used to subsidize the purchase of commuter rail equipment and the consolidation of mass transportation facilities.[23] After ten months, the commuter crisis of 1958–59 was over, although the New York region's suburban rail problems were far from being resolved.

The Commuter Crisis and Federal-Metropolitan Politics

Action by the states, not the federal government, terminated the emergency on the New York area's suburban rail system in the spring of 1959. None the less, the crisis, triggered as it was by the Transportation Act of 1958, greatly increased regional interest in the federal government's commuter-railroad role. The activities of all participants in the post-Transportation Act commuter politics of the region were affected by Washington's heightened visibility. Characteristically, the responses of the various metropolitan actors reflected the fragmented institutional base of the metropolis and the particularist perceptions of its components. Suburbia, reacting in typical remedial and localistic fashion, clamored for changes in the Transportation Act, the seeming cause of the grass roots' distress. In the state capitals, wariness of direct federal-local relationships led the states to look to Washington only for facilitation of state efforts, primarily in the form of approval of federal tax measures. New York City, joined by other metropolitan centers and the commuter railroads, was spurred by the crisis to turn to Washington for federal mass transportation assistance. Finally, the New York area's congressmen, newcomers to the region's commuter politics, attempted with varying degrees of interest, ability, and success to satisfy the federal level commuter objectives of their constituents in the suburbs, cities, and state capitals.

The next four chapters examine the federal-metropolitan relations which grew out of these fragmented responses of the suburbs, states, central cities, and regional congressmen to the commuter crisis during the twenty months following the passage of the Transportation Act. It is not a success story, for these varied urban efforts bore little fruit in Washington until mid-1960. Neither the ICC nor the Eisenhower Administration changed its negative attitudes or policies toward mass transportation. Congress did not amend the Transportation Act, facilitate state commuter programs with federal tax benefits, nor enact an aid program. Not until the introduction of federal mass transportation assistance legislation in March, 1960, by New Jersey Senator Harrison Williams did urban interests embark on a course of action that was to produce changes in federal urban transportation policies. Yet this period is instructive for the light it sheds on the characteristic behavior of the various participants in federal-metropolitan politics. Moreover, as Part Three—which examines the politics of commuter aid during the fifteen months following the introduction of Senator Williams' bill—indicates, the factors which shaped these initial responses to federal involvement in the commuter issue continued to influence participation in the federal-metropolitan politics of mass transportation long after the original stimulus had disappeared.

CHAPTER IV

Suburbia: Remedialism and Localism

We all know that the closer we can spend a tax dollar to
the point it was raised by taxation, the better the value we
will get for it, and I think the same thing applies to the
regulation and setting of service for railroad passenger service. Since conditions vary so much between areas on a single
railroad, and within one state, I doubt if it is practical for
any Washington agency to get down to the grass-roots and
meet local needs.   MAYOR THOMAS TABER

Nowhere in metropolitan America is the impact of governmental
fragmentation on political values and behavior more striking
than in the suburbs.[1] Unlike the central city, which constitutes
a single political system, suburbia is fragmented into numerous
small units. As a result, suburban government is on a modest
scale, relatively simple in structure, and close to its citizens.
Within these small communities, public energies are focused
on local questions, particularly those dealing with the home and
the child, suburbia's overriding concerns. Consequently, the
prime issues at the urban grass roots are land-use controls, education, the property tax, and related local matters affecting the
environment and image of the suburban community.

Dedication to the maintenance of local control over the vital
parameters of community life commits most suburban units to
the preservation of the fragmented institutional status quo of the
metropolis. Opposition is almost automatic to entangling regional arrangements which imperil local self-determination,
threaten unequal costs and benefits, or imply "reunion . . . with
the central city and its corrupt politics, its slums, immigrants,
criminals, and various elements from which [the suburbanites]
had only recently escaped."[2] Inevitably, the narrow institutional

base and the political values of suburbia produce responses to metropolitan issues that are localistic and remedial, designed to serve particular community interests with minimum disturbance to existing governmental and fiscal arrangements. As will be seen, these factors also shape the suburban aspects of federal-metropolitan politics into a similar remedial and localistic pattern.

Another factor conditioning suburban-federal relations is the lack of involvement of the smaller units of the metropolis at the national level. Although the average suburbanite probably owns a home financed by a federally guaranteed mortgage, drives his car to work over a federally aided highway, and perhaps has his wastes processed at a federally assisted sewage-treatment plant, Washington is not recognized as a major factor in his political life. Preoccupation with local issues dims suburban interest in national politics. Affluent and thus heavily taxed suburbs are skeptical of federal assistance programs, often administered under need formulas, which do not return benefits commensurate with their costs to sububan taxpayers.

When the suburbs seek outside help, as in education, where demand constantly threatens to outrun the local tax base, or in emergencies, when outside assistance offers an alternative to institutional changes which might erode local independence, they usually are more favorably disposed to state assistance than to federal aid. The state is considered closer to home and thus more responsive to local needs than the distant leviathan in Washington. The vocal opposition of suburban conservatives to new federal spending programs creates negative attitudes toward national aid despite possible local benefits. The result, as Hacker notes in commenting on suburban diffidence toward congressional underrepresentation, is that suburbanites are "relatively unconcerned with the federal government's role in their continued existence."[3] As a consequence of this outlook, suburban involvement with the federal government is likely to be sporadic and crisis-oriented.

New York's Suburbs and the Commuter Problem

Commutation has been a particularly vexing problem for the

residential suburbs of the New York region. The interests of commuters, merchants, real estate brokers, and developers, as well as property owners in general, argued for strenuous local efforts to preserve suburban rail service. Yet the cherished suburban approach of unilateral local action offered no assurance that commuter service could be maintained. Viable plans to keep the trains running involved unpleasant proposals, such as drastically higher commutation fares, tax relief on rail properties, local subsidies, or regional instrumentalities empowered to levy taxes in which an individual suburb would have little influence. Since these alternatives were unpalatable, most of the region's local governments confined their activities to the rail line serving their own communities.

Involvement was normally stimulated by crisis, usually resulting from railroad proposals for fare increases and rarely persisting past the termination of the emergency. Limited resources and the narrow institutional base restricted suburban leaders to reiteration of the necessity of local rail service, sporadic pressures on state legislators and congressmen for help, and periodic appearances before regulatory bodies to defend the commuters' interest in lower rates and better service.

To enhance their limited capabilities, suburban governments created official and semi-official railroad service groups. The oldest of these was the Inter-Municipal Group for Better Rail Service (IMGBRS), founded in 1945 by the communities served by the Jersey Central. Through negotiations with the railroad and participation in the regulatory process, IMGBRS sought to preserve passenger service deemed vital by the member local governments. While the committee had some success in accommodating community and carrier interests, it lacked the means to tackle the Jersey Central's underlying problems. Subsidization and local tax relief were beyond the ken of IMGBRS, which made no financial demands on its members beyond assessments for its nominal administrative and legal expenses. In northern New Jersey, the long fight to save the West Shore prompted the creation of the quasi-official Bergen County Transit Committee, a group composed of both local government and commuter representatives. After the onset of the 1958 crisis, similar organizations were formed along other threatened rail lines. The most active of these was the Morris County Railroad Transportation Association, an official arm of county government.

Limited resources and capabilities also shaped the pre-crisis political behavior of suburbia's most direct beneficiaries of rail service, the commuters. While the average commuter has a strong interest in preserving and improving his means of transport to the city, he reacts to discomfort in typical consumer fashion with numerous complaints but negligible collective action. In 1958 fewer than 10 percent of the region's commuters belonged to one of its two dozen commuter groups. And less than 5 percent of these played an active role. Significantly, none of the commuter leaders came from the fairly large pool of suburban rail users who are influential in the business and political affairs of the region. Few of these busy men apparently attach sufficient importance to their daily journey to employ their influence for better rail service. Nor do the folkways of commuting encourage the face-to-face contacts and the intercommunication essential to grass-roots organization. Commuters on the same line "have very little in common with one another, except for a time-table and a powerful feeling of self-pity." [4] Those riding on different lines could be on separate continents as far as collective experience and action are concerned.

Commuter groups generally were organized in the wake of a crisis, such as an abandonment notice, a drastic fare increase, bankruptcy, or an accident. Organization was primitive and financing sporadic. Rarely were there more than two dozen active members, and a number of groups were one-man operations. Contributions and rank-and-file interest waned once the immediate threat had passed. The key problems of all the commuter groups were similar: obtaining relevant data to battle the railroads on fares and service, securing the services of a lawyer competent in rate and regulatory litigation, and raising funds to cover legal expenses.

Remedial activities preoccupied the local user groups. The railroads were berated for poor service, dishonest accounting, and an allegedly calculated policy of discouraging commuter traffic.

While each commuter group had its favorite solution, none possessed sufficient resources to promote it effectively. In their contests with the railroads, the commuters' allies were the suburban governments, local business groups, and the rail unions, who opposed service cuts in order to protect jobs. The alliance with the brotherhoods was uneasy, since most commuters were convinced that high labor costs and the inflexibility of the unions with respect to the elimination of unnecessary personnel were major causes of the passenger deficit.

Little in the behavior of the region's commuters during the pre-crisis period supports Wood's hypothesis that "The only identifiable metropolitan political community at present is likely to be found, in H. G. Wells' happy phrase, among the delocalized inhabitants, popularly known today as the commuters."[5] While New York's commuters perhaps formed an identifiable "political community," it was hardly "metropolitan" in outlook. Their focus was subregional, rarely extending beyond the particular railroad or branch on which they rode to work. Each of the commuter groups was organized along a single rail line; activities were universally keyed to the specific problems faced by this limited population of riders. There was relatively little effective coordination or cooperation among commuter groups. Periodic attempts at wider groupings failed because of the lack of perceived common problems and objectives among the commuter leadership.

Although suburbanites normally eschew involvement with the federal government, the preoccupation of grass-roots interests with commuter fares brought them into regulatory proceedings before the ICC throughout the postwar period. In fact, the suburban-ICC relationship was the only functioning federal-metropolitan channel on the commuter issue in the New York region prior to congressional consideration of the Transportation Act of 1958. Local groups unsuccessfully protesting rate increases before the ICC found the relationship unrewarding. Suburban leaders scored the Commission as pro-railroad, "constantly giving in to the railroad's demands."[6] Most resented was the failure of the ICC to check the fare spiral. One suburban spokesman, noting that ICC examiners always asked each commuter representative contesting fare hikes what his solution was, protested that "This is not a problem for the average man, the average commuter, to solve. Did not Congress create the ICC for this purpose?" [7]

Suburban exposure to the ICC had made federal regulatory reform the only grass-roots commuter rail objective at the national level in the pre-Transportation Act period. The IMGBRS sought changes in ICC policy throughout the postwar period.[8] In 1954 the New Jersey legislature asked Congress to revise the federal law to permit the ICC to attempt a solution of the commuter problem.[9] Local politicians took campaign potshots at the commission for its failure to hold down fares and maintain adequate service.[10] By 1957 commuter demands for regulatory changes were widespread. In New Jersey, a number of groups expressed the general suburban feeling when they wrote to Senator Clifford Case urging an investigation of the ICC because "commuters feel they stand no *chance at all* before [the] ICC." [11]

The Suburban Response to Crisis

A week after the announcement of the discontinuance of the West Shore and Erie ferries, Long Island commuter Nathan Klein, whose appearance earlier in the year before the Smathers subcommittee had done little to further the suburban cause, expressed the local reaction to this disturbing development. "There is nothing but trouble in the future for commuters under the new railroad bill," wrote Klein in a letter to the New York *Times.* "The swiftness with which the railroads have responded to the new bill calls for action at once by Congress to repeal it." [12] To the suburbanite, federal intervention had precipitated the crisis and threatened the continuation of vital local services. The immediate need was to remove this potent weapon from the railroads' hands. The result of this crisis-stimulated grass-roots concern with the federal role in rail commutation was the campaign to amend the Transportation Act of 1958—suburbia's chief contribution to the federal-metropolitan politics of mass transportation.

Because the source of their trouble appeared to come from Washington, commuters and local leaders turned to their congressmen for help. For the congressmen, it was the old story of constituents being threatened by federal action; their mandate was to try to help. As with most locally inspired remedial legislative efforts, such as campaigns to prevent the closing of a military base or to halt the construction of a highway or an airport, there was a marked tendency to focus completely on local interests and to ignore more general considerations. Parochial efforts of this sort usually obtain only very limited support outside the affected regions; the train-service campaign was no exception.

Initially, congressmen from the region sought assurances from the ICC that essential commuter services would not be discontinued. These efforts, however, had no effect on the rapidly deteriorating situation in New Jersey. After the Supreme Court's refusal to reopen the West Shore ferry case, regional congressmen, led by the New Jersey delegation, turned to legislation to provide relief for their beleaguered suburban constituents. On March 9, Senator Case, joined by all the region's senators except Williams of New Jersey, introduced a bill which replaced the train-service provisions of the 1958 law with procedures for passenger-train discontinuance similar to those in effect for line abandonments under the Transportation Act of 1920. Railroads seeking to eliminate passenger service or facilities were required to obtain affirmative authority from the ICC. The public was assured the right of appeal, and the burden of justifying discontinuance was placed on the carrier. Public hearings were made mandatory, and the four-month time limit on the ICC for investigation was abolished.[13] Considerations of political feasibility led Williams to offer legislation which sought only to remove the four-month time limit and to make ICC hearings mandatory in train-service cases.[14] Companion measures to both rail bills were introduced in the House of Representatives by a number of congressmen with suburban constituencies, primarily in New Jersey.

Local preoccupations restricted suburban interest in the federal train-service issue to those areas in New Jersey threatened by the abrupt termination of service. By spring Rockefeller's program had turned the New York suburbs to pleasanter thoughts than the end of rail service. Although the New Haven was soon to totter on the brink of financial collapse, Alpert had temporarily shelved his threats. As a result, discontinuance was not yet a sufficient danger in Connecticut to spark widespread public interest in amending the Transportation Act. While New Jersey was fighting to preserve service itself, Fairfield County's prime worries were untidy, tardy, and unsafe trains. Early in 1959, the Connecticut legislature asked the Public Utilities Commission to investigate the "serious deterioration of service and the large number of complaints of late and dirty trains." [15]

Because of the prolongation of the crisis in New Jersey, the June, 1959, hearings marked the high point of grass-roots interest and involvement in the federal side of the commuter issue. The prevailing sense of urgency prompted leaders of almost every major New Jersey commuter group and local governments transportation committee to testify or to insert statements.[16] Except for the commuters and the congressmen, no other regional actors —either state, city, or suburban—were represented.

In the absence of other metropolitan interests, the aggrieved New Jersey suburbs had the stage to themselves in Washington. As a result, this fragment of the metropolis set the tone of the hearings on the Case and Williams bills. With the normal grass-roots preoccupation with local matters heightened by the ongoing rail crisis, the tone, predictably, was one of remedialism and localism. Reciprocating the rest of the region's lack of interest in their plight, the New Jersey suburbanites largely ignored other sectors of the metropolitan area. For the most part, their attention was centered on the immediate problems of the railroads, and usually only on the one serving their own communities.

The suburban spokesmen argued that federal control over train service was inconsistent with the local solutions called for by Congress and the Administration. Reminding the Smathers subcommittee of its finding that the problem was essentially local, one commuter leader voiced a common suburban sentiment:

We appreciate your recognition of the fact that the problems confronting us are local. They are our problems and we are doing our best to solve them. We would be in a much better position to solve these problems if all our time were not taken up with continual battles and litigation with railroads which are attempting to discontinue the trains which we need and must retain.[17]

Few grass-roots leaders disagreed with Mayor Thomas Taber of Madison, founder of the Morris County Railroad Transportation Association, who believed that "the public interest . . . should first be established by local 'watchdog' committees, such as the county, municipal, and other organized and recognized commuter associations," which, after discussions with the railroads, would pass "their recommendations to the State utility commission, which could review and, if necessary, alter or amend them." [18] Given these views, the suburbanites found neither the Case nor the Williams bill very satisfactory. They preferred the outright elimination of the discontinuance provision and congressional action to whittle down ICC powers to regulate commuter fares. Much of their testimony was devoted to cataloguing the alleged bias, unfairness, and injustice suffered by New Jersey commuters at the hands of the ICC.

Among the New Jersey suburban interests represented at the hearings, there was little interest in positive federal action to help preserve commuter rail service. Some emphasized that financial assistance and tax relief were "purely state matters," others the need for action by the Port Authority, which had "refused . . . to take a single concrete step to solve a problem that is a matter of concern to the port of New York." [19] The question of federal responsibilities for mass transportation was left unanswered by the suburbanites, who perceived their difficulties almost completely in a local commuter railroad rather than a metropolitan mass transportation frame of reference.

Because of their railroad perspective, suburban thoughts ran along the lines of bolstering the individual carrier's financial position, of internal railroad reform, and of the necessity to preserve private enterprise on the rails. Such views reflected the prevailing values of suburbia. Mayor Wagner's urban-oriented idea of a regional mass transportation system, publicly controlled and perhaps federally assisted, did not. Since the grass roots focused on the railroad rather than on the urban aspects of the problem, they emphasized that the commuter rail situation could be improved measurably by more beneficial federal railroad policies. Thus, although commuters and the Eastern carriers were bitterly opposed over the issue of federal regulation, they tended to see eye to eye on the need for the elimination of subsidies to competing modes of transportation, for a maximization of the railroad's role in mail-carrying at equitable rates, and for federal action to insure adequate rail passenger facilities for national defense purposes.[20]

National Politics and Suburban Interests

From the beginning, suburbia's weakness in the national political arena burdened the campaign to amend the Transportation Act. The localism, narrow objectives, and commuter railroad focus of the New Jersey grass roots left the suburbs with few influential allies and many powerful antagonists. In the New York region, as the next two chapters indicate, differing perceptions of the problem and objectives led the states and the central cities to ignore the crisis-stimulated efforts of the suburbanites and their congressmen. Since rail commutation is limited to a few metropolitan areas and the suburbs failed to frame the issue in terms of general mass transportation needs, the train-service campaign drew little support from other urban areas. Of the central cities with an interest in rail transport, only Philadelphia and Milwaukee endorsed the legislation. Aside from Senator Clark, a former mayor of Philadelphia, and California's Senator Thomas Kuchel, urban congressional support from outside the region was not forthcoming. In addition, a handful of states seeking a return to the pre-1958 passenger-train regulatory situation of state control favored the pending legislation.

Also damaging the suburbs' cause was a failure to mobilize potential resources. The lack of national organizations defending the interests of suburbanites contributed to the localization of support, as did the absence of any groups in Washington dedicated to protecting the interests of public transportation users or railroad passengers. The NACO, which aspired to be the voice of suburbia in Washington, concentrated its transportation energies on highways and took no position on the train-service issue, which was of interest to only a small minority of the nation's suburbanites. Within the New York region, the crisis orientation of local involvement limited grass-roots participation to the threatened areas in New Jersey. And even here, the suburban leaders were unable to employ the latent political influence of commuters who possessed direct channels to congressional and Administration leaders. This failure resulted from the political naïveté of the commuter leadership and its isolation from influential commuters.

As a result of the suburbs' restricted resources, lack of lobbyists, limited contacts with federal officialdom, and infrequent involvement in issues at the national level, the channels on the train-service question were simple and direct—grass roots to Congress—and appear typical of the federal-suburban relationship. Lacking alternative means of access, the durable and traditional congressional channel served as the suburbs' main pathway for information and influence.

Although the commuter leaders were influential in setting the tone of the dialogue in Washington in 1959, their limited capabilities prevented them from playing a significant role in the events that followed. When it came to preparing legislation and securing support in Congress, the superior legal and lobbying resources of railroad labor, the suburbs' chief allies on the train-service issue, were far more valuable to the congressmen than the underfinanced and understaffed efforts of their suburban constituents.

Railroad labor's interest in protecting jobs led it to join the New Jersey commuters in seeking changes in the Transportation Act of 1958. The brotherhoods opened their campaign in January, when twenty-three railway unions announced a fight against "unjustified" discontinuances of passenger service. Throughout the commuter crisis railroad labor criticized Congress, the ICC, and the railroads for neglecting the public interest in continued passenger service. For example, on the day the train-service hearings opened, the unions wrote to Governors Rockefeller, Ribicoff, and Meyner and Mayor Wagner charging the railroads with deliberately ruining their passenger business. A week later the Brotherhood of Locomotive Firemen and Engineers claimed that all the New York area railroads except the Long Island were following a calculated policy of discouraging commuters with poor service, filth, and safety hazards.[21]

At the hearings, the RLEA offered to present the public's case for continued passenger service because of "the nonexistence of any nation-wide passenger groups or civic associations which have as a particular function the presentation of the national effect of section 13a on the members and the immediate need for curative legislation."[22] But railroad labor's interests were hardly altruistic. The Case bill was written in large part by an RLEA attorney, and it gave the rail unions procedures in discontinuance similar to those in effect for abandonments. The Supreme Court had ruled that the ICC could condition its approval in proceedings which required certification of carrier actions, as did abandonments under the Transportation Act of 1920.[23] At the discretion of the ICC, such conditions might also include employee protection provisions. While extraneous to the continuation of commuter service, the employment issue motivated the strong support that railroad labor gave the Case bill at the hearings.

Labor's participation was a mixed blessing. Job security, the unions' prime concern, obscured the urban aspects of the train-service issue. Many congressmen from metropolitan areas, including some from New York, viewed the Case bill as an episode in the perennial tussle between the railroads and the brotherhoods. These demands also exacerbated the opposition to change in the Transportation Act in Congress, the Administration, the railroad industry, shipper groups, and business associations. Led by Senator Smathers, this alliance easily bested the far weaker suburban–railroad labor bloc, a defeat which illustrates a key feature of the federal-metropolitan political process: issues are decided by the interplay of national rather than local or metropolitan factors.

Leading the national grouping opposed to the train-service bills were the railroads. Executives of the AAR and of a number of carriers, most of them with suburban services,[24] defended the discontinuance procedures in the 1958 act as fair, equitable, and absolutely essential to the survival of the rail industry. They emphasized that the train-service provision was having the very effect on the states and local communities that the Smathers subcommittee intended it to have: after years of inaction New York and New Jersey were finally coming to grips with their commuter rail problems.

The commerce nexus of the ICC, the Department of Commerce, and the Commerce Committees held firm in defense of the principle of federal control over interstate passenger service. Support for minor changes in the Transportation Act came from both the ICC and the Department of Commerce. On the basis of its experience in administering the law, the ICC recommended increased time limits and placement of the burden of proof on the carriers. The Commission opposed mandatory hearings, however, claiming that suburban criticism of ICC procedures based on the exceptional West Shore case was unfounded. Commissioner Anthony Arpaia explained that the Transportation Act requirement that the public convenience and necessity be considered was an ample safeguard of the public interest.[25] Procedural changes were acceptable to the Commerce Department as long as they did not "further delay the granting of relief from the operation of unprofitable trains or ferries." [26]

Most important for the fate of the train-service amendments were the views of Senator Smathers. He and his colleagues were sympathetic to the personal plight of the commuter and to the constituency pressures on the suburban congressmen. In an article which appeared after the hearings, Smathers termed the commuter "long-suffering" and characterized suburban rail service as essential.[27] But nothing that happened in 1959 convinced Smathers or a majority of the subcommittee that substantive changes were needed in the Transportation Act. When the urban senators launched their effort, Smathers announced that he did not "believe the answer to the problem . . . will be to pass the stopgap bill which they have introduced today." [28] During the hearings he repeatedly expressed satisfaction with the working of the discontinuance section, claiming that it enabled the ICC to protect the public and the national interest in maintaining a healthy railroad industry. Only with respect to the time limits did Smathers see any possibility of altering the Transportation Act of 1958.

Like the commuters, Smathers and his colleagues perceived the suburban rail question almost entirely in railroad terms, evidencing little interest in metropolitan transportation. Unlike the suburbanites, however, the subcommittee was interested primarily in the economic health of the railroad industry rather than the preservation of suburban service. Commutation was a railroad liability before it was an essential public service. Also, like the commuter leaders, Smathers believed the problem must be solved at the local level. But again the difference was crucial. The subcommittee wanted national regulation to insure that local solutions would be forthcoming and would not burden interstate commerce. Commuters and their representatives sought local regulation to deter the railroads from eliminating their means of transport. "Railroad orientation" and "grass-roots solution" thus had quite different meanings to the two major participants on the train-service issue.

In the hope of getting some protection against abrupt termination of rail service for their suburban constituents, senators from the New York region, led by Case, sought a compromise. To mute the opposition provoked by what they now called the extraneous issue of job protection, the certification procedures favored by the rail unions were dropped. But without the support of labor, which had no interest in a bill that would not safeguard passenger-train employees, Case and his colleagues were unable to force Smathers' hand; and no changes were made in the Transportation Act in 1959.

The Passenger-Service Issue Fades

Few suburbanites shed tears over the death of the train-service amendments in the Smathers subcommittee. Crisis alone had

brought the grass roots to Washington; by September, 1959, the
emergency was over, and the New Jersey suburbs were paying
little attention to Senator Case's futile efforts on their behalf. Instead, the various suburban groups turned to more immediate
tasks. Top priority went to the November election, when the
state would pass judgment on Governor Meyner's plan to use
the surpluses of the New Jersey Turnpike Authority to subsidize
mass transportation programs. Although there was some grum-
bling about the failure to involve the Port Authority, most of the
local rail leaders joined the railroads, bus lines, civic groups, and
the RPA in support of the proposal. But the opposition, led by
Hudson County leaders fearful over the possible loss of taxes on
rail properties, the New Jersey automobile clubs and other highway interests, and organized labor, was too strong and prevailed
in the referendum by a four-to-three margin.

The stage appeared set for another commuter crisis. Governor
Meyner's pessimistic public statements on the suburban rail issue
were reminiscent of the previous winter. For example, in February, 1960, he spread gloom in the suburbs with an announcement
that the railroads could expect no aid, since the commuters had
failed to convince the public of their needs in the November
referendum.[29] Commuter discontent rose as fares went up around
the region. In October, the Erie increased rates 15 percent. Two
months later Long Island fares were raised 4.3 percent. February
brought a 28 percent hike on the Pennsylvania and a 10 percent
boost on the New Haven. However, although the Erie continued
to discontinue off-peak trains throughout the winter and the
Susquehanna sought permission in December to terminate all its
passenger service, the major New Jersey railroads, looking ex-
pectantly toward Trenton for another proposal, had not revived
their threats to terminate all service. But the situation was
charged with uncertainty, since no one knew how long the railroads would wait.

At the same time, a major crisis was brewing on the New
Haven, whose position deteriorated in the fall of 1959 despite
some benefits from Governor Rockefeller's tax relief program. At
the beginning of October, New Haven president Alpert an-

nounced that unless the road was granted fare hikes to eliminate
its $5-million passenger deficit, he would be forced to employ the
Transportation Act to discontinue the New York commuter operation. In January Alpert said that the alternatives to $8.4 mil-
lion in federal, state, and local subsidies and tax relief were a 70
percent fare increase or the abandonment of the service under
the provisions of the Transportation Act of 1958.[30]

Despite the tense situation in New Jersey and the fact that
communities along the New Haven, according to Westchester
County Executive Edwin Michaelian, were "faced with a specter
of complete and irrevocable discontinuance of service," [31] the
events of the previous year were not repeated. In 1960, the suburbs failed to turn en masse to their congressmen for help. One
reason was their dismal experience with the Smathers subcommittee, which did not appear likely to change its position on the
commuter question. Of greater significance was that after a year
of living with the situation created by the Transportation Act,
Smathers' law was less fearsome than in the days of its initial
impact. Despite the threats and the strain, suburbanites still had
most of their rush-hour commuter trains.

Most important, however, in explaining the dormant suburban
interest in the federal aspects of the issue was the new climate in
the region with respect to governmental action. New York's actions and New Jersey's search for a formula to preserve essential
service removed the cloud of uncertainty which had sent suburbanites scurrying to Washington in 1959. Now that state action
was expected, the federal government's role became unimportant.
Despite the surface pessimism in New Jersey, by the time hearings on the new train-service legislation opened in early March,
it was reliably reported that Trenton had a new plan. The previous month, hopes of New Haven riders were buoyed when
Chairman Eugene Loughlin of the Connecticut Public Utilities
Commission announced that he felt "confident that if the [New
Haven] demonstrated that it had no other course than to stop
service, then responsible governmental officials would step in and
come up with some solution." [32]

The anticipated moves to avert another commuter crisis materialized quickly. In March the ICC guaranteed the first of a series of loans to the New Haven, which postponed the railroad's financial collapse for more than a year, while the following month New Jersey Highway Commissioner Dwight Palmer announced that the Division of Railroad Transportation would contract with the commuter railroads for the subsidization of suburban services deemed essential by the state.

In the absence of an atmosphere of crisis, the suburbs largely ignored efforts in 1960 to change the passenger-train provisions of the Transportation Act. Only Taber of the Morris County group made the trip to Washington to "plead for the governing bodies of the many suburban municipalities which are dependent on their reliable railroads for safe transportation to and from the metropolitan area." [33] Although a few congressmen from the region co-sponsored the train-service bill of 1960, amending the Transportation Act was now clearly a railroad union rather than a suburban enterprise. Administration opposition and Smathers' continued hostility killed the Passenger Train Service Act of 1960 in committee. With it died the major suburban effort on the mass transportation issue at the federal level.

The passenger-service campaign was a product of suburban discontent with the Transportation Act of 1958. Suburban interest in Washington was a function of federal involvement in a crisis situation. When the railroads employed the Transportation Act to threaten or carry out service cuts, pressures were exerted on the region's congressmen for help. Once state initiative eased the grass roots' anxiety over their commuter trains—or, as happened on the West Shore, when a *fait accompli* faded into the past—suburban interest in the federal government's role evaporated. Neither the train-service issue nor the suburbanites played an important role in the federal-metropolitan politics of mass transportation in 1960 and 1961. Nor, as the next three chapters indicate, did the commuters show much interest in efforts launched during 1959 by the states, central cities, and regional congressmen on other federal aspects of the commuter rail issue.

CHAPTER V

The States: A Wary Eye on Washington

There is no greater challenge in our age to the inventive-
ness of the federal idea than the surging tide of urbanism.
And here—while all three levels of government in the
United States are necessarily involved—the states have a
crucial role. Regrettably, they are only now coming to
recognize it.   GOVERNOR NELSON ROCKEFELLER

Metropolitan development poses formidable challenges to state
government. The states are the legal masters and traditional over-
seers of local government in the United States. Political considerations impel the states, particularly their chief executives, to
tackle metropolitan problems. The governors of urbanized states
are among the most visible and influential participants in regional politics. Only at great risk does the metropolitan governor
ignore the needs and demands of his urban constituency. As a result, concludes Wallace Sayre,

The governor, like the president, is an asset of urban America. Urban
influence is great in his nomination and election in every urban state;
he cannot escape his urban commitments at home, and if he aspires
to the presidency he cannot afford even the inevitable wish to escape.[1]

Yet many of the states have been reluctant or unable to meet
the challenges of urban society. Rurally dominated state legislatures, competing demands on chronically overburdened fiscal systems, and the lack of capabilities for dealing with complex metropolitan questions hinder state efforts. During the depression
the failure of almost all the states to meet urban needs turned
the cities to Washington for assistance. Direct federal aid to the
local governments has not been welcomed at most statehouses.

State influence in local affairs is decreased and local dependence upon the states weakened by relations between the state's subdivisions and Washington which bypass the state capital. One response has been state efforts to block direct federal aid. Most of the states with large metropolitan areas, however, have realized that they cannot retain urban allegiances with purely negative reactions to the pressing problems which turn their local subdivisions to Washington.

More common have been state efforts to retain the upper hand in intergovernmental relations by having federal aid for urban areas channeled through the states. From the states' point of view, the highway program offers the ideal format for federal aid. The rural origins of national highway assistance led to a close relationship between the federal roads agency and the state highway departments, in which the latter were senior partners, long before Washington became involved in urban road-building. As a result, the cities receive no direct federal aid highway funds, and local officials and interests play a far less important role in relations with the federal government on highways than they do in direct federal-local programs such as urban renewal, public housing, or hospital construction. The subordinate position of the cities in the development and implementation of highway policy explains a good deal of the urban dissatisfaction with the federal highway program and the cities' opposition to its use as a prototype for other federal ventures in metropolitan areas.

Finally, the availability of the national government as a source of direct assistance to the cities, as well, of course, as pressures from the cities and suburbs, have prompted the urban states to undertake a rapidly growing list of responsibilities in metropolitan areas. This development, however, increases rather than decreases the conflicts and complexities inherent in the triangular federal-state-local relationship. State assistance, however welcome, is not likely to deter the cities from their profitable relationship with the national government. Instead, a competitive situation is produced, since, as Sayre and Kaufman note, "It seems inevitable that cities will call for more direct federal aid in the hope that they can thus extract compromises from their increasingly anxious states, or perhaps get help from Washington, or both." [2]

The context of state involvement in urban problems also keeps the larger local units looking toward Washington. No matter how urban-oriented the governor or how desirous he may be of shortcutting (or supplementing) federal assistance with state programs, like all metropolitan actors he perceives regional issues in a frame of reference strongly conditioned by his institutional base. Although his problems may be largely urban and his debt to metropolitan constituencies great, the governor is a state official. His public image, party role, and political reputation depend fundamentally upon his ability to obtain results in the state arena. To deal effectively with the state legislature, which is almost always less responsive to urban needs, the governor must place the interests of the state above those of its local subdivisions. Nor can he neglect the nonmetropolitan remainder of his constituency, particularly since malapportionment usually gives it considerably more legislative influence than mere numbers would warrant.

Consequently, the governor must deal with metropolitan problems in state terms. Wood emphasizes this point in his conclusions on metropolitan northern New Jersey's search for new sources of water in the 1950s:

In New Jersey, the halfway house of state government had to deal with an emerging water shortage in essentially non-Regional terms. People outside the New York Metropolitan Region made the key decisions; an electorate [the entire state] much broader than the Region delivered the final approval.[3]

Since the governor is an urban asset in terms of this state frame of reference and since the cities rarely fare well in the state political arena, the mayors have strong reasons to maintain their political friendships in the nation's capital.

Fiscal problems also condition the state's role in intergovernmental politics. As long as metropolitan governors are unable or unwilling to raise sufficient taxes from a reluctant electorate to meet the burgeoning requirements of their urban constituents, federal aid will continue to be attractive to the cities and not without appeal to some hardpressed governors, who, of course, hope that the aid will be channeled through the statehouse.

The interplay of all these factors—state power, the gubernatorial constituency, the threat of direct federal-local relations, the statewide institutional base, and the fiscal and rural restraints on state action—underlie the characteristic behavior of the states in federal-metropolitan politics. The remainder of this chapter examines their effect on the political strategies of the states of the New York region once the federal government became an active participant in the area's commuter politics.

The States and the Crisis

Vast powers over their local subdivisions, relatively wide territorial jurisdictions (compared with any of the region's local governments), and superior fiscal resources provide the states with considerable capabilities for action on the transportation problems of the New York region. The state highway departments and the state-created and -controlled toll authorities (the New York City Triborough Bridge and Tunnel Authority is an exception) are the dominant participants in the region's transportation politics. State regulatory commissions help to determine rates and standards for the common carriers serving the region. Railroad taxation is subject to control by the state legislatures. In addition, state law prohibits the New York City Transit Authority from incurring an operating deficit, as well as stipulating that the governor of New York appoint one of the authority's three members. Finally, any significant change in the decisional or financial system for transportation in the region requires state approval, as did the MRTC proposals, which were accepted in Albany but rejected in Trenton.

Despite this impressive potential for action on the commuter rail problem, the states, like the federal government, had not ventured beyond their customary regulatory role in the years before the commuter crisis. Nor were they particularly anxious to get involved in expensive alternatives to the traditional system of private operation of suburban rail lines. Only after a prolonged crisis did New York State join with New York City and other local governments in 1954 to provide tax relief to insure the continuation of commuter service on Long Island. In the same year, joint action by New York and New Jersey created the MRTC. For four years, the MRTC diverted attention away from the states' responsibilities for preservation of rail service in the region. When the MRTC's recommendations faltered in New Jersey in 1958, pressures for state action to forestall an emergency mounted. But Governors Harriman and Meyner resisted, arguing that budgetary constraints made commuter railroad tax relief, much less state subsidies, a fiscal impossibility. Action to head off the commuter crisis was limited to the efforts of Harriman and Feinberg to alter the Transportation Act's train-service provisions and New Jersey's unsuccessful court action in the West Shore ferry case.

With the emergency commenced stronger and more urgent pressures for state action. Solutions to the commuter problem clearly were beyond the capabilities and jurisdiction of the localities. Despite the endorsement of a locally controlled tri-state instrumentality by New York City and the MRC, the MRTC experience indicated that the fear of regional ventures and unequal costs and benefits was greater than the desire to preserve commuter service. Besides, there was not time to negotiate an acceptable regional arrangement. Amending the Transportation Act would not come to grips with the underlying problems of the commuter railroads. And federal aid, little more than a big-city dream at the time, could not overcome the immediate difficulty. Thus, the burden of ending the crisis came to rest on the states.

Of the region's governors, only Rockefeller, elected three months after the enactment of the Transportation Act, viewed the commuter crisis as an opportunity for state leadership in metropolitan affairs. As the February, 1959, meeting indicated, the chief concern of Governor Ribicoff was to limit Connecticut's liability to those measures necessary to insure the continuation of rail service in Fairfield County. Governor Meyner, haunted by fiscal problems, clung to his precrisis policy of minimizing New Jersey's role in stabilizing the commuter situation, while suggesting that the preservation of suburban service was primarily a railroad, a tri-state, or a federal responsibility. Rockefeller, on the other hand, welcomed the opportunity to deal with a crisis. The governor advocated immediate state action to end the emergency. Such initiative, he emphasized at the February meeting, should be based on the efforts of individual states rather than those of the region as a whole. Where necessary, as with the trans-Hudson problem, cooperation should be between the two states involved rather than among the local governments as proposed by the MRTC.

Rockefeller's position on the commuter issue was a natural product of his institutional base and his political ambitions. Assuming his first elected post with well-publicized presidential aspirations, Rockefeller was eager to build a reputation as a successful and decisive political leader. Obviously, the main arena in which to accomplish this objective was New York State. What better way to maximize his political exposure than to assert state responsibility for a knotty problem like the commuter rail question, which had defied solution for decades? Moreover, Rockefeller had strong views on the need for competent and activist state governments. His plans for capturing the 1960 Republican presidential nomination called for putting these ideas to work. Conservative skepticism about Rockefeller's liberalism could be put to rest by having the Governor underscore his devotion to state prerogatives in comparison with the Democrats, who, he claimed, looked to Washington for the answers to all domestic problems.

Rockefeller made it clear, however, that the states could play a meaningful role in an urban society only if their outlook was positive, as he intended New York's to be. And he said three years later in his Godkin Lectures at Harvard, "The preservation of states' rights depends on the exercise of states' responsibilities." Therefore, the states "must fully awaken to—and act on—their responsibilities and opportunities." [4] Rockefeller's aim upon taking office in January, 1959, was to demonstrate how this could be done, and the commuter problem was one of his first opportunities.

In capitalizing on this opportunity, a commuter railroad policy emerged which reflected the state's stakes and capabilities far more than it did the region's needs. To maximize the Governor's ability to undertake speedy and effective action, the program recommended by transportation adviser Robert Purcell, a Rockefeller business associate and former vice-president of the Chesapeake & Ohio Railway Co., concentrated on the suburban rail problem in New York. Making this unilateral state approach politically feasible, of course, was the absence of large numbers of interstate commuters in Rockefeller's constituency. Maintenance of New York's freedom of action and avoidance of heavy drains on the state budget were paramount in Purcell's mind when he recommended against entangling regional arrangements which threatened to involve New York in New Jersey's more expensive suburban rail problems. The heart of the proposal was an improvement program that involved relatively little cost to the state, since it called for financial help for the railroads through local tax relief and a Port Authority-administered program under which repayable state funds would be used to purchase new commuter cars for lease to the railroads.[5]

Later there would be complaints that New York's program and that of New Jersey, which followed it by a year, were stop-gaps which, according to the RPA, failed to "do much to promote a future system that would be less costly to operate and would handle increased volume with better service." [6] And New York City's planners would argue that tackling the problem on a unilateral state basis resulted in "well-intentioned but conflicting programs which are threatening to prevent the formulation of a rational transportation policy." [7] But in the midst of the emergency in early 1959 immediate political considerations predominated. For the crisis-stimulated public in the suburbs, it was a local commuter railroad problem rather than one of regional mass transportation. Long-range implications were of little interest as long as the trains were kept running. Moreover, in Rockefeller's constituency, no one was upset because the program concentrated on the suburban rail problem in New York State.

Nor did the Governor and his aides have any reason to be unhappy over the course of action they had chosen. To the accompaniment of a chorus of praise for his decisive leadership, Rockefeller speedily terminated the commuter crisis in New York through the exercise of state power. Before the end of March, the legislature had authorized $1.5 million in local tax relief on railroad properties (to be increased tenfold by 1963), a $100-million referendum for the commuter car program (plus a $20-million loan to finance the purchase of new equipment in the interim before the electorate could vote on the required constitutional amendment in 1961), the creation of a state transportation office, and the establishment of a bi-state agency to coordinate the commuter rail programs administered in Albany and Trenton.

Rockefeller and the Federal Government

Washington did not loom large in Governor Rockefeller's conception of the suburban rail problem. One of the reasons he moved swiftly to end the commuter crisis was his conviction that state inaction on urban problems created a vacuum which the federal government inevitably filled. He regarded "federal-local action bypassing the states" as an "ever-present danger" because it was a "giant step toward unitary, monolithic government." [8] Rockefeller's fear of direct federal-local activities led him to undercut Mayor Wagner's suggestion that the February conference endorse federal aid for commuter railroads. A week before the meeting he insisted that the time was past "for calling on Washington or someone else to solve the problem." [9] Although numerous urban leaders were attracted to the federal aid idea during 1959, Rockefeller did not change his mind. In February, 1960, he declined an invitation to join a group composed of mayors, railroad presidents, and Pennsylvania's Governor David Lawrence in an attempt to persuade congressional and Administration leaders to support federal mass transportation loans.[10]

Rockefeller's distaste for involvement with Washington extended to the campaign for a train-service amendment. In failing to offer encouragement to the efforts of the New Jersey congressmen and their suburban constitutents, he ignored the advice of the New York Public Service Commission. Two weeks before the February, 1959, session, the NYPSC termed the discontinuance provision an "all pervading sword of Damocles." After registering its shock at the ICC's handling of the West Shore ferry case, the NYPSC called for amendment of the law or "marked caution" in its administration. The commissioners believed that, without an immediate change in the situation, "Any State and local governmental assistance which might conceivably be extended to the industry pales into insignificance and perforce becomes the essence of futility." [11]

Rockefeller and his advisers did not concur, since they were convinced that state and local action programs would nullify the effect of the 1958 act. Besides, in New York only those commuters who used the New Haven were threatened by the interstate discontinuance provisions. As a result, the train-service provisions were not on the agenda at the February meeting. In his report to the Governor, Purcell ignored the Transportation Act, except to note that it served to translate the railroads' continuing financial emergency into a "service crisis for the people." [12] By the time the hearings on the passenger-service bills opened in Washington, the commuter crisis was a fading memory in New York State. Despite an invitation from Senator Javits, no one from Albany made an appearance before or submitted a statement to the Smathers subcommittee.

New York's lack of interest in both federal aid and the discontinuance measures was apparent in a set of proposals for federal action to help preserve passenger service developed by Rockefeller's aides. Announced during the train-service hearings by the New York Congressional Steering Committee, the program did not mention federal assistance, the Transportation Act, or the legislation pending before the Smathers subcommittee. Instead Rockefeller called for the exemption of federal taxation of railroad income derived from state and local tax relief, elimination of the 10 percent federal excise tax on railroad passenger fares, greater military use of passenger trains, and interrailroad agreements to cut duplicating services.[13] Designed to facilitate the state's program and to avoid direct federal involvement with the suburban railroad problem, these suggestions reflected the limited

nature of Rockefeller's federal level commuter rail objectives and
the focus on railroads rather than mass transportation in New
York's approach.

Among these proposals, Albany assigned the highest priority
to legislation to exempt tax relief savings from the 52 percent
federal corporate income taxes. Without such action, aid to
commuter railroads operating at a net profit would provide only
48 cents of help per dollar of tax relief or subsidy. Recognition
of this problem had led the Smathers subcommittee to suggest
in 1958 that, in the event of state and local tax relief, "The Federal Government should likewise give a proportionate remit-
tance of Federal income taxes to allow the amount of such local
and state tax reductions to be retained by the railroads." [14]

At the time of the passage of the Transportation Act, Senator
Javits of New York introduced legislation to prevent tax relief
assistance from being absorbed by increased federal taxes too late
for action in the Eighty-fifth Congress. Reintroduced in 1959, the
measure was supported by Mayor Wagner, the NYPSC, Governor
Rockefeller, and the New York Congressional Steering Committee. Despite the unanimity in New York, the Javits bill ran into
trouble in Washington. The Eisenhower Administration, which
normally extolled the virtues of state and local initiative and
federal facilitation of such activities, refused to support the measure because it would decrease federal tax revenues, and it died
in committee.

Rockefeller was no more successful in 1959 with his other
federal tax objective: elimination of the 10 percent excise levy
on rail passenger travel. Although the tax did not apply to regular commutation tickets, it was included in other suburban fares.
Repeal, the Governor argued, would help relieve pressure for commuter service cuts through higher general passenger revenues or
increased ridership. Although Rockefeller was supported by the
railroads, Mayor Wagner, the New York delegation, and some
New Jersey congressmen, the proposal attracted little attention
during 1959. Not until 1962 did Congress, on the recommendation of President Kennedy, eliminate the tax on passenger tickets.

Only on the establishment of a bi-state transportation agency to coordinate policies with New Jersey, which required an inter-state compact and congressional approval, did Rockefeller receive any satisfaction in his dealings with Washington in 1959. That spring New Jersey acceded to New York's proposal for a state-controlled bi-state new agency headed by the chiefs of the state railroad transportation offices, responsible only to the governors, and with no local representation. State officials took the lead in securing congressional approval of the New York–New Jersey Transportation Agency (NY-NJTA) compact. Enabling legislation was drafted by state officials and presented to members of the state delegations for introduction. As with all the state relations with Washington on the commuter issue during 1959, the channels were direct, from statehouse to Congress. All four senators and a number of representatives from the region sponsored the compact bill. Aside from the congressmen, the governors and their aides were the only regional actors to take an interest in the proposal.

In spite of the preeminent role of state figures, indirect regional pressures played a part in shaping the final version of the bi-state compact. One of the objectives of the growing anti-Port Authority alliance was a congressional investigation of the PNYA's failure to assume a share of the responsibility for commuter rail operations in the region. Early in 1959 a number of New Jersey congressmen queried Representative Emanuel Celler, chairman of the House Judiciary Committee, about the possibilities of an investigation of the Port Authority. Celler, who had been at odds with the Authority for a number of years over his contention that Congress had the right to oversee the operations and pass on changes in the powers of agencies created by interstate compacts, was unable to drum up support within his committee for an investigation of the Authority in 1959; but he did insist that the NY-NJTA compact be amended to provide for congressional clearance of any augmentation of the power of the NY-NJTA, congressional access to all its records, and congressional approval of any long-range plans prepared by the NY-NJTA and adopted by concurrent legislation of the compacting states.[15]

Thus, regional concern, growing out of the campaign for a

Port Authority commuter rail responsibility, indirectly altered Albany's handiwork, upgraded the federal role from passive approval to potential active supervision of the new bi-state transit agency, and illustrated again for Rockefeller and his aides the perils of pursuing his commuter railroad objectives at the federal level.

Trenton and Washington

Governor Meyner's perspective on the commuter problem differed significantly from that of his colleague across the Hudson. In office since 1954, Meyner did not see the crisis as an opportunity to bolster his image. Instead it was another potential burden on New Jersey's already overloaded fiscal system. A unilateral state approach was without appeal, since most of the region's interstate commuters lived in New Jersey. Insuring their access to Manhattan was by far the most expensive aspect of the regional mass transportation problem. Meyner was not anxious to seek New Jersey's first broad-based tax, especially for a service used by less than 5 percent of the state's population. Nor was Rockefeller's happy alternative of local tax relief available to Meyner, since the lion's share of New Jersey's rail taxes went to local communities in Hudson County, a pillar of the Governor's Democratic Party.

Lack of confidence about New Jersey's ability to resolve the crisis made Meyner far more receptive to the idea of outside assistance than Rockefeller had been. In addition, as a Democrat Meyner did not share all Rockefeller's qualms about the perils of federal aid bypassing the states, particularly if such assistance would relieve the state of what might otherwise be an expensive responsibility. And if New Jersey had to assume a fiscal role, which became unavoidable after Rockefeller dashed all hopes for a regional approach in February, Meyner had no hesitation about reducing the state's burden with some federal-state commuter rail assistance.

New Jersey's interest in federal aid dated to the precrisis period,

As the clouds darkened on the commuter horizon in the spring of 1958, the possibility of the Smathers subcommittee considering federal financial help for the suburban railroads was explored with members of the New Jersey congressional delegation. Meyner's counsel, Vincent Biunno, argued that the unique interstate nature of the problem in the New York metropolitan region required a positive national role. After some inquiries, the congressmen advised Trenton that federal aid would not be recommended by Smathers and his colleagues nor supported by the Administration. From then on, although Meyner continued to call for federal assistance, especially when the New Jersey commuter situation turned bleak, he entertained few illusions about the probability of help materializing in Washington. As a result, Trenton's political investment in the federal aid cause was light.

The immediate effect of the Transportation Act was a surge of interest in federal aid in New Jersey. Momentarily forgetting their local preoccupations, worried commuter groups called on Governor Meyner to give "very serious consideration . . . to State or Federal subsidy." [16] On the day after the death of the MRTC proposal in the New Jersey legislature, Meyner called for federal aid, claiming that "This is as much a problem of the Federal Government as it is of New Jersey or New York. If we are going to keep the railroads moving the Federal Government has got to participate." [17]

Throughout 1959 Meyner periodically reiterated his support for some positive action on the part of the national government. At the February meeting, he endorsed federal assistance. During the turnpike referendum campaign, he declared that New Jersey could not solve all the problems of the passenger railroads and that the federal government must play a financial role.

The defeat of the turnpike plan convinced Meyner that the federal government would have to enter the picture. His 1960 annual message called for national commuter rail aid similar to that given highways. On television the following week, in conjunction with his campaign for the return of the federal telephone tax to the states, Meyner stressed that the national government would have to help the states if it was going to monopolize revenue sources.[18] However, because of his pessimism about the political feasibility of federal aid, Meyner was content to publicize his views and let it go at that. No legislation was prepared, nor did he seek to have New Jersey's congressmen act on his suggestions. Support was neither solicited nor received from New Jersey's sister states.

As with federal aid, Meyner thought changes in the Transportation Act of 1958 to be in New Jersey's interests, but not worth the expenditure of any political capital. Prior to the rejection of the turnpike referendum, he had been content to remain aloof and let the state's congressmen fight the train-service battle. After the referendum defeat Meyner announced that he planned to work closely with both senators "in pressing for amendments to the Federal Transportation Act of 1958" because its provisions on train service gave too little consideration to the commuter and to the general public.[19] As was his practice on suburban rail ventures involving Washington, however, the Governor failed to follow up his words with action.

Meyner was unwilling to invest time and effort in federal aid or the train-service issues because Trenton realized that the prospects for success were slim. Moreover, with respect to the Transportation Act, after seeing how quickly New York's program had ended the emergency and how fast the Lackawanna and Jersey Central Railroads had shelved their threats once the initial promise of state aid had been made in mid-1959, Meyner's transportation advisers ceased to share the worry of the congressmen and the commuters that service might disappear before positive measures were implemented. Despite the defeat of the referendum proposal, they were confident that something would be arranged that would keep the threat of discontinuance in the background.

Like New York, New Jersey was interested in insuring that state commuter aid was exempted from the federal corporate income tax, but there was no community of interest on the matter, since the Javits bill provided for federal exemption only in the event of tax relief. For policy and political reasons, once Rockefeller's actions committed New Jersey to a state program, Trenton preferred direct subsidies to tax relief. Jersey officials

felt that subsidies were more flexible than tax relief, which because of its blanket effect was difficult to apply with precision for
a specific purpose, such as insuring the continuation of commuter
service. They also argued that subsidies lent themselves more
easily to the imposition of conditions through contractual agreements. As Jean Gottmann has pointed out, when New Jersey's
plan finally was ready in April, 1960, it stipulated "two essential
conditions" which New York's tax relief scheme had omitted: "the
maintenance of existing commuter services at a standard satisfactory to the state . . . and no increase in existing fares." [20] An
even more powerful argument in New Jersey was that cash subsidies avoided the serious political problems that would result
from an attempt to alter the tax base in Democratic Hudson
County.

Since the Javits bill offered New Jersey nothing, Meyner's
transportation aides sought to substitute legislation broad enough
to subsume all varieties of state commuter aid programs. However, the absence of a sense of urgency—financial conditions on
the New Jersey railroads were so depressed that none was likely to
insure federal tax obligations in the near future—resulted in a
lack of congressional interest in Trenton's proposal. And because
Governor Rockefeller was interested only in safeguarding New
York's tax relief program from federal taxes, the two states failed
to get together to present a joint proposal in 1959 or 1960.

The Other States

Aside from New York and New Jersey, only Pennsylvania and
Connecticut played a part in the federal-metropolitan politics of
mass transportation between August, 1958, and March, 1960.
Elsewhere the absence of constituency concern or pressing problems resulted in a dearth of interest among the urban states in the
federal govenrment's metropolitan rail role. Of the half-dozen
states that supported the train-service legislation, only Pennsylvania did so for commuter rail purposes. In addition, Pennsylvania's David Lawrence, a Democrat and former mayor of Pitts-

burgh, was the only governor besides Meyner to endorse federal mass transportation aid during this period. In both instances, Lawrence's activity was in response to requests from Philadelphia's Mayor Richardson Dilworth and marked the extent of Harrisburg's involvement with Philadelphia's expensive public transportation problems.

Connecticut's relations with Washington were also limited. At the time of the February meeting, Governor Ribicoff had asserted that the federal government "could not wash its hands of this thing." [21] But after throwing in his lot with Rockefeller, whose New York program promised to help the New Haven without any cash contributions from Connecticut, Ribicoff ignored the federal government's role. He did not endorse a state legislative committee report, which, after concluding that state assistance for the New Haven was politically unfeasible, recommended federal aid while cautioning that "The practical difficulty of persuading Congress to help may make Federal aid in time to save the [commuter railroads] a vain hope." [22] Not until the New Haven tottered on the brink of bankruptcy in 1960 did Ribicoff look to the Washington and the ICC for help; and, as will be seen in Chapter VIII, he did so primarily at Rockefeller's instigation.

The Pattern of State Action

Choice in New York's case and necessity in that of New Jersey left the states largely dependent upon their own resources in tackling the commuter railroad problem. Once Governor Rockefeller established the basic pattern of commuter policy in the region, Washington's role was not a central concern of either state. Both agreed that the federal task was to facilitate state action rather than to resolve the problem. Fiscal and political considerations, however, led Meyner, a Democrat, to define facilitation more broadly than Rockefeller, a Republican. Because their suburban rail objectives at the national level had a relatively low priority, the states' political investment in such efforts was marginal. The result was a lack of success in securing federal facilitation of the two states' programs.

Apparent in the states' activities during this period is the role of the institutional base in shaping federal-metropolitan politics. The commuter rail programs developed in Albany and Trenton were the product of state perspectives, requirements, and capabilities. In both states they leaned heavily toward the traditional state concern with railroads and eschewed the broader mass transportation focus of the central-city and the urban planners. State dealings with Washington, particularly in New York, reflected this railroad orientation. Fear of direct federal-local relations also shaped state policy, again much more noticeably in New York during 1959. Particularism deriving from the fragmentation of the region, in this case the cleavage caused by the Hudson River, hindered interstate cooperation on a number of matters, including the proposals for changes in federal tax policy. All these factors —the state institutional base, focus on railroads, dislike for direct federal-local relations, and parochialism—were to play an important part in the involvement of both states in the politics of federal aid for mass transportation in 1960 and 1961, as will be seen in Chapters VIII and IX.

CHAPTER VI

The Cities: The Quest for Federal Aid

The city is a kind of island surrounded by a body of deep water called state government. For Federal help to reach these islands, it must find its way past the often unfriendly reefs and shoals of state bureaucracy.

MAYOR ROBERT WAGNER

Central-city participation in federal-metropolitan politics is strongly conditioned by the cities' positive orientation toward Washington. Metropolitan development, particularly the flight of the white middle classes to the suburbs and their replacement in the urban core by largely nonwhite groups at the lower end of the socio-economic scale, has increased the costs and decreased the revenues of big city governments. An inability to tap regional resources for problems like public transportation and dissatisfaction with the response of state governments to their requests for help have led the large cities to look on the national government as "the only medium with sufficient tax resources or sufficient flexibility to give the cities the aid which they need and deserve." [1]

Also attracting the cities to Washington has been the growth of urban influence in national politics. Cities are better represented in the House of Representatives than in most state legislatures, and more than half the Senate comes from constituencies dominated by urban populations. As a result, urban spokesmen have plotted their intergovernmental strategies reasonably confident that "If the states cannot or will not heed the cities' pleas and warnings . . . Congress will." [2] Moreover, the greatest prizes of the American political system, the presidential nominations and the presidency, are urban-based in the national conventions and in the Electoral College, a fact that has led one observer to conclude that "The growth of Presidential power and the intimate relation of urban political parties to that power . . . may be the central political phenomena of our time." [3] No presidential hopeful can ignore the potent influence of the cities, as John F. Kennedy indicated in late 1959, when he told the nation's mayors that "The overall outcome of the 1960 campaign is going to be decided in the cities of the United States [since] most of the votes in both the conventions and the electoral college will be [from] those states with great urban areas." [4]

Another reason the cities come to Washington is their capability for effective action at the national level. Alone among the local components of the fragmented metropolis, the central city is big government. It commands the largest bloc of personnel and of technical, financial, and political resources in a metropolitan area. Paramount among its political resources is the mayor. In terms that describe most big city chief executives, New York's mayor has been called "the central focus of responsibility and accountability for all that occurs in the city; . . . the problemsolver, the crisis-handler, the man-to-blame for all the defects of the governing process in the city." [5] The political capabilities of the mayor are far greater than those of any other local leader in the metropolis. He is the region's most visible political figure, commanding more public and mass media attention than most of his local counterparts combined. "Insofar as there is a metropolitan community," writes Scott Greer, the central-city mayor "is its highest elected official." [6] Except for the governors and congressmen, the mayor normally is the only metropolitan actor with significant influence in the national political arena.

Central-city interest in federal aid is enhanced by the regional perspectives of the urban core. Location, the headquarters economy, and dependence on a commuter network rather than on a single line as in the suburbs compel the city to view mass transportation in a regional frame of reference. Another factor is the desire of the central cities, already bearing the burden of subsidizing public transport within the city limits, to tap regional resources for new and expensive responsibilities like rail commutation or areawide rapid transit. Political considerations also urge a regional outlook. The prospect of local control through areal approaches is far more tempting to the powerful central city, which would play a major role in any regional instrumentality, than to a suburban village with 10,000 residents, a part-time mayor, and little hope of even being directly represented on a regional body. Moreover, regional statesmanship often is a requisite of the central-city mayor's broader political roles. If a leader of his party in the state and nation is eager for personal advancement to the state capital or Washington, the mayor, like Chicago's Richard Daley, "must show the suburbanites that they have nothing to fear and much to hope for from . . . the central city." [7] At best, federal aid could help provide a bypass around the conflict-laden question of the sources and allocation of local financial support, certainly the most formidable barrier to regional cooperation on a costly issue like mass transportation. And if federal aid failed to induce suburban participation in a regional venture, it still would help the hard-pressed cities to improve mass transportation and commuter rail facilities within the city limits.

Philadelphia's Initiative

Of the handful of great cities dependent upon rail commutation, Philadelphia was the first to turn its attention and resources to the development of a federal financial role in mass transportation. In the early 1950s, Philadelphia's rail transportation story was familiar: service was deteriorating and patronage declining on its rapid transit and commuter rail systems. The Pennsylvania and the Reading Railroads, which carried over 100,000 riders in the region daily, were talking of the impossibility of private corporations continuing to provide unprofitable services. In response to this situation, Mayor Joseph Clark in 1953 created an Urban Traffic and Transportation Board (UTTB) to develop an overall transportation program for the city. Composed of representatives of the railroads, downtown commerce and finance, rubber interests, and civic leaders, the UTTB studied the governmental, fiscal, and physical aspects of the transport systems of the city and the metropolitan area. In December, 1955, the UTTB recommended a coordinated rail-rubber development program for the region with extensive renovation of the existing subway and commuter lines.[8]

Clark's successor, Richardson Dilworth, endorsed the plan and assigned a high priority to its implementation. A comparison of the costs of building expressways and renovating rail facilities made it clear that the smaller investments required for rapid transit and commuter rail improvements would bring greater returns, in terms both of transportation outlays and of preserving downtown Philadelphia. It was estimated that mass transportation rehabilitation within the city would cost upwards of $25 million, while $65 to $80 million would be required to modernize the transit and commuter rail network in the entire metropolitan area.[9] This appeared to be a bargain, with urban expressway costs averaging well over $4 million a mile. Yet, bargain or not, the city, which already was putting $4 million a year into its rapid transit system, could not undertake a program of this magnitude on its own. The UTTB had concluded that Philadelphia's transportation woes were inseparable from those of the region; but the suburbs, fearful of unequal costs and benefits and central-city domination, showed no interest in an areawide attack on transport problems. Because Pennsylvania's rurally dominated legislature foreclosed state help, thoughts naturally turned to the federal government. Since Washington was already underwriting much of Philadelphia's urban renewal, why, thought city officials, shouldn't it get involved in mass transportation, which was equally important to the survival of the central city?

At first, federal highway aid appeared to be the most likely source of funds for mass transportation. Even before the passage of the Federal Highway Act of 1956, Philadelphia proposed that federal support of transit "could best be achieved through the inclusion in any federally-supported urban highway [of a] provision for dedicating a portion of the right-of-way for public transit."[10] Powerful highway and automobile-user interests were, however, opposed to the diversion of federal highway funds, and Dilworth made little headway. At a 1957 conference in Chicago on the coordination of metropolitan transportation, highway spokesmen rejected Dilworth's proposal that the federal government "make it possible to include in the financing of the highway system provisions for improving our mass transportation system." [11]

By the end of 1957, Dilworth was seeking to sidestep the opposition of rubber interests by de-emphasizing federal highway funds as a source of national mass transportation assistance. From the AMA, an organization of over 13,000 cities dedicated to safeguarding "the interests, rights, and privileges of municipalities as they may be affected by federal legislation," [12] Dilworth secured approval of a proposal which asked that federal highway funds be used only for "plans and specifications for the construction of high-speed mass-transit" along highway rights-of-way. Roads funds would not be used for mass transportation capital costs. Instead, Washington was urged to "establish a Federal lending agency similar to the Federal National Mortgage Association in the transit field." [13]

To implement the transit loan proposal, legislation was prepared in Philadelphia to create a federal lending corporation in the Department of Commerce with a financing capability of $500 million. Loans would be made to public and private transit operators, commuter railroads, and local governments in metropolitan areas to improve services.[14] Representative William Green of Philadelphia introduced the bill in the House, but the measure died in committee without attracting much notice. Efforts the following year by Dilworth and by Clark, who was elected to the U.S. Senate in 1956, to interest the Commerce Department and the Smathers subcommittee in the proposal proved equally fruitless.

Dilworth also faced the problem of preserving commuter trains until federal funds were secured to renovate them. Late in 1946, Pennsylvania Railroad president James Symes indicated that declining patronage and increasing losses left the railroad no alternative but to discontinue unprofitable trains as quickly as possible. While informing Symes that the city would oppose such action, Dilworth reminded him that they had a mutual interest in maintaining the vitality of the central business district. Symes agreed that commuter services were a necessary public service but argued that he could not ask the Pennsylvania's directors and stockholders to subsidize unprofitable suburban trains forever. He did, however, indicate a willingness to sit down with city officials to discuss alternatives to discontinuance.[15]

In the talks that followed, Philadelphia's immediate objectives were to keep the trains running and to increase their utilization. The goal of the Pennsylvania and the Reading Railroads, on the other hand, was to displace the burden of commutation losses on the public. While the city and the railroads agreed that an area-wide approach was required, the commuting suburbs were not interested in regional ventures which would cost them money. After protracted negotiations, whose completion was spurred by the enactment of the Transportation Act, Philadelphia contracted with the railroads in the fall of 1958 for increased service at reduced fares on three commuter lines wholly within the city. The program would cost the city from 6 to 9 cents a ride, less than half its outlay for expressways and parking facilities for each downtown automobile trip.[16] The experiment was an immediate success and reinforced the conviction of Dilworth and his aides that the downward trend in railroad commuting could be reversed. It also increased their desire to obtain federal help for capital improvements which would cut operating costs and provide more attractive service.

Philadelphia's bargaining sessions with the Pennsylvania Railroad had revealed a common interest in federal aid. Unlike the Southern and Western railroads, which feared federal intervention, the mounting troubles of the Eastern carriers had drawn them toward Washington for help. A passenger-subsidy trial balloon launched in 1955 by the ICC produced favorable responses from the Pennsylvania and the New York Central.[17] Upon taking command of the New Haven in 1956, George Alpert opened a campaign for local, state, and federal subsidies, arguing that "Most other forms of transportation in the United States require and get a subsidy. Since the public is demanding better commuter service, it would make sense to provide the necessary subsidies here as well." [18] At the Smathers hearings in 1958, both Alpert and Symes proposed federal aid for commuter railroads and mass transportation. While nothing came of these suggestions, the Eastern carriers, led by Symes, did secure in the Transportation Act $500 million in federal loan guarantees, under conditions, however, which precluded their use for improving commutation services.[19]

The failure of these sporadic efforts by Philadelphia and by the Eastern railroads to arouse interest in Washington prompted Dilworth and Symes to consider how urban and railroad influence could be put to better use in the future. As concern over the commuter situation mounted in the wake of the emergency in the New York area, the two Philadelphia leaders decided to bring together the big cities and the railroads to promote public and congressional acceptance of the idea of federal mass transportation assistance. In December, 1958, Dilworth and Symes invited a group of mayors and railroad executives to a meeting in Chicago the following month to discuss their urban rail problems.

Precrisis Views on Federal Aid in New York City

The central city's resources, capabilities, and positive attitude toward the national government guarantee neither action nor leadership on an urban issue at the federal level. Although New York City was the greatest municipal beneficiary of Washington's largess, was served by the nation's largest commuter rail network, and contributed over $100 million annually to its public transport system, federal aid for mass transportation did not attract serious attention until pressures for action on the commuter rail front mounted sharply during the summer of 1958. Historically of low priority in the city compared with the question of subway fares and subsidies, the suburban rail issue has had to compete for the mayor's attention with scores of other problems and contant ceremonial, civic, and political demands on his time. Too busy reacting to problems to indulge often in the luxury of anticipating them, New York's mayor, like most political executives, normally takes on new burdens only in the wake of a scandal, disaster, or crisis, which, on the commutation question, did not occur until 1958.

Four years before the commuter crisis, a federal aid proposal failed to attract serious attention in the city. Councilman Morris Stein, a Brooklyn Democrat hopeful of avoiding future subway fare increases, secured City Council approval of a resolution calling for federal assistance for the city's subways, bus lines, and commuter railroads.[20] However, none of the city's key political leaders, congressmen, or transportation spokesmen took notice of the proposal. In the years that followed, Mayor Wagner and his aides paid little attention to the federal aid schemes promoted by Dilworth, Symes, and Alpert. For example, in an appearance before a House subcommittee in 1957, on the same day that Dilworth argued that the federal government was "throwing money down the drain . . . by just building highways, unless they also take into account . . . mass transit," Wagner omitted mass transportation from a long list of areas of present and possible future national concern, which included urban renewal, public housing, planning, civil defense, water and air pollution, and juvenile delinquency.[21]

By July, 1958, however, the deteriorating commuter rail situation prompted Wagner to ask City Administrator Charles Preusse and four other top city officials to explore all aspects of the commuter rail question.[22] Meetings were held with executives of the New York Central, the New Haven, the Pennsylvania, and the Long Island Railroads, who insisted that the only alternative to governmental assistance was discontinuance of unprofitable services.[23] After listening to the railroads, the Preusse committee concluded that the city could do little to preserve commuter service on its own. Unilateral action would be fruitless because the problem had to be attacked regionally, and subsidies beyond New York City's means were essential to preserve service. This much of the committee's findings was old hat. Wagner repeatedly had claimed that the city was doing its share on regional mass transportation, pointing to the Transit Authority subsidies and the Long Island Railroad and Staten Island Rapid Transit tax relief. And in opposing the trans-Hudson scheme of the MRTC, Wagner had endorsed a tri-state approach.

There was, however, one new wrinkle in the advice the committee gave Wagner. Preusse and his associates convinced themselves that the interstate nature of the problem and, more important, its magnitude required a federal financial role. New York, the city official agreed, could not foot the bill for the needed regional solution. The suburbs, in the light of their reaction to the MRTC's locally based financing plan, were pretty poor prospects. Although Wagner had told the MRTC in 1957 that "primary responsibility for financing should be assumed by the two states," [24] Preusse doubted if sufficient cash could be pried loose from the state capitals under conditions favorable to the city. That left the federal treasury as the only politically convenient source of funds. At the time the Preusse committee's conclusions were being considered, Dilworth's letter inviting Wagner to attend the Chicago meeting arrived at City Hall.

The Chicago Conference

Representatives of twelve cities and seventeen railroads met in Chicago on January 13, 1959, to discuss urban rail problems.[25] In bringing the mayors and the railroad presidents together, Dilworth and Symes hoped to broaden support and build a consensus for a national mass transportation program. It was clear that political activity in Washington on the sporadic and uncoordinated basis that had prevailed before 1959 was not likely to secure enactment of a federal aid program. Another objective was to extend the Dilworth-Symes cooperative relationship into a national coalition of railroad presidents and mayors which would increase the bargaining strength of each. After winning urban-rail acceptance of the general concept of federal aid, the Philadelphia sponsors of the conference planned to have specific proposals drafted, approved by the mayors and railroad presidents, and endorsed by the AMA, the AAR, and other interested groups. Once their position was consolidated, support would be sought in Congress and the Administration.

Considerable harmony prevailed among the mayors who journeyed to Chicago. Central-city concerns were foremost, since no suburban representatives had been invited. To preserve the core, the big cities realized that regional action and large capital outlays would be needed. The mayors were sure that city voters would not approve large-scale transportation schemes without some outside assistance. They had no illusions about what the suburbs would contribute unless induced or coerced, and most doubted that their states would help. Few had specific proposals, but all were willing to call on Washington.

Among the big-city leaders without a detailed plan, but prepared to endorse federal aid, was New York's Mayor Wagner. Drawing on the conclusions of the Preusse committee, Wagner recommended coordinated regional approaches to the commutation problem with aid from all levels of government. For the New York region, Wagner urged the creation of a locally controlled tri-state agency but insisted that "The burden of commuter railroad deficits . . . cannot be borne by the local communities alone." While the states had a role to play, "most important of all" for Wagner was the federal stake in rail commutation. However, except for the novel suggestion that regional bodies like his proposed tri-state agency, rather than Congress, develop an equitable sharing formula for all levels of government, Wagner offered no federal aid proposals.[26]

Despite the consensus among the mayors, dissenters in the railroad camp prevented the Chicago conference from agreeing on an overall objective. Rather than federal assistance, Perlman of the New York Central preferred an improved regulatory climate and the elimination of advantages to other forms of transportation. More adamant opposition came from the Chicago rail group led by Clair Roddewig, president of the Western Association of Railroads. To Alpert's question—"Why are subsidies moral for other forms of transportation and so immoral when it comes to railroads?"—Roddewig answered that "subsidies seldom solve anything" and could "irrevocably start the railroads on a short cut to government ownership." [27]

Because of this railroad opposition, the only tangible product of the Chicago meeting was the formation of a twelve-member working committee. Representing the cities were Mayors Dilworth of Philadelphia, Wagner of New York, Richard Daley of Chicago, Anthony Celebrezze of Cleveland, Frank Zeidler of Milwaukee, and Raymond Tucker of St. Louis, who was also president of the AMA, as well as Robert McLaughlin, president of the District of Columbia Commission. Except for Roddewig, the five railroad members of the committee were from the Eastern commuter roads—Symes, Alpert, Perlman, and Henry von Willer of the Erie. The committee's task was to settle the differences which were voiced at Chicago and to recommend an action program for adoption by the AMA and AAR. [28]

Development of the Urban-Rail Program

Two months after the Chicago conference the working committee convened in Mayor Dilworth's office in Philadelphia. Three issues prevented the mayors and rail executives from reaching agreement. First, and most important, was the continued opposition of Roddewig and Perlman to federal aid. Second, supporters of a federal aid program differed on the type of assistance that should be sought in Washington. While Dilworth and Symes argued for federal grants similar to those available for urban renewal, Mayor Celebrezze of Cleveland and City Administrator Preusse of New York insisted that the recommendation be limited to low-interest loans. [29] Finally, Alpert wanted direct federal aid to the commuter railroads, which would avoid the inevitable delays of a city-administered program. However, a desire to insure that federal mass transportation aid served public policy led the mayors to demand a program in which assistance was channeled to the railroads and transit operators through local public agencies.

Failure to resolve these differences threatened to doom urban-rail cooperation. To buy time, Dilworth suggested that the AMA analyze the problem for the working committee. However, the resultant study of the five metropolitan areas with extensive rail systems—New York, Chicago, Philadelphia, Boston, and Cleveland—was a Philadelphia rather than AMA effort, undertaken by three men strongly committed to federal aid—John Bailey, Dilworth's chief transportation adviser; Walter Patchell, the Pennsylvania Railroad's vice-president for passenger service; and Patrick McLaughlin, an AMA official who also served as Philadelphia's Washington lobbyist. In addition to gathering information, the three drummed up support among the city officials, planners, railroad men, and transit executives in the cities they visited. In keeping with the central city-railroad orientation of the campaign, neither suburbanites nor state officials were consulted.

The result was a short study entitled *The Collapse of Commuter Service,* designed to convince doubters like Roddewig and Perlman of the need for federal aid. Written by Bailey, the report demonstrated that over $3 billion was needed in the five areas to modernize commuter rail and rapid-transit facilities. Highways of equal capacity would cost approximately $17 billion. Federal financial help was essential because "equipment needs alone are much too large for cities, railroads or transit organizations to finance as quickly as needed to halt the loss of ridership." [30] In an attempt to break the deadlock on the working committee, Dilworth and Symes shelved their proposal for federal grants. Instead, the report recommended that the $500-million mass transport loan bill prepared in Philadelphia in 1958 form the basis of a federal aid program.

Denver was the scene of the AMA's December, 1959, American Municipal Congress and "Better Urban Transportation" was the theme. Meeting during the session, the working committee hammered out a four-point compromise based on the guidelines set forth in *The Collapse of Commuter Service.* Two recommendations were largely for the benefit of the railroads, calling on Congress to establish a national policy for a balanced and coordinated transportation system and on all levels of government to develop rational tax policies for the railroads. The remaining proposals dealt with the more controversial question of federal mass transportation assistance. After the Eastern roads, led by AAR chairman Symes, promised to support the Western carriers on some noncommuter matters in dispute between the geographical railroad blocs, Roddewig finally gave his reluctant endorsement to a loan program. In addition, Alpert acquiesced to the demands of Preusse and Mayor Tucker of St. Louis that aid not go directly to the railroads and transit companies.[31]

The recommendation that emerged from this bargaining session urged that long-term low-interest "Federal loans be made available where necessary to municipalities or publicly constituted bodies for new commuter equipment and improved facilities and for the improvement of intracity mass passenger transportation facilities." In deference to Roddewig and Celebrezze, who refused to go along unless the recommended program was limited to loans, the policy statement suggested only that

a study be made of grants-in-aid by the Federal Government to communities or duly constituted public bodies which have a sound plan for the permanent improvement of commutation or other intracity transportation facilities, this to be modeled on the present urban renewal program.[32]

Strong endorsements from its top officials and its staff led the membership of the AMA to adopt unanimously the urban-rail proposals as part of the national municipal policy. However, the rail focus of the four-point program precluded much personal interest among the hundreds of municipal officials who gathered in Denver to discuss "Better Urban Transportation." The few cities with urban rail systems, all of whom had been represented on the working committee, were even a minority on the "big-city" panel at the meeting. Despite persistent efforts by moderator Dilworth to introduce commuter rail and rapid transit problems into the discussion, the panel devoted most of its attention to buses, parking, and expressways.[33] Obviously, the urban-rail program was too narrow an approach to public transportation to win the active support of the nonrail cities.

None the less, one half of the Chicago conference's objective, formal AMA backing, had been achieved. Symes, however, was unable to secure the other half, support by the AAR. The Southern and Western railroads would not accept the compromise on loans and grants. Roddewig had both second thoughts and constituency pressures. As a result of these developments, the AAR board of directors failed to endorse the program at their January, 1960, meeting. However, in announcing that the AAR would not participate, Symes stressed that "All Eastern lines will cooperate with the American Municipal Association in seeking the necessary legislation to make effective the four point program recently adopted by that group." [34]

Building a Federal Aid Coalition in the New York Region

Achievement of internal consensus and a solid urban-rail alliance were the primary objectives of the federal aid forces in 1959. As has been seen, Philadelphia provided both the leadership and the staffwork in this effort. Publicizing federal mass transportation assistance and broadening the base of support beyond the mayors and the railroads was a secondary goal. In this sphere, Mayor Wagner was quite active. His aim was to bring the familiar central-city cluster of governmental, civic, business, and newspaper interests, as well as the region's other large Democratic cities and the MRC, into the federal aid camp. By promoting federal assistance and a tri-state approach as a package, Wagner saw an opportunity to win backing for federal aid from the New York newspapers and conservative downtown business and civic groups which were regionally oriented but normally less inclined than Democratic politicians to call on Washington for help with "local" problems.

For his tri-state proposal, Wagner already had considerable press support. At the beginning of the commuter crisis in 1958, the New York *World-Telegram & Sun* had called for a tri-state authority, and the New York *Journal-American* had nominated the MRC for the job.[35] Federal aid, however, was a new idea for the New York newspapers, and Wagner's Chicago speech received a mixed reaction. The *Journal-American* applauded the Mayor for offering a "simple, concrete plan for solving the commuter transportation crisis" with the added benefit that the "burden would not fall heavily on any one level." A favorable response also came from the New York *Daily News,* which thought that the "Mayor rates thanks from the commuters and the rails for having given some real thought to this problem and come up with some concrete proposals." But criticism came from more influential editorial pages. The *Herald Tribune* scored Wagner for trusting "to apportioned subsidies from every level of government," and for not being "keen about having the bill come close to home." The New York *Times* concurred, depreciating Wagner's proposal for federal aid in an editorial entitled "Let George Do It," which complained that "When it comes to the hard question of counties, cities, towns, villages granting tax relief or providing subsidy by taxation, everybody runs away like mad." [36]

Discussions by city officials with members of the *Times* editorial board failed to change that influential newspaper's views on federal mass transportation assistance. Its next comment on the subject was in connection with the ICC's May, 1959, passenger deficit report. "One of the most striking features of the report," said the *Times* in an editorial, "is the paucity of significant suggestions for Federal action. But this gets us closer to the heart of the matter: the most important remedies, particularly for the commutation problem, lie with the state and local governments." [37] Nor was editorial comment on Wagner's effort to win support for federal aid at the February, 1959, meeting encouraging. A typical reaction was the satisfaction of the *World-Telegram & Sun* that the region's political leaders had reached a "realistic agreement that turning to Washington for a handout isn't the answer." [38]

Despite the unfavorable press and his failure to secure an endorsement of his tri-state federal aid package at the February conference, Wagner and his aides sought to keep federal mass transportation assistance in the news during 1959. In April, at a Fordham University panel on commuting problems, City Administrator Preusse called for a bold program encompassing subsidies from all levels and a tri-state coordinating agency.[39] In mid-November, Wagner presented the case for federal aid at the National Conference on Government of the National Municipal League.[40] Assisting in these efforts was George Alpert, who took to the luncheon circuit seeking business support for a federal commuter rail program. Alpert also provided some additional publicity for federal aid when he answered a *Time* magazine article entitled "How Not to Run a Railroad" [41] with full-page advertisements in the New York press which declared: "We have been proclaiming repeatedly that a federal subsidy is the only remedy." [42]

The missionaries activities of Wagner, Preusse, and Alpert won few converts to federal aid among the central-city business and civic groups, which were favorably inclined toward a regional approach to the commuter problem. The Commerce and Industry Association, the Citizens' Union, the Citizens' Budget Commission, the Fifth Avenue Association, the RPA, and the New York Real Estate Board all remained silent. A more positive reaction to Wagner's proposals came from the region's Democratic subcentral cities, particularly Newark and Jersey City. Already the beneficiaries of many federal aid programs, the older cities did not share the doubts of central-city business interests of the propriety of enlarging Washington's urban responsibilities.

Supported by Newark and Jersey City, Wagner secured in January, 1960, an endorsement of the urban-rail federal aid program from MRC's Traffic and Transportation Committee, headed by Jersey City's Mayor Charles Witkowski, a Democrat. At the same meeting, Witkowski and two suburban Republicans were named to seek the concurrence of the three governors on the creation of a tri-state agency to accept any federal aid that might become available.[43] Reacting to the referendum defeat in New Jersey and to Alpert's threat to terminate the New Haven's commuter services, Governors Meyner and Ribicoff agreed to a tri-state approach if New York would go along.[44] Although Rockefeller's negative response dashed hopes for an immediate change in regional commuter policy, the MRC heeded the advice of its big-city leaders and in February, 1960, unanimously reaffirmed its support of a tri-state agency and endorsed the AMA-Eastern railroad federal mass transportation program.[45]

The Urban-Rail Program Falters

At the same time Wagner was winning regional backing for the urban-rail mass transportation program, the Philadelphia leaders of the federal aid movement prepared to enter the national legislative arena. Given the Eisenhower Administration's opposition to new federal spending programs, the mayors and railroad presidents faced an uphill fight in the Eighty-sixth Congress. Their immediate objective was to publicize the program and to build congressional and group support so as to insure favorable action when the climate in Washington for expanding federal responsibilities had improved, which the Democratic mayors hoped would occur after the presidential election in November, 1960. To fulfill these goals, the urban and railroad lobbyists sought commitments from strategically placed congressmen to introduce legislation embodying the urban-rail program and to secure prompt and sympathetic hearings.

Although their mass transportation program had been developed without congressional participation, the urban-rail allies had two latent sources of legislative support. First, many senators and representatives from metropolitan areas could be expected to back an urban assistance program vigorously promoted by the AMA. Congressmen friendly to the railroads provided a second, if smaller, reservoir of potential support. Even without the backing of the AAR, the Eastern railroads would get some help from conservative congressmen who normally opposed new federal ventures. In addition, the presence of numerous White House hopefuls in the Senate presented opportunities to capitalize on the augmentation of urban political influence in a presidential election year.

Responsibility for drafting legislation to implement the urban-rail program was delegated to Dilworth and Symes by the working committee. Actually, the new legislation was no more than a

minor revision of the $500-million transit loan bill introduced by
Representative Green in 1958. The only important change produced by the year of negotiations was the deletion of the provision for direct loans to the carriers. Under the new bill, $500
million in low-interest loans were to be made available by the
Department of Commerce to municipalities, states, and authorities
in standard metropolitan areas for the acquisition, maintenance,
and improvement of mass transit and commuter rail facilities and
equipment.[46]

As the urban-rail forces soon discovered, the bill had a fatal
flaw: it assigned the program to an agency opposed to federal
involvement in mass transportation and would be referred to
congressional committees which were convinced that urban rail
transportation was a state and local responsibility. Although the
positions of the Department of Commerce and the Commerce
Committees were matters of public record, the Philadelphians
continued to cling to the commerce approach developed in their
1958 proposals. It was an understandable error. The Department
of Commerce was the federal government's key transport agency.
Initially, Dilworth had sought mass transportation aid from federal highway funds, which were under the control of the Secretary
of Commerce. And the rail attorneys who helped draft the loan
bills in 1958 and 1960 almost automatically thought in terms of
the commerce nexus of the federal government. Finally, urban
congressmen who might have helped the Philadelphia leaders develop a more feasible legislative strategy were consulted after,
not before, the bill was drafted.

These difficulties became apparent when the draft bill was circulated to members of both Commerce Committees, the House
Banking and Currency Committee (which has jurisdiction in the
House over all federal lending programs), and individual members of Congress with an interest in metropolitan problems. Senator Smathers and most of his colleagues were not interested in the
bill. Senator Case, the most urban-minded member of the Surface Transportation Subcommittee, was not sure of the wisdom
of federal aid for mass transit. The subcommittee staff opposed
the draft on the grounds that it established a new loan program
in the Department of Commerce rather than building on the ICC

loan guarantee plan created in the Transportation Act of 1958. Equally dispiriting reports came from the House Commerce Committee. Because of the dismal committee prospects, most urban congressmen shied away from the proposal.

Although the initial plans called for holding the mayors and railroad presidents in reserve until hearings were scheduled, the negative response to the draft legislation prompted a change in tactics. The Philadelphia group decided to delay the introduction of the bill pending direct lobbying by the mayors and railroad presidents. A series of conferences with key congressional and executive figures was arranged for mid-February. A week before the delegation arrived in Washington, however, a freshman member of the House of Representatives from the New York area, Donald Irwin of Fairfield County, ignoring the AMA's request that the legislation be withheld until endorsed by congressional leaders, introduced the urban-rail bill. Although annoyed by Irwin's precipitous action, Dilworth and Symes proceeded to implement their plan to secure top-level backing for the federal aid proposal.

On February 16, 1960, eight mayors, including Wagner and Newark's Leo Carlin (who were accompanied by MRC executive secretary Maxwell Lehman), Governor David Lawrence of Pennsylvania, and officials of twelve Eastern railroads came to Washington. They discussed their proposals with the Secretary of Commerce, Frederick Mueller, Bureau of the Budget aids, majority and minority leaders of both Houses, the House Commerce Committee, the Smathers subcommittee, and the chairman of the House Banking and Currency Committee. The purpose of the meetings, as Wagner explained, was "to meet these leaders face to face and let them know what our problems are." As the New York *Times* noted, the delegation "did not pretend to expectations of any action on the problem by Congress this year," but, as Wagner told reporters after the round of conferences, "Even if we don't get it this year, they will have an opportunity to study it and get to work on it next year." [47]

The delegation received few promises of support. Commerce Secretary Mueller declined to take a position, indicating that any decision would have to come from the White House. The Bureau of the Budget also was noncommittal. Smathers and most of the subcommittee reiterated their conviction that commuter aid was a state or local rather than federal responsibility. As one member of the subcommittee, Senator Frank Lausche of Ohio, later explained, the delegation "found there was an adverse attitude in the committee toward the proposal to subsidize the railroad[s]." [48] On the other side of the Capitol, Smathers' counterpart, Representative John Bell Williams of Mississippi, was "not ready to start putting Federal money into the operation of a commuter service to meet what is obviously a local problem." [49] It was clear to the urban-rail delegation that their program was tactically weak and that a sympathetic hearing was unlikely to be afforded by the Smathers or Williams subcommittees, both of which were largely immune to urban pressures and could afford to ignore the pleas of the segment of the rail industry involved, particularly in light of the failure of the AAR to endorse the federal aid program.

One key figure on the Washington scene, however, was impressed by the political influence of the urban portion of the delegation which came to Washington in mid-February. Senate majority leader Lyndon Johnson bent a receptive ear to the mass transportation plaints of the urban leaders. In quest of the Democratic presidential nomination, Johnson desperately needed urban support to slow the pace of front-running Senator John F. Kennedy, whose dogged pursuit of urban delegates had been highlighted by a bold bid for urban support at the AMA meeting in December. Kennedy had declared that "The cities of America, their problems, their future, their financing, must rank at the top of any realistic list of 1960 campaign issues. This is the great unspoken, overlooked, underplayed problem of our time." [50] Needing little encouragement from his rival, Johnson let it be known that he would be receptive to measures of interest to big-city leaders.

The urban half of the February delegation, all of whom were Democrats, were conscious of the leverage implicit in the situation. Governor Lawrence made the trip to Washington for his political weight rather than because of a compelling interest in mass transportation. In firm control of his state's 81 uncommitted convention votes, Lawrence, like Kennedy a Catholic, had serious reservations about Kennedy's ability to win a national election. In addition, Wagner, who, as a Catholic, could hardly expect to have his vice-presidential ambitions satisfied by a place on the same ticket as Kennedy, wielded considerable influence in New York's 114-member delegation. The upshot of this encounter between presidential ambition and urban political power was a commitment from the majority leader to get the $500-million transit loan bill through the Senate. Speaker Sam Rayburn, who was supporting Johnson for the nomination, promised to do his best to secure favorable action in the House. Thus, the result of the February 16 meetings was a somewhat anomalous situation. The urban-rail alliance had a program which interested neither the recipient department nor the responsible congressional committees. Yet they had commitments from the two most powerful men in Congress that action would be forthcoming.

To avoid the hostility of the commerce nexus and to capitalize on the pledges of support from the majority leader and the speaker, the urban-rail mass transportation program was in need of a transfusion. The cities had gone as far as they could on their own. Despite the delay in developing a program acceptable to the diverse interests involved and a flawed bill resulting from an inadequate appraisal of the political situation in Washington, the large cities and Philadelphia in particular had pursued their interests with considerable success between January, 1959, and February, 1960. Widespread urban acceptance of the idea of federal aid had been achieved, including strong support from all the urban centers with rail systems and an endorsement by the AMA. An alliance between the cities and the commuter railroads, both nationally and locally, promised to bring normally antagonistic congressional groups together in support of urban rail assistance. Finally, urban political influence, enhanced in a presidential year, had secured a significant beachhead for federal aid in Washington. Now it was time to turn to the urban congressmen for legislative leadership. As will be seen in the next chapter, a strategically placed U.S. senator from a large urban state, Harrison Williams of New Jersey, by tailoring the urban-rail proposal to fit political realities and personal necessities, capitalized on this opportunity.

CHAPTER VII

The Congressmen: Direct and Indirect Constituency Pressures

Throughout our community there is a grim anxiety hanging over our commuter communities and this is felt by the young and the old, the rich and the poor. Our mail reflects even the anxiety among children who hear the talk at the dinner table of their parents who have invested in a home out in the suburbs and now wonder just how they are ever going to get to work if the discontinuances continue at the rate they have been proceeding.

SENATOR HARRISON WILLIAMS

Like most participants in metropolitan politics, urban congressmen rarely view the fragmented metropolis in a regional perspective. The institutional base of representatives in the larger multimember metropolitan areas is subregional, while senators, like governors, have a superregional electoral base. Since most residents of the metropolis perceive their difficulties in a subregional frame of reference, pressures on urban congressmen for federal action on an areawide basis are infrequent. Moreover, congressmen have many identities and interests. Loyalties to party, faction, constituency, programmatic and group interests, and committee are more important and self-evident than ties to the metropolitan area in which their district happens to be located. As a result, the forty-one representatives and six senators with all or part of their constituencies in the New York area are far more aware of being Democrats or Republicans, liberals or conservatives, members of the Commerce or Appropriations Committees, New Yorkers or New Jerseyites, or ambassadors from Bergen or the East Bronx than of sharing a nebulous community of interest arising from the fact that they represent a part of the New York region.

Reflecting the urban congressman's nonmetropolitan outlook

and the dearth of constituency pressures for federal help with regional problems is the lack of coordination among congressmen from a particular metropolitan area. In this respect, state ties, because of the institutional focus of state government, the state base of political party organization, and the senatorial constituency, are stronger than identification with the metropolitan area, which is no one's constituency. While the New York delegation has a steering committee to handle matters of common interest and the New Jersey delegation meets regularly, including an annual breakfast session with state officials, congressmen from the New York region have created no functional equivalent of the MRC to facilitate the exchange of information and the coordination of activities on questions of general interest to the metropolis.

As congressional behavior on the mass transportation issue indicates, the paucity of regional perceptions and pressures are not the only obstacles to cooperation among congressmen on a matter of interest to a metropolitan area. Institutional factors play a part, including the "undercurrent of institutional hostility between the House and Senate" [1] and the coolness between senators from the same state arising in large part from the "competition for publicity in the same arena." [2] Another damper on coordinated efforts is the congressman's almost perpetual quest for a place in the sun. One of the prime reasons for investing time and effort in an issue is the opportunity for individual leadership and publicity. In addition, consensus among regional congressmen is impeded by differences rooted in party affiliation and political philosophy. Federal actions to ease a constituency crisis, such as the Transportation Act amendments, or to facilitate state and local programs, such as exempting state railroad aid from federal corporate taxes, are much less likely to conflict with party positions and personal views on the "spending" issue and with adverse constituency pressures than new federal ventures involving sizable commitments, such as a mass transportation assistance program.

Urban congressmen's perspectives and capabilities on metropolitan issues also are shaped by the committee system and the resultant congressional specialization. For most congressmen, opportunities for effective legislative action are limited to matters which come before their committees. Major investments of political capital on matters requiring legislation which are outside the jurisdiction of a member's committee rarely pay dividends. As a result, such involvement is limited, tending to be a function of the severity of the problem in a constituency and fading quickly when the situation in the district eases. Since the combination of committee assignment, personal interest, and constituency concern will give only a few congressmen from a large metropolitan area the potential for effective leadership on an urban issue, most will do little more than handle constituency pressures in routine fashion, by making inquiries, issuing an occasional statement for consumption back home, or introducing legislation. Letters and mimeographed releases require no political investment, and, as Bertram Gross has noted, "introducing a bill is easy and painless," constituting "no commitment as to whether its sponsor will ever lift a finger to advance its progress on the legislative highway." [3]

Another important feature of congressional participation in federal-metropolitan politics is the greater capabilities of senators for effective action on metropolitan questions. The statewide constituency gives the senator a broader view of the urban landscape than the House member, at least in the larger metropolitan areas, where the far smaller House districts produce a concentration on submetropolitan matters. The breathing space of a six-year term permits senators to look beyond narrow constituency concerns, while representatives' submetropolitan preoccupations are heightened by the two-year term. Larger staff allowances enhance the senator's capacity to deal with complex metropolitan issues. In addition, the senator functions in an environment more hospitable to innovation and leadership. Since the depression the Senate has been more receptive to the expansion of the domestic responsibilities of the federal government than the House, a consequence in large part of the urbanization of a majority of senatorial constituencies.[4] Moreover, operating in a smaller chamber, the senator has much greater scope for individual influence and leadership. In the more hierarchical House, the junior member's role is severely circumscribed. Rural and small-town representatives control most of the lower chamber's major levers of power.

Urban members among the House's leadership are from the big-city one-party districts, holders of safe seats with subregional outlooks and little interest in metropolitan problems.

Congressmen and the Commuter Crisis

Prior to the enactment of the Transportation Act of 1958, few urban congressmen had paid much attention to mass transportation problems. In 1957, the developing plans of the San Francisco Bay Area Rapid Transit Commission for a regional rail system led Representative William Mailliard, a Republican from San Francisco, to propose the creation of a select House committee to study the metropolitan mass transportation problem in order to determine "whether Federal technical assistance and coordination of mass transportation . . . would be of value" and "what, if any, Federal financial aid is necessary to assist in solving these problems." [5] At the Chicago conference on the coordination of metropolitan transportation held that spring, Mailliard urged the urban and transportation spokesmen present to use their influence in Congress to get the resolution out of the House Rules Committee in order to permit hearings which would "throw the spotlight" on the metropolitan transportation problem.[6] However, little urban congressional support materialized, and the proposal died in the Rules Committee. The following year, at Mayor Dilworth's request, Representative William Green of Philadelphia introduced the original $500-million urban mass transportation loan bill. But Green did nothing to promote the measure, and it failed to attract the attention of congressmen from the large metropolitan areas.

Before the crisis, constituency pressures on the commuter issue in the New York region were limited to occasional suburban complaints about rail service and the ICC. Too sporadic and isolated to merit more than a nominal investment of time and effort, this murmur of grass-roots discontent aroused little congressional interest in the problem. Since no one back home was promoting federal mass transportation ventures, congressmen from the tri-state region ignored the Mailliard resolution and the Green bill, except for a suggestion from Senator Javits that Mailliard's inquiry might prove more useful politically if undertaken by a joint Senate-House select committee.[7] Like their constituents, almost all of the region's congressmen were unaware of the threat to commuter service posed by Senator Smathers' legislation in 1958. Cries of alarm, particularly from Feinberg of the NYPSC, it will be remembered, had been necessary to prompt a belated response from a few congressmen from the area who were able to eliminate the net-loss provision but who could not forestall the crisis.

After the implementation of the Transportation Act of 1958, congressmen from the New York area with suburban constituencies found it necessary to look at the commuting problem in a new light. Congressional mail on the subject, particularly from New Jersey, reflected mounting anxiety about the future of suburban rail service. After the West Shore action and the Lackawanna threats, Congresswoman Florence Dwyer found that the commuter rail question had become the prime issue in her Union County district. Representative Peter Frelinghuysen received hundreds of letters from Morris County constituents stating that they would be forced to sell their homes and move elsewhere if service on the Lackawanna were eliminated.[8]

Congressmen from the New York region initially responded to this crisis-stimulated constituency concern by seeking assurances from congressional leaders and the ICC that suburban interests in continued rail service would be respected. A few days after the ferry announcement, the area's six senators, as well as Clark and Martin of Pennsylvania, wrote to Senate Commerce Committee chairman Warren Magnuson to express their concern about the future of commuter service. Congress, they insisted, did not intend in 1958 that the ICC "preside over the liquidation of vital railroad services."[9] Two months later, Senator Case, who quickly moved to the forefront of the commuters' champions in Congress, queried the ICC on discontinuance procedures but received little satisfaction, since the commission would guarantee only that commuters would be informed about procedures for filing objections.[10] In February, the deteriorating situation in New Jersey led Case to charge the ICC with a failure to consider the interests of the commuting public and to call for a Senate investigation of ICC procedures in the handling of commuter cases.[11] When these and similar routine congressional efforts on behalf of the beleagured commuting suburbs failed to check the crisis or alleviate the local pressures for help, the congressmen turned to legislation.

The severity of the situation in New Jersey was evident in the sources of congressional support for amending the Transportation Act. In the Senate, Case and Williams were the prime sponsors of the 1959 passenger-service legislation. In the House, five of the six representatives who introduced train-service bills were from New Jersey, four suburban Republicans—Florence Dwyer (Union County), George Wallhauser (Essex County), Frank Osmers (Bergen County), and William Widnall (Passaic and Bergen Counties)—and a Democrat, Dominick Daniels, who numbered many commuters, particularly on the Hudson and Manhattan Tubes, in his Hudson County district. The sixth was another New York area suburbanite, Westchester County Republican Edwin Dooley.

The paramount interest of the New Jersey suburbs in the train-service issue was also apparent at the 1959 hearings before the Smathers subcommittee. Except for New York's Senators Javits and Keating, co-sponsors of the Case bill, who appeared to bolster the cause of their fellow liberal Republican, all the congressional supporters of changes in the Transportation Act present at the hearings were from New Jersey. This group included Senators Case and Williams and three representatives from suburban districts—Dwyer, Osmers, and Frelinghuysen. Reflecting their constituencies' lack of interest in the troubles of the New Jersey suburbs, other New York area congressmen failed to put in an appearance.

Since constituency pressures generated congressional action on the train-service issue, congressional involvement was keyed to suburban concerns. At the hearings, the New Jersey delegation echoed the grass roots in concentrating on the local situation, focusing on the commuter railroad aspects of the metropolitan transportation problem, and stressing the need for federal action to remedy the unfortunate situation created by the Transportation Act of 1958. They readily admitted that their proposals constituted remedial action, a "mild . . . but sorely needed antidote," in Representative Wallhauser's phrase, which, according to Senator Case, would not by "itself solve the commutation problem." [12] Like the commuter spokesmen, they emphasized that suburban service had to be safeguarded until state and local programs could be implemented. Since the main theme of the grass roots was to reduce the national government's role in commutation, little was said about positive federal mass transportation programs. Most of the congressmen followed their constituents' lead because they shared the perceptions and prescriptions of the commuter leaders on the suburban rail question. Typical was suburban Republican Frelinghuysen, whose "political affiliation" made him "not anxious to inject the Federal Government into areas where it logically could be kept out." [13]

Except for Mrs. Dwyer and New Jersey's senators, the suburban congressmen did not make sizable political investments in the commuter issue. Disadvantageous committee assignments, lack of personal interest in the problem, the apparently dismal prospects for success, and more pressing legislative and political concerns limited their activities to making a satisfactory record for the folks back home. Rarely does this involve more than it did on the commuter issue—making inquiries to the ICC, co-sponsoring a bill, putting in an appearance at a legislative hearing on the day when a delegation of constituents has journeyed to Washington, and echoing their complaints. Seldom do such activities get bills passed or solve local problems, but they are essential aspects of the congressman's relationship with his constituency.

Other congressmen from the New York region, of course, did far less. Where constituency pressures were light or nonexistent, as within New York City's large delegation, involvement for the most part was confined to endorsing the federal level commuter rail proposals developed at the state capitals, such as the tax measures and the NY-NJTA compact.[14] During 1960 and 1961, as Chapters VIII and IX show, congressmen from the region's heavily Democratic districts would give the same kind of inactive support to the federal mass transportation assistance program backed by Mayor Wagner and the MRC.

In a few instances, however, committee assignment, reelection prospects, special constituency situations, the opportunity to provide leadership and obtain publicity, or personal interest in the mass transportation problem led to involvement in the commuter issue on the part of congressmen from the New York region transcending the normal requirements of local pressures. During the period under study, the four most active congressmen on the commuter issue, all suburbanites from the New York area, were Senators Clifford Case and Harrison Williams and Representatives Florence Dwyer and Donald Irwin. Although the two senators found leadership far easier to come by than the pair of representatives, and while Senator Williams was the only one of the quartet to achieve legislative success on the commuter issue, the behavior and experience of each sheds light on the question of congressional leadership in metropolitan affairs.

Senator Clifford Case

In his first twelve years in Congress, four in the Senate and eight in the House representing suburban Union County, Clifford Case had taken little interest in the metropolitan transportation problem, except for occasional routine inquiries to the ICC prompted by commuter complaints. Although he was engaged in the effort to eliminate the net-loss provision from the Transportation Act, his involvement on the suburban rail issue really began with the ICC's failure to investigate in the West Shore ferry case. A liberal Republican whose political appeal was strong in New Jersey's sprawling suburbs, Case was the natural focus of commuter complaints about the "Senate" law that was threatening local rail service.

Sensing a relatively rare opportunity for leadership on a federal question of interest to large numbers of New Jersey voters, Case moved quickly to capitalize on constituency unrest and establish himself as the champion of the commuters' cause in Congress. A senator's superior staff resources and the visibility afforded by his broader constituency put Case in a better position to assume leadership than his House colleagues, while his party affiliation gave him a fundamental advantage over his Democratic colleague, Harrison Williams, in dealing with the Republican suburbs. To enhance his capabilities on the passenger-service issue, Case used his seniority to obtain a place on the Senate Commerce Committee and its Surface Transportation Subcommittee at the opening of the Eighty-sixth Congress in January, 1959. For the next two years Case's principal activity on the committee was to champion the commuters' cause in Congress.

Former commuter Case brought to the Smathers subcommittee views similar in many respects to those of his suburban constituents. He perceived the mass transportation problem largely in commuter railroad terms, a frame of reference which was reinforced by his Commerce Committee assignment. Like the commuters, he felt that the suburban carriers were performing an essential public service which should not be terminated merely because it failed to return a profit. As Case put it, "I do not believe that mass transportation services, operating under a public franchise, should be permitted to be dropped solely because the carrier sees fit to do so." [15] He also shared the suburbs' wariness of greater federal involvement in the commuter problem. His federal-level objective was to preserve facilities in being while "long-range efforts to solve the problem of continuing commuter service on a permanent basis [were] being made at the state and local level." [16] Federal mass transportation assistance, in Case's view, was not desirable because it would reduce the pressures on the states and local governments for meeting their commuter responsibilities.

Case's views, his constituents' interests, and his committee assignment led him to concentrate his energies in 1959 on the train-service aspect of the commuter issue. His capabilities and interests permitted him to play the dominant role. With Javits, he organized the Northeastern senators' August, 1958, protest to Commerce Committee chairman Magnuson over the ICC's inaction on the ferries. With the deepening crisis in New Jersey and Case's acquisition of a place on the Smathers subcommittee, Javits passed the mantle of leadership on the commuter issue to Case, who maintained a steady flow of criticism of the ICC throughout the winter. After the Supreme Court's ruling on the ferries, Case cemented the suburban-railway labor alliance on the passenger-train issue and became the prime sponsor of the bill prepared by the RLEA. At the 1959 hearings, Case was the leading defender of suburban interests. Case's role involved him in frequent verbal parries with Senator Smathers, who was not overjoyed at the presence on his subcommittee of an articulate spokesman for the commuters, especially one who called the Transportation Act of 1958 "an illogical, confused, screwball law." [17]

Senator Case's efforts and his espousal of the grass-roots view-point won him considerable favor in the commuting suburbs of New Jersey, but few victories in Washington. Despite his strategic committee assignment, his legislative capabilities were limited. The remedial and commuter railroad frame of reference Case adopted from his suburban constituents precluded support from urban congressmen who had no interest in rail commutation. Labor's support and the charges of "featherbedding," as well as criticisms that Case favored "forced business-at-a-loss" for the commuter railroads,[18] made it difficult to win over fellow Republicans. Most important, Smathers, a member of the Senate's inner circle, or "establishment," [19] had far more influence in the upper chamber than Case, a member of the Senate's small outcast band of liberal Republicans.

The political realities of the situation led Case to conclude that "if the Senate is to approve legislation so badly needed for the protection of the public, some modifications are desirable in my bill as originally introduced." [20] Case's changes did not advance his cause, however, since they were insufficient to please Smathers and involved dropping the provisions favored by rail labor, caus-ing the loss of the only significant group backing for substantial changes in the Transportation Act. As a result, Case was forced to accept Smathers' offer of a bill providing for only minor changes in the time limits in discontinuance proceedings. Lacking an alternative, Case unhappily went along with Smathers, de-claring that he was "not at all satisfied with this bill," while ex-plaining that "It is the best bill we can get at this stage." [21] Case's weakness became glaringly evident a few days later, when Smathers, piqued at the New Jersey senator's public statements, reneged on his promise to get the emasculated train-service bill out of committee. Powerless to retaliate with anything but words, Case ended his 1959 efforts on behalf of the commuter with a sharp attack on the leadership of the Senate Commerce Committee, accusing it of "deliberately blocking all efforts to ease the commuter rail situation." [22]

Despite this setback, Case continued to tailor his commuter activities to fit his constituency interests, committee assignment, and personal views. Although he still believed that it was essential to amend the Transportation Act to provide more effective safeguards against discontinuances not in the public interest, declining constituency pressures on the train-service issue led Case to play a less active role in 1960. He did not participate in the preparation of the Passenger Train Service Act of 1960, nor was he enthusiastic about the RLEA's embellishments, emphasizing that his "chief interest [was] in the provisions of the new bill . . . which embody the provisions of my earlier bill." [23]

With the fading of suburban interest in train service, Case turned in 1960 to other aspects of the commuter problem with constituency appeal which could be pursued with profit from his committee vantage point. One idea, which reflected his "railroad-commerce" frame of reference, was to help the commuter railroads through the establishment of a federal Department of Transportation which would focus national responsibilities for urban transportation in a single agency. New Jersey commuter leaders were enthusiastic about the proposal because it suited their railroad perspective on the commutation issue. An endorsement was forthcoming from Governor Rockefeller, who also saw the commuter question as a railroad rather than an urban transportation matter; but other support did not materialize and the legislation introduced by Case died in the Commerce Committee.

Another promising venture was a Senate Commerce Committee study of the commuter railroad problem in the New York region. It offered the possibility of fostering a tri-state solution with Case as the catalyst. Following a preliminary study, Case hoped to draw "together the Port Authority, the railroads, appropriate municipal and state officials and other interested parties" in a "hard-hitting public hearing" which would lead to the development of "a master pilot plan in [the] tri-state area." [24] Such a study also could satisfy the growing grass-roots demands in New Jersey for an investigation of the Port Authority's failure to play a role in the New York area's rail transportation problem. Early in 1960, Case told commuter spokesmen that he favored a "friendly" Senate inquiry "to get on the public record a clear understanding of what it would take for this job to be done by Port Authority." [25] However, Case had no desire to antagonize the influential PNYA. A few days after announcing his plans, he made it clear that he was "a great admirer of the Port Authority" and that "This would not be a punitive or an unfriendly inquiry at all." [26]

As Chapter IX indicates, the resulting Senate Commerce Committee investigation neither bothered the PNYA nor set the stage for a tri-state solution to the region's commuter railroad woes. Instead, to Case's disappointment, it recommended a massive program of federal aid for New York's suburban rail lines. However, as happened on most of Senator Case's unsuccessful ventures on the suburban rail issue, his efforts were well received where it counted, among his constituents in New Jersey. Typical of the local reaction to the announcement of the PNYA investigation was the IMGBRS's commendation of Case "for taking the initiative in recommending a hearing for the purpose of publicly recording the Port Authority's reasons for not complying with its statutory duty in the field of rail passenger transportation." [27] Later in the year, when Case ran successfully for reelection, he was strongly endorsed by the leadership of the suburban rail groups because of his persistent efforts in Washington on behalf of New Jersey's commuters.[28]

Representative Florence Dwyer

Senator Case, with his prominence, superior staff resources, and committee assignment, was far more successful in capitalizing on the commuter issue than any representative from the New York area. Only one House member from the region, Representative Steven Derounian, filled the appropriate committee slot, in this case on the Commerce Committee's Subcommittee on Transportation and Aeronautics; but he was from Nassau County, the suburban area least threatened by the Transportation Act of 1958. Supporters of the passenger-service amendments were unable even to secure House hearings in 1959 on the bills introduced by Representatives Dwyer, Osmers, Wallhauser, Widnall, Daniels, and Dooley. Of this group, the most enthusiastic and persistent booster of the train-service legislation was Florence Dwyer, a Union County Republican; but her committee assignments—she was a member of the Banking and Currency Committee and the Government Operations Committee—denied her a central role like that which Senator Case was playing in the Senate.

Given her interest in the commuter problem, its importance in her district, and her limited capabilities on the train-service aspect of the issue, Mrs. Dwyer sought, as congressmen seeking to lead and obtain publicity often do in such situations, to turn her committee assignments to advantage. For this purpose, her membership on the Government Operation Committee's Intergovernmental Relations Subcommittee, which had a long-standing interest in the intergovernmental aspects of metropolitan problems, seemed fortunate. Like Senator Case, Mrs. Dwyer believed that New York's commuter rail difficulties required a regional approach. What better way to discover one than an investigation by the Intergovernmental Relations Subcommittee, which also, of course, would place Mrs. Dwyer in the limelight?

Early in 1959, Mrs. Dwyer asked the subcommittee chairman, Representative L. H. Fountain, to hold hearings on the New York transportation crisis as soon as possible. She suggested that the problem would provide excellent material for a case study in intergovernmental relations because the situation was "confused, especially in the minds of the general public, by the vast proliferation of state, regional, county, and local units of government." [29] Before scheduling hearings, Fountain, a cautious Democrat from rural North Carolina whose interest in New York's transportation problems was purely academic, wanted to insure that state and local officials would welcome a congressional forum in which to air their views. Leaders in New York, Albany, and

Trenton were sounded out late in January, 1959. Since the prevalent attitude in the region on the eve of the meeting between Rockefeller, Ribicoff, Meyner, and Wagner was one of hopeful expectancy, Fountain was advised that it might be judicious to wait until the direction of public policy in the region was clarified. On the basis of this information, the chairman decided to drop the matter, much to Mrs. Dwyer's disappointment.

Despite this setback, Representative Dwyer did not abandon her plans for a federal investigation of the intergovernmental aspects of the New York region's mass transportation problem. Along with Fountain and Maine's Senator Edmund Muskie, she played a key role in the establishment in September, 1959, of the Advisory Commission on Intergovernmental Relations (ACIR), which was empowered to "encourage discussion and study at an early stage of emerging public problems that are likely to require intergovernmental cooperation." [30] One of the three House members appointed to the ACIR,[31] Mrs. Dwyer proposed in December, 1959, that the ACIR "undertake [as] a matter of first priority . . . a study of the intergovernmental aspects of the commuter transportation crisis, especially as it concerns the major metropolitan areas of the country and as it involves passenger transportation by railroad." [32] Support from the proposal came from a number of urban members of the ACIR, including the mayors of Los Angeles and Cleveland, Governor Ribicoff of Connecticut, and Westchester County Executive Edwin Michaelian. In mid-1960, the ACIR voted to sponsor a study of metropolitan mass transportation problems. However, the ACIR rejected Mrs Dwyer's recommendation that the New York region's commuter rail problem be the subject of an intensive case study, thus depriving her of an opportunity to serve as a lightening rod for regional transportation sentiment in the tri-state area.

Representative Donald Irwin

The limited capabilities of junior House members and the liabilities of not having a strategic committee assignment are even more apparent in the case of Representative Donald Irwin.

Elected to the House in the 1958 Democratic sweep in Connecticut, the thirty-four-year-old Irwin broke a two-decade Republican hold on the Fairfield County seat. Suburban rail problems on the New Haven were a major item in the mail from back home, and Irwin, eager to consolidate his position in his normally Republican district, made commutation one of his high-priority concerns. He acted as a channel for commuter complaints to the ICC and personally protested New Haven fare increases before the Commission. Irwin also demanded investigations of the New Haven by the ICC, by the House Commerce Committee, and by the Special Subcommittee on Legislative Oversight. In addition, he introduced legislation to improve safety conditions on passenger trains and supported the New Jersey congressmen's efforts to amend the Transportation Act of 1958.[33]

Yet from his seats on the District of Columbia Committee and the Post Office and Civil Service Committee Irwin could do little to advance his proposals. As a result, the freshman congressman's dogged efforts had little effect on the fortunes of the moribund New Haven and its unhappy customers. But Irwin's activities did win him publicity, both in Fairfield County and in the metropolitan press.[34] This attention prompted the AMA to provide Irwin with a copy of the $500-million Commerce loan program bill early in 1960. Irwin had already indicated an interest in a positive federal role in mass transportation. In October, 1959, he asserted that the possibility of federal assistance must be faced. Two months later he suggested that federal aid might be necessary. By January, Irwin was emphasizing "the need and inevitability of a Federal mass transportation policy to embrace all metropolitan regions." [35] The AMA-railroad bill represented an ideal vehicle for Irwin's personal and constituency interests. Claiming it as his own, he introduced the measure without obtaining clearance from the AMA. Lacking committee access, leadership backing, and group support, however, Irwin was unable to move the bill. As a result, he saw the mantle of congressional leadership on federal aid pass to the far better equipped Senator Williams of New Jersey. Nor did Irwin's earnest but fruitless efforts help him

much in Fairfield's Republican suburbs, since he was defeated in
his bid for reelection in 1960.

Senator Harrison Williams

Like Case, Dwyer, and Irwin, New Jersey's junior senator, Harrison Williams, was in the market for a salable item in the metropolitan transportation field, something which would help solve
his constituency's commuter problem, permit him to assume
leadership, and generate publicity. A resident of suburban West-
field, Democrat Williams, like Republicans Case and Dwyer, was
from Union County. In fact, he had succeeded Case in the House
in 1953, only to be defeated in 1956 by Mrs. Dwyer, two years before he made a successful race for the Senate seat being vacated
by retiring Republican H. Alexander Smith.

Although Williams and Case shared the same constituency, they
did not experience similar grass-roots pressures during the commuter crisis, nor did they perceive the problem in the same manner or have equal capabilities for action. When their trains were
threatened during the winter of 1958–59, suburbanites naturally
turned to Republican Case, who had been in the Senate for four
years, rather than Democrat Williams, who had not even been
elected when the emergency began. While Williams did not ignore the train-service issue—he initially introduced legislation
proposing less far-reaching changes in the Transportation Act in
the hope of persuading fellow-Democrat Smathers to support him
and later gave Case his full backing [36]—he was content to take a
back seat to Case. A member of the Banking and Currency Committee and Labor and Public Welfare Committee, Williams recognized that Case's position on the Smathers subcommittee put
him in a far more strategic position to provide leadership on the
passenger-service aspect of the commuter issue. In addition, Williams was aware that as a Democrat he was not as likely to get as
much political mileage as Case out of an issue like the Transportation Act amendments, which had appeal only in the suburbs.

More fundamental differences between the two senators derived from dissimiliar perceptions of the commuter issue. Unlike Case, Williams inclined to the view that the federal government's responsibilities for mass transportation should encompass more than a redressing of the regulatory balance upset by the Transportation Act. As early as April, 1959, Williams raised the possibility of low-interest federal loans for mass transportation capital improvements.[37] Throughout 1959 he expressed interest in a positive federal program. As a result, the senator was receptive to the draft legislation circulated by the AMA early in 1960. In February, while Irwin prematurely introduced the Commerce loan bill and the urban-rail delegation attempted to round up support, Williams commandeered a small task force to refashion the legislation in order to improve its political appeal and to make it more uniquely the "Williams bill."

Williams' background and constituency—he was a liberal Democrat from the nation's largest metropolitan area and represented the state with the most acute commuter rail problem—conditioned his receptivity to the idea of federal mass transportation assistance and enhanced its political attractiveness for him. Yet background and constituency do not completely explain Williams' decision to commit a significant portion of his senatorial resources to this proposal. At this time, early 1960, aside from Governor Meyner, who never pressed Williams or any other New Jersey congressman for action on his federal aid ideas, practically no one in New Jersey was promoting federal mass transportation assistance. Commuter and local groups were not demanding federal aid; in fact, most suburban leaders concurred with Senator Case and Governor Rockefeller that commuter railroads were a state and local problem. Although Mayor Wagner and the MRC were publicizing the AMA-rail plan, little energy was expended securing regional congressional support, which the mayors assumed would be forthcoming when required. The urban-rail strategy at this stage, as revealed in the February, 1960, sessions in Washington, was to secure backing from influential congressmen, a category which did not include freshman Senator Williams.

As a result of this dearth of constituency pressures, the factors influencing Williams were more internal than external. A compound of personal interest, ambition, and opportunity, conditioned, of course, by the broader context of his metropolitan background and generalized constituency concern, led him to make a bid for leadership on the federal aid aspect of the commuter issue. Such a move also fitted in with a notion developing in the mind of the Senator and his aides that Williams, representing the nation's most urbanized state, had a golden opportunity to enhance his position by specializing in metropolitan problems, up to this time a neglected area of congressional concern. When the AMA-railroad bill arrived in his office, Williams already had taken a step in this direction by obtaining a place on the Banking and Currency Committee's Housing Subcommittee, the natural focus of a great deal of the Senate's urban activities.

The task of shaping the AMA-railroad draft to meet Williams' needs and capabilities was given to ArDee Ames, a young former newspaperman on the Senator's staff. Assisting Ames were two urban transportation specialists from the Senate Commerce Committee's Special Study Group on Transportation Policies,[38] Ralph Rechel and Richard Heilprin, both of whom had participated in the urban-rail commuter policy meetings in 1959. For Ames and his co-workers, as for the proponents of any controversial piece of legislation, "Proper committee referral [was] a matter of high strategy." [39] The surest way to avoid unfavorable consideration by the Smathers' subcommittee was to shift the program from the Commerce Department to the HHFA. Referral would then be to the Banking and Currency Committee with hearings before its Housing Subcommittee, which, with its strong urban and liberal representation, promised a far more hospitable climate. Even more important, referral to the Housing Subcommittee would permit Williams to assume direct leadership of the bill. Programmatic as well as political logic dictated the maneuver. Mass transportation, Williams and Ames soon convinced themselves, was more an urban than a commerce or transportation problem. Location within HHFA dovetailed with the long-range objective of Mayor Dilworth and other urban leaders of mass transportation renewal grants, similar to the urban renewal grants already administered within HHFA.

In *Congress Makes a Law*, Bailey notes that of the governing rules of strategy, "In preparing controversial legislation, by far the most important is that a bill must be made to appeal to the widest possible group of potential supporters." [40] This dictum governed much of the surgery performed on the AMA-railroad proposal in Williams' office. To increase the bill's palatability among economy-minded congressmen, the loan authorization was pared from $500 million to $100 million. Rather than create a new program within HHFA, the mass transportation loans were grafted onto the public facilities loan program. Two considerations motivated this maneuver. First, expanding an existing program rather than establishing a new one removed some of the onus attached in conservative quarters to new spending programs. More important, Williams' version proposed to lower the interest rate for *all* public facilities loans. Since loans under the existing program were earmarked for small communities, this logroll was designed to secure rural and small-city support for the mass transportation program. Another innovation was a section on urban transportation planning, a subject ignored in the bills prepared in Philadelphia, designed to enhance the bill's appeal among professional planners and urban transportation specialists. [41] Finally, the bill emphasized the overall urban public transportation problem, as compared with the urban-rail program, whose focus was the rail situation in the great metropolitan area. Williams and his aides believed this broader approach was essential if support was to be secured from urban congressmen whose constituencies had public transportation problems, but no commuter railroads.

These efforts were crowned with success when the AMA decided to throw urban-rail support behind the Williams bill. Although the urban-rail alliance was not especially eager to have the very junior senator from New Jersey as the principal sponsor of "its" federal aid bill, there was no viable alternative. The Commerce Department approach had come to a dead end in the House and obviously had no future in the Senate. Furthermore, Williams was determined to introduce and push his version regardless of the municipal and rail leaders' course of action. Given this situation, and not unimpressed with the political improvements fashioned in Williams' office, the AMA agreed to mobilize the mayors and railroad presidents behind the revised bill. This decision marked the passing of leadership on the federal aid issue from the big cities and the commuter railroads to an urban congressman. It also set the stage for a full-fledged campaign to win congressional and Administration support of federal aid for urban mass transportation.

PART THREE

The Politics of Federal Aid

CHAPTER VIII

Federal Aid in the Congressional Arena

Senator Williams has done a wonderful job here in developing this case. It is something more or less new, and I think everyone who sat here has come to realize the necessity of something being done in this field.

SENATOR JOHN SPARKMAN

On March 24, 1960, Senator Williams introduced his mass transportation bill in the Senate. Terming the $100-million HHFA loan proposal a "modification and conceptual expansion" of the AMA–Eastern railroad program, the freshman senator from New Jersey justified the legislation on grounds which were to become familiar during the campaign to secure federal aid. He stressed the welfare of 100 million Americans dependent upon urban transportation, the need to protect the federal investment in urban highways, and the threat of traffic congestion and transit deterioration to the economic welfare of the nation's major wealth-producing centers. Williams also emphasized the bill's "symbolic value," arguing that enactment would represent "an important recognition on the part of the Federal Government that it, too, has a stake in the survival of our major metropolitan areas—a survival that will in no small part depend on the establishment of good, modern mass transportation systems." He concluded by telling the Senate that "The time for this recognition is now." [1]

As this and the following chapter indicate, Williams had considerable success in securing recognition of mass transportation as a national problem and a federal responsibility. In 1960, he staged Senate hearings which impressively documented the public transportation needs of the larger metropolitan areas. Williams also won Senate approval of his proposal, although opposition from the Eisenhower Administration and the lack of urban leadership in the House of Representatives precluded further action. Before the year ended, the efforts of Williams and his big-city supporters put mass transportation in the front rank of national urban issues. Strong endorsements of the federal aid proposals were obtained from the Democratic party and its victorious presidential candidate, John F. Kennedy. And in 1961, less than fifteen months after the introduction of the original Williams bill, a federal mass transportation program, albeit a far more modest one than the Senator and the urban-rail alliance sought, was initiated in the Housing Act of 1961.

However, the emergence of federal aid as the key aspect of the mass transportation issue in Washington had relatively little impact on the patterns of federal-metropolitan politics. The fragmented interests of the metropolis did not rally around the federal assistance legislation. Instead, as during the period between the passage of the Transportation Act of 1958 and the introduction of Senator Williams' bill, differing perceptions, capabilities, and objectives led the various metropolitan actors down separate paths. Suburban interest in the national government, largely dormant since the easing of the commuter crisis, was not revived by the sudden prominence of federal aid. Nor did Williams' proposal cause the states to reassess the low priority they had assigned to the federal government's role in commuter transportation.

The main sources of support for positive federal involvement continued to come from central-city political leaders and the Eastern commuter railroads. In 1960, planners, metropolitan transportation experts, and urban specialists from the academic community were added to the ranks. The following year, increased publicity and the efforts of Williams, Dilworth, Wagner, Symes, and Alpert brought the transit industry, central-city business interests, and the metropolitan press aboard the bandwagon. By the spring of 1961, the federal mass transportation coalition bore a close resemblance to the familiar urban alliance of "downtown stores, real estate interests concerned with central city property values, commuter railways, central city banks, central city and other politicians concerned with the implications of the worsening of the central city tax base," making "common cause with the press, university professors, the foundations and the civic leaders in a crusade to save downtown." [2]

Metropolitan congressional behavior reflected the changing importance of various federal aspects of the commuter issue. In 1959 suburban Republicans had occupied the Washington stage on the commuter rail question; in 1960 and thereafter urban Democrats played the key roles. Declining suburban interest in the federal government's commuter role reduced the activity of the suburban Republican congressmen who had contested the train-service issue. Further discouraging Republican involvement was the "spending" aspect of the Williams bill, the opposition of the Eisenhower Administration in 1960, and the use of the federal aid issue for partisan purposes by the Democrats. On the other hand, with crystallization of support for federal mass transportation assistance in the large cities and in the top echelons of the Democratic party came widespread congressional support from urban and liberal Democrats. And, as he had planned it, leading this coalition was the junior senator from New Jersey.

The 1960 Hearings

Given the urban and liberal strength in the Housing Subcommittee and Lyndon Johnson's pledge to get a mass transportation bill through the Senate, Williams was optimistic about securing committee backing and vote on the floor.[3] The chief problem was to find time for an adequate hearing on the subcommittee's crowded calendar. After some prodding from Williams and the majority leader, however, subcommittee chairman John Sparkman of Alabama, a long-time supporter of urban legislation, agreed to schedule three days of hearings beginning May 23.

In arranging the hearings, Williams sought to impress Congress with the national impact of the mass transportation problem by inviting witnesses from outside the large Eastern metropolitan centers. He was particularly eager to avoid a preponderance of participants from the New York region, as had occurred during the train-service hearings. And to broaden his base of support in Congress, Williams wanted the hearings to draw attention to all aspects of the mass transportation problem, rather than just the woes of the commuter railroads.[4] Yet this careful planning could not disguise the fact that support for the bill was concentrated almost exclusively in the central cities of the large metropolitan areas. While only two state officials put in an appearance and no suburbanites were present, the big cities, led by Mayors Dilworth, Wagner, Tucker, and Celebrezze, were out in force.

Williams' striving for geographical balance was reflected in the presence for the first time at a federal mass transportation assistance conclave of representatives from the West Coast. Both the general manager of the San Francisco Bay Area Rapid Transit District and the executive director of the Los Angeles Metropolitan Transit Authority were on hand to endorse Williams' program. The presence of the heads of the proposed Los Angeles and San Francisco rapid transit systems, as well as of the chairman of the Chicago Transit Authority, also indicated the broadening of the base of support for federal aid beyond its commuter rail origins. Even New York City, which had originally geared its approach to federal assistance on a commuter railroad rationale, now was talking in terms of federal aid for the city subway system.[5]

The mayors' appetite for federal mass transportation assistance —Cleveland wanted $129 million and Philadelphia $80 million for a single project—led them to express disappointment over the paltry $100 million in loans proposed by the bill. Mayor Wagner pointed out that the legislation called for less than the annual subsidy paid by New York City's taxpayers to maintain their transit system. None the less, the big-city leaders concurred with Williams that it was a symbolic beginning. "More important than the specific sums of money that would be available to local governments," declared Mayor Wagner, "is that Senator Williams' bill establishes the interest and involvement of the Federal Government in a very vital field."[6] AMA president Tucker agreed, terming the hearing "an historic occasion," marking the first time Congress had granted "official recognition . . . to one of the most pressing domestic problems" facing the nation.[7]

Echoing the views of the big-city leaders were Williams' two most vocal boosters on the Housing Subcommittee, Philadelphia's Senator Clark and Chicago's Senator Paul Douglas. Expert support came from Luther Gulick, a former City Administrator of New York and president of the Institute of Public Administration (IPA), an urban research organization based in New York City, and Detlov Bronk, president of the National Academy of Sciences. Alpert and Symes, as usual, carried the ball for the Eastern railroads, both emphasizing that the legislation was designed primarily to benefit the metropolitan areas rather than the carriers. Railroad support of the bill also won an endorsement from the ICC, which noted that the proposal seemed consistent with the 1958 report of the Smathers subcommittee "in that it would provide Federal assistance to State and local governments in attempting to solve what is essentially a local problem, but one in which the Federal Government has a real concern." [8]

Aside from the commuter railroads, however, the more conservative elements of the central-city coalition were not yet in the federal mass transportation camp. Little editorial support was forthcoming from the metropolitan press, particularly in the New York region. Except for the past chairman of the National Retail Merchants Association's downtown development committee, representatives of central-city business and civic organizations and the private transit industry did not endorse the Williams bill at the 1960 hearings. Moreover, fear that the private capital market for municipal improvements would be damaged by the lower interest rates for mass transportation and community facility loans proposed by Williams led three influential national business groups—the U.S. Chamber of Commerce, the American Bankers Association, and the Investment Bankers' Association of America —to submit statements opposing the legislation.

As expected, an unfavorable response also came from the Eisenhower Administration. Four years before, MRTC fiscal consultant William Miller had explored the possibilities of federal aid, only to learn that the Administration opposed the use of federal funds for local functions such as mass transportation.[9] Subsequent inquiries by Dilworth and Clark and the efforts of the February, 1960, urban-rail delegation produced similar responses. However, the White House's election-year desire to avoid fueling the recurrent Democratic charge of Republican neglect of urban problems prompted it to soft-pedal its opposition to the Williams bill by having no spokesmen appear at the hearings. Instead, comment was confined to negative reports on the proposal filed with the committee by three federal agencies. Treasury's statement set forth the Administration's basic feelings about federal transit aid, declaring that "Federal participation in programs which are more appropriately the responsibility of States and local authorities must be held to an absolute minimum if budget expenditures are to be kept within reasonable limits in the years ahead." The Department of Commerce objected to the establishment of a transportation program in the HHFA, while the HHFA protested that the interest rate formula proposed by Williams would "result in a program far exceeding any proper Federal responsibility in this field." [10]

Success in the Senate and Failure in the House

The Senate hearings marked the arrival of the mass transportation issue at the federal level. Under Williams' skillful management, the prime objective of the urban-rail alliance had been achieved, as a persuasive political case was made for a positive federal role. A keen observer of the legislative process has noted that while the enlightenment of "judicious and detached Congressional minds" is not their main function, hearings can have "valuable byproducts." [11] In this case, the byproduct exceeded expectations. Senators were impressed by the testimony; congressional interest was aroused. At the conclusion of the hearings, Senator Sparkman told Williams he had never heard "so much dramatic testimony speaking to a need in a program." [12] Even Senator Styles Bridges, the chairman of the Republican Policy Committee, after a nudge from New England rail interests, endorsed the bill.

In an interesting twist on the usual conservative outcry against the federal octupus choking local initiative, Bridges, normally no friend of liberal legislation, declared that there was "only one agency big enough and powerful enough and with facilities sufficient to deal successfully with the octopus that is strangling the lifeblood of our metropolitan cities, and that agency is, of course, the Federal government." [13]

Bipartisan support moved the bill quickly through the Housing Subcommittee with only one major change: the low interest rate was limited to mass transportation loans. The deletion was made because Senator Sparkman thought the extenison of lower interest rates to all public facility loans would make it easy for the Administration to justify a veto should the bill get through Congress. [14] In mid-June, the Banking and Currency Committee favorably reported the revised bill. In a report prepared in Senator Williams' office, the arguments for active federal participation in mass transportation were restated. To counter the Republican contention, heard in the New York area from Senator Case and Governor Rockefeller, that federal aid would result in a relaxation of local efforts, the report emphasized that the program was "intended to sitmulate the maximum degree of concern, involvement, and initiative on the part of the State and local governments, which in the long run will be as important as the dollar volume of the assistance given." [15]

One month after the end of the hearings, the Senate passed Williams' bill. Senator Johnson's pledge, urban political power, Williams' skill and able staffwork, the impact of the hearings, and the political influence of the railroads greased the legislative skids. [16] Also helping the mass transportation cause in the Senate was the political situation in a presidential year. Although not particularly enthusiastic about Williams' bill, conservative and nonurban Democrats were willing to boost the party's metropolitan appeal in a presidential election year, particularly since it was not likely to cost anything. The bill's prospects were dim in the House. Even if the House passed it, a presidential veto appeared to be a strong possibility. Only archconservative Strom Thurmond of South Carolina dissented on the Senate floor, protesting that the national government had no business aiding local matters such as mass transportation. On June 27, the Senate passed the Williams bill by a voice vote.[17]

Commenting on the Senate's approval of the $100-million loan program, the New York *Times* noted that the "bill now goes to the House, where no action is likely." [18] This proved to be an accurate forecast for two reasons: first, the Administration remained opposed, and, second, sustained leadership for the measure was lacking in the House.

Williams' attacks on the Administration—at the Senate hearing he had accused it of permitting the mass transportation crisis to worsen "by engaging in a prolonged Alphonse and Gaston routine" [19]—and the hope of sidestepping an "anti-urban" veto by killing the bill in the House produced a change in Administration tactics. On hand at the House hearings to deprecate the need for federal aid were HHFA Administrator Norman Mason and Urban Renewal Commissioner David Walker. The urgent requirement was "for stimulating and coordinating the planning of transportation systems, for integrating transportation planning with comprehensive planning, and for designing transportation systems that will help create the sort of urban communities in which we want to live and work." Until this sort of planning was undertaken, there would be "no real measure of the need for metropolitan transportation facilities." Another Administration argument for inaction was the lack of public bodies "equipped to finance and develop coordinated transportation systems for our metropolitan areas." When these planning and organizational tasks were completed would be the time to judge "whether Federal assistance is needed in financing the construction of such facilities, or whether, as we firmly believe, the facilities for mass transportation can better be financed from State, local, and private sources." [20]

Aside from the testimony of the HHFA officials, aides of Wagner and Dilworth, Symes of the Pennsylvania Railroad, and Senator Williams, the House hearings were given over to brief endorsements of the bill by nineteen urban congressmen, most of whom were rounded up by the AMA and the mayors. Except for

Delaware's Harris McDowell, they all came from major metropolitan areas—six each from New York and Philadelphia, three from Pittsburgh, and one each from Boston, Cleveland, and San Francisco—and two-thirds were from large cities within these areas. Only five were Republicans, all with relatively liberal voting records and none with misgivings about supporting a bill opposed by the Eisenhower Administration.[21]

Despite this turnout, the lack of a House counterpart to Senator Williams was apparent at the hearings. The burden of answering the Administration's criticism fell on Williams, who counter-attacked with the claim that the need for federal aid had been amply documented. He agreed that comprehensive planning must be encouraged, "but first you have to give the communities some incentive, which can't be accomplished by noble words alone." Giving priority to aid applicants with workable plans for coordinated transportation systems, declared the Senator, was the most effective method of spurring planning. Belittling the Administration's "policy of delay," he warned that

If we keep procrastinating until all our metropolitan areas come up with full-blown plans, we may find that we have waited too long, with the result that we will find ourselves called upon to spend far greater sums to provide alternative forms of transportation for those lines going out of business in the meantime.[22]

Representative Irwin, who had hoped to play a leading role in the House, found his junior status and lack of a place on the Banking and Currency Committee insuperable hurdles. All he could do was introduce a companion bill to Williams' measure and endorse the legislation at the House hearings. With Irwin out of the picture, the task of leadership fell upon the metropolitan area representatives on the Banking and Currency Committee. Eighteen of the twenty-nine members of the committee represented urban or suburban districts, and eight actively supported the Williams bill,[23] but none were able to provide sustained leadership on the issue. Florence Dwyer and Newark Democrat Hugh Addonizio were among the bill's staunchest supporters within the committee, but both were hampered in their efforts to steer the legislation to the floor. Addonizio was not a member of the subcommittee which considered the bill, and Mrs. Dwyer, although on the subcommittee, was excluded from a leadership role because the Democrats, in an election year, did not want a Republican floor manager for "their" legislation.

This lack of effective leadership, a persistent urban malady in the lower house, prevented the bill from coming to the floor for a vote. No one was able to secure the coordinated action on the part of three House patriarchs—Sam Rayburn, Brent Spence, and Howard Smith—necessary to get the bill out of committee. Although unimpressed by the legislation, Speaker Rayburn had assured the urban and rail leaders, as well as Senator Johnson, that he would try to get the bill through if it reached the House floor. Banking and Currency chairman Brent Spence, the oldest member of the House, had no strong feeling about the bill. But he did have a busy calendar and a sharp ear for grass-roots sentiment. A few hostile press notices and the silence of the commuters on the issue troubled him. Spence was also unhappy because the Senate dropped the public-facilities-loan interest-rate extension which appealed to his rural Kentucky constituency interests. Refusing to be rushed, Spence awaited assurances that Rayburn and Rules Committee chairman Howard Smith would act on the bill. Although a favorable vote in the Rules Committee was likely because the railroads had been able to persuade two Republicans to support the legislation, chairman Smith declined to take up the proposal until it was reported from Spence's committee. Combined with the pressure of time in the hectic days before adjournment, the absence of urban leadership to get Rayburn, Spence, and Smith together finally killed the 1960 mass transportation legislation in committee.

The Democrats Embrace Federal Aid

While Congress was considering the Williams bill, the big-city mayors continued to provide the chief source of support and publicity for federal mass transportation assistance. In a presidential election year, with all eyes on the convention and Electoral College strength of the urban states, it was not difficult either to keep the commuter aid issue alive or to make it part of the national legislative objectives of the urban bloc and the presidential wing of the Democratic party.

In May, the U.S. Conference of Mayors, representing cities of over 50,000 and with roughly the same leadership as the AMA, had asked Congress to "give its prompt approval to pending proposals with respect to financing capital improvements for improved commuter service." [24] Late in June, Mayor Wagner called a press conference to preview his presentation to the Democratic platform committee. A federal loan program was needed immediately, declared the Mayor, and federal subsidies were a definite possibility for the future. Advocating a tri-state tri-level approach, he emphasized that not too much of the burden should fall on the cities. Wagner also called for a Department of Urban Affairs to provide leadership, planning, and coordination in the attack on the commuter and other urban problems.[25] Testifying before the Democratic platform committee, Wagner, Dilworth, and Mayor Daley of Chicago, representing the AMA and the U.S. Conference of Mayors, called for a mass transit federal aid plank. In August, as hopes faded for the Williams bill in the House, Wagner joined municipal officials from Philadelphia, San Francisco, and other cities in an effort to secure action before adjournment, urging "immediate, decisive action" on the mass transportation legislation.[26]

The year 1960 marked the coming of age for urban problems in the national party platforms. To no one's surprise, Wagner, Dilworth, Daley, and their friends fared well at the hands of the Democratic platform writers and nominee John F. Kennedy. Never before had a party platform treated urban areas and their problems as a major national issue. Among a number of planks on cities and their suburbs, the Democratic platform pledged "federal aid for comprehensive metropolitan transportation programs, including bus and rail mass transit, commuter railroads as well as highway programs and construction of civil airports." Urban problems received a briefer and more general treatment in the Republican platform. Ignoring commuter aid, they promised only a "stepped up program to assist in urban planning, designed to insure farsighted and wise use of land and to coordinate mass transportation and other vital facilities in our metropolitan areas." [27]

The stronger statement in the Democratic platform reflected the sources of support for mass transportation aid from its inception. Most of those connected with the development of the AMA-rail program and the Williams bill were Democrats. Equally important, Kennedy, having secured the nomination in the urban states and planning to win the election in them, desired a strong urban plank. He had often repeated the view that "We must increase the amount of the Federal appropriation . . . going to meet our urban problems." [28] The Republican statement, on the other hand, was a product in part of the Eisenhower Administration's opposition to new domestic spending programs. Another factor was nominee Richard Nixon's lack of interest in urban problems, which he had ignored in the year prior to the convention.[29] Moreover, Governor Rockefeller, the prime urban influence brought to bear on the Republican platform, was opposed to federal mass transport aid to the cities. Finally, and perhaps most important, Nixon made no effort to match Kennedy's promises to the metropolitan areas because he was convinced that he could not win a campaign based on domestic issues.[30]

Kennedy made his major campaign speech on urban problems in October. Over 500 Democrats, including Wagner, Jersey City's Mayor Witkowski, and Newark's Mayor Carlin gathered in Pittsburgh to hear Kennedy heap scorn on the Eisenhower Administration's "shameful record of neglect" on urban problems. Echoing Williams, he characterized the Republican attitude on mass transportation as "ignore it" and called for federal aid to commuter transportation, conditioned on unified transportation planning.[31] Also in October, in a campaign statement addressed to the transportation industry, Kennedy declared that "the Democratic party knows of no wiser investment that this nation could make" than federal aid to urban transportation.[32]

The Suburbs and Federal Aid

Senator Williams had initially attempted to cultivate suburban support for his proposal. Early in 1960, he emphasized that federal aid was not a substitute for the train-service amendments pending before the Smathers subcommittee.[33] For home consumption, he pointed out that agencies such as the Port Authority would be eligible for aid under his bill.[34] Despite these efforts, federal assistance attracted little attention in the suburbs. None of the grass-roots groups which had set the tone for the 1959 train-service hearings journeyed to Washington to comment on Williams' proposals. Many suburbanites opposed new federal spending programs on principle. For example, two weeks before the hearings on the mass transportation bill commenced, Representative Dwyer reported that only 40 percent of her Union County constituents favored federal assistance to insure continued passenger service.[35] Political factors also played a part in shaping suburban attitudes. Reflecting Governor Rockefeller's distaste for federal aid, local Republican leaders in Westchester and Long Island informed Senator Javits that their only concern was with aid from Albany. Even where there was suburban interest in federal help, it was shaped by suburbia's railroad-oriented perceptions and preoccupation with the local situation. In a statement submitted to the Housing Subcommittee, Thomas Taber, the tireless publicist of the Morris County Railroad Transportation Association, suggested that the Williams bill be modified so "that these funds . . . be used for the maintenance, improvement, rehabilitation, and extension of existing lines; and that they not be made available for new railroads not as yet built and in service." [36]

A few New Jersey newspapers attempted to arouse suburban interest in federal aid. The New Brunswick *Daily Home News* thought the "bill introduced by Senator Williams seems to hold great hope for the future of mass transportation in the Nation," while the Bergen *Evening Record* found the Senate committee report on the mass transportation legislation encouraging because it bolstered the case for decisive action on federal aid without delay.[37] But more common was skepticism, particularly concerning the Democratic platform's "strong pitch to the commuter." The Newark *Evening News* reminded suburbanites that the Democrats' two "contributions to the commuters' welfare" were the Smathers subcommittee recommendations and the Transportation Act of 1958.[38]

Sharing the suburbs' lack of enthusiasm about Williams' proposal was the commuter's champion, Senator Clifford Case. Throughout 1959 Case had stressed the need for state and local solutions to the suburban rail problem, arguing that federal moves in the direction of subsidy would remove the pressure from local units to solve the problem. As a member of the Surface Transportation Subcommittee, Case had consulted with the delegation of urban and rail leaders in February. Although not convinced of the wisdom of their proposal, he agreed to join Senator Magnuson in sponsoring the Department of Commerce mass transport loan bill. However, Case was not informed by the AMA and the railroads of the shifting of support to the Housing Subcommittee–HHFA approach of the Williams bill. Taken by surprise when Williams suddenly emerged in command of the federal loan program, Case quickly cooled to the idea. He declined to cosponsor or testify in favor of the legislation. Case also cautioned that federal aid without regulatory reform, that is, his Transportation Act amendment approach, would be extremely unwise.[39]

The States and the Williams Bill

Like the suburbs, New York and New Jersey—the only states with direct mass transportation responsibilities in 1960—paid little attention to the efforts of Senator Williams and his central-city allies to initiate an urban-oriented federal transit program. The states' commuter railroad focus, their dislike for direct federal-local ventures, and their preoccupation with the immediate problem of keeping the suburban lines running—solutions to which could not await the enactment of the Williams bill at some distant date—combined to produce disdain for federal transit aid in Albany and only peripheral interest in Trenton.

Governor Rockefeller's negative attitude toward federal financial involvement in the commuter problem remained unchanged. In February, 1960, he turned down an invitation to join the delegation of mayors and railroad presidents which journeyed to Washington to promote mass transportation assistance. The following month, the head of the State Office of Transportation resigned after the Governor failed to release his recommendation that the state seek federal subsidies for the commuter railroads.[40] Declining to appear at the Williams bill hearings, Rockefeller indicated to Senator Javits that the legislation was of no concern or importance to the state. In July, while the Democrats were giving commuter aid a prominent place in their national platform, Rockefeller declared that he was a "little skeptical of passing the whole thing to the federal government and some federal authority which would subsidize everybody." [41]

Although the Democrats in Trenton had a less negative outlook on federal aid than the Republicans in Albany, the Meyner administration, busy with plans to preserve vital commuter service in the state, had little time for the Williams bill. At the Senator's request, Governor Meyner journeyed to Washington to tell the Housing Subcommittee that the transit legislation "will not cause New Jersey's transportation problems to vanish, but it would be a start on the road back." [42] Six weeks before, however, Highway Commissioner Dwight Palmer had indicated that federal aid did not figure prominently in New Jersey's plans. In recommending a $6-million state subsidy program, Palmer emphasized that "Action at the Federal level aiming to preserve the commuter lines . . . will be time consuming in accomplishment," and concluded that "Emergency State action of some character appears as the only immediate course to prevent complete breakdown of suburban rail service." [43]

Moreover, state officials in New Jersey, like their suburban constituents, considered the Port Authority a far more likely source of help than the national government. While the state's lobbying in 1960 for federal transit aid began and ended with Governor

Meyner's trip to Washington in May, Palmer worked for months to bring the PNYA into the commuter rail picture. These negotiations produced an agreement in September, 1960, that the PNYA would purchase, improve, and operate the bankrupt Hudson and Manhattan Tubes, conditioned on a guarantee that it would be saddled with no other rail responsibilities. In announcing that the PNYA would assume deficit-producing commuter rail responsibilities, executive director Austin Tobin indicated that one of the alternatives of Port Authority operation of the tubes considered and rejected during the negotiations was federal aid, since both Trenton and the PNYA "agreed that the possibility of immediate financial assistance from the Federal Government was unlikely." [44]

The New Haven Loan Guarantee

Another 1960 venture involving New York area actors and Washington—Governor Rockefeller's successful bid to secure help for the New Haven from the ICC—also sheds light on state participation in federal-metropolitan politics. In March, 1960, the failure of New York's commuter program to resolve the New Haven's financial difficulties led George Alpert to obtain a $10-million loan guaranteed by the ICC so that the railroad could meet its operating expenses. The ICC program, established at the urging of the Eastern railroads in the Transportation Act of 1958, involved federal guarantees of loans made to the railroads at commercial interest rates by private lending institutions.[45] By late September, the New Haven again tottered on the brink of bankruptcy, unable to meet its operating expenses for more than 30 days. Alpert sought to float a $6-million federally guaranteed loan to provide desperately needed working capital, but the ICC balked at this new request, since the New Haven's prospective earning power did not furnish reasonable assurance that another loan could be repaid.

The ensuing crisis led to the creation of a committee—headed by Rockefeller's chief transportation adviser, William Ronan, with other members representing Connecticut, New York City, and Westchester County—which recommended a program of additional tax relief, local subsidies, and ICC approval of the New Haven's pending application for a $6-million loan guarantee.[46] Despite his strong aversion to a federal financial role in the commuter problem, Rockefeller found a number of appealing features in the ICC program. It fit New York's "railroad-commerce" approach to the commuter problem, in comparison with the "mass transportation–urban" orientation of the Williams bill forces. Moreover, by making funds directly available to the railroads, it avoided the problem of federal aid bypassing the states, Rockefeller's chief objection to the urban-rail alliance's transit legislation. Finally, and most important in the crisis context of the New Haven situation, financial help was available immediately under the ICC program.

To implement his New Haven program, Rockefeller organized a delegation of officials from New York, Connecticut, Massachusetts, Rhode Island, New York City, and Westchester County which journeyed to Washington to persuade the ICC to reconsider the New Haven's application. While sympathetic, the commissioners pointed to the legislative prohibition against backing loans when there was no apparent ability on the part of the carrier to repay. Perhaps, the ICC members suggested, bankruptcy would provide a more effective solution than loans which merely extended a hopeless situation. New York officials disagreed, arguing that another loan, coupled with state and local tax relief, could save the day. Only after receiving assurances that substantial tax relief and fare increases would be forthcoming did the commissioners reluctantly agree to approve the application. The following day the ICC guaranteed a $4.5-million loan to the New Haven from the Chase Manhattan Bank, but withheld a guarantee of the remaining $1.5 million until the various state legislatures and regulatory commissions had fulfilled their part of the bargain.

Patterns of Action: 1960

A comparison of state and suburban behavior in 1960, particularly the New Haven loan episode, and the campaign for the Williams bill brings into sharp focus the basic differences between the federal mass transportation perceptions and objectives of the states and suburbs, on one hand, and the central-city cluster of interests on the other. The former turned to Washington during emergencies for help with their immediate difficulties and perceived the problem largely in limited commuter railroad–commerce terms. By contrast, the latter grouping adopted a broad mass transportation–urban focus and, as in urban renewal, sought to enlist Washington as a long-term ally in the preservation of the urban core. Thus, behavior on the federal aspects of the mass transportation issue, particularly of the participants from the New York area, suggests that federal-metropolitan political interaction tends both to reflect and to reproduce the cleavages between the central city and its traditional antagonists, the suburbs and the state.

CHAPTER IX

Federal Aid on the New Frontier

> The administration is fully cognizant and very much concerned with the problem of mass transportation. . . . There is also, I think, agreement that further action is required. There has not yet been a determination as to what that further action should be.   ROBERT WEAVER

Urban hopes for the enactment of mass transportation legislation were buoyed by the election of John F. Kennedy. The President-elect's record, campaign pledges, and urban political support all seemed certain to insure active White House backing for a federal commuter aid program in 1961. As for Congress, the Senate emerged from the 1960 election with its liberal majority intact, and repassage of the transit bill appeared assured. Although the election had reinforced the House's anti-spending bloc, thus endangering many of the new President's programs, the urban-rail alliance was confident that railroad-inspired Republican votes would provide the margin of victory on mass transportation. Thus, Senator Williams and his supporters had every reason to believe that federal transit aid would be one of the more easily reached sectors of President Kennedy's New Frontier.

Developments in the pre-inaugural period bolstered these expectations. Early in December, Kennedy cited mass transportation as one of the five most important problems requiring attention by a Department of Urban Affairs. Once again he supported federal help for commuter railroads and transit systems.[1] A month later the President-elect's task force on housing policies endorsed the $100-million mass transportation loan program proposed by

Williams in 1960.[2] Although differing with the urban approach of the Williams bill, two studies released at the end of the year reinforced the case for federal commuter aid. In a report to Kennedy on the regulatory agencies, James Landis recommended federal loan guarantees for the commuter railroads.[3] And a study undertaken for the Senate Commerce Committee—the so-called Doyle Report—documented the transportation crisis in the major metropolitan areas. However, the Doyle Report's commerce origins restricted its prescriptions to an ICC loan program for the suburban railroads.[4]

Cheered by these favorable omens, Williams introduced the Urban Mass Transportation Act of 1961 a week before Kennedy's inauguration. The anticipated support in key decision-making centers resulted in the elimination of the interest-rate logroll of the previous edition and an increase in the loan authorization from $100 million to $250 million. The new bill also required the HHFA to give priority to those loan applicants developing a transit program within the framework of a comprehensive regional transportation plan. In addition to the loans, the proposal authorized $75 million in matching grants for comprehensive urban transportation planning and pilot demonstration projects. The demonstration grants—an innovation of Senator Williams and his assistant ArDee Ames—were to be awarded for projects which

would make a significantly important contribution to the development of research data and information of general applicability relating to the improvement of mass transportation service and the contribution of such service toward meeting total urban transportation needs at minimum costs.[5]

Spurred by his success with the mass transportation issue in 1960, Williams also broadened his urban horizons, seeking to bolster his claim to metropolitan leadership in the Congress. Taking his cue from *The Race for Urban Space,* a study prepared by New York's Regional Plan Association (RPA),[6] Williams and Ames readied a program of federal grants and loans for open spaces. The Senator also became one of Congress' most vigorous advocates of a Department of Urban Affairs, arguing that a de-

partment was essential so that urban issues like mass transportation would have a "partisan" at the highest federal level, a secretary representing a clientele, able to "do battle for cities and
suburbs in much the same way the Secretary of Labor or the
Secretary of State do battle for programs in which they have
faith." [7]

However, when the new Administration took office, Williams,
to his surprise, was unable to find any "partisans" at the other
end of Pennsylvania Avenue willing to "do battle" for his mass
transportation bill. The urban-rail alliance learned to their cha-
grin one of Washington's oldest lessons: it is much easier to win
an endorsement from a candidate on the stump than it is to secure
the backing of a President burdened with budgetary headaches,
internecine warfare among the executive departments, and complex questions of foreign and defense policy. Unable to resolve
the conflicting views of his advisers and the mass transportation
assistance partisans, President Kennedy sought refuge in a proposal for further study of the problem.

This unexpected turn of events set the tone for the federal-
metropolitan politics of mass transportation in 1961. Although
the states and the suburbs continued to play a peripheral role,
the federal aid coalition was reinforced, particularly through the
addition of organized labor and the central-city business and
civic interests that had been missing in 1960. Drawing on this
broadened base of urban support—which included many congressmen and groups whose help was vital to the Administration
—Williams and the urban-rail leaders pressured President Kennedy to honor his mass transportation commitments. First, they
attempted to negotiate a satisfactory settlement with Administration officials. These efforts failing, hearings were staged in the
Senate to demonstrate the strength of the mass transportation
alliance. Finally, persistent urban pressures, skillful legislative
maneuvering, and the Administration's desire not to alienate the
large segment of its housing coalition seeking transit action produced a compromise victory for the urban-rail alliance. A federal
mass transportation assistance program was established in the
Housing Act signed by President Kennedy on June 30, 1961.

The Dispute with the White House

President Kennedy himself had no quarrel with Senator Williams' proposals; but with little time to give to relatively minor issues like transit and the need to maintain harmony in his official family, he was not prepared to override his advisers' numerous objections to the bill on personal grounds alone. The Bureau of the Budget was unhappy about the financing provisions of the legislation. While loans might be more palatable to Congress, Budget officials pointed out that they would offer little incentive to communities which had reached their debt limit or which could float municipal tax-exempt bonds at a lower interest rate than federal loans. They also emphasized that the only criteria in the Williams bill for setting the magnitude of federal financial participation had been how much Congress might be persuaded to accept. These considerations led Budget Director David Bell to argue that it would be premature to initiate a transit aid program in the absence of a comprehensive study of urban transportation needs.

The logic of assigning mass transportation to the HHFA was also questioned within the new Administration. Secretary of Commerce Luther Hodges argued that mass transportation should be given to his department, since it already administered the federal highway program and was charged with the development of national transportation policy. Hodges' vigorously advanced claims were enhanced by the failure of HHFA Administrator Robert Weaver to defend the Williams bill. Like his predecessor in the Eisenhower Administration, Weaver felt that the lack of comprehensive metropolitan transportation plans in most of the larger urban areas made federal aid premature. In addition, Weaver, whose background was in housing, approached the transportation problem with caution. He feared that "deficit-ridden transit networks [might gobble] up all the funds communities earmark for housing." [8] Finally, after weathering strong Southern opposition in the Senate to his appointment, Weaver, a Negro, had no desire to engage in a public dispute with Hodges, a former governor of North Carolina. [9]

Commerce's jurisdictional challenge was far more important to Williams and his urban allies than Budget Director Bell's financial objections. By 1961, the tactical considerations which had caused the transit loan program to be shifted by Williams from Commerce to HHFA had hardened into fundamental urban doctrine. At issue was a basic question of federal policy: Would new urban programs be centralized in a single agency or would they be scattered all over the Washington landscape? The same issue was posed on open spaces, where a fight was developing between the HHFA, which would administer the program under Williams' bill, and the Department of the Interior, which claimed jurisdiction on the basis of its responsibility for the national park system. Unless new programs went to the HHFA, Williams argued, urban interests would obtain little benefit from President Kennedy's plan to make the housing agency a Department of Urban Affairs.

Personal considerations were closely interwoven with matters of principle for Williams. Mass transportation was his issue; to lose control over the transit bill would be a serious blow to his prestige. The Senate Housing Subcommittee could not function as the legislative focus of federal urban activities unless the HHFA's role were broadened to include programs like mass transit and open spaces. If mass transportation went to the Department of Commerce, the bill would go to the Smathers subcommittee and Williams would be out in the cold. With his budding future as a congressional spokesman on metropolitan problems at stake, Williams was prepared to fight the President if Hodges convinced the White House to assign mass transportation to the Department of Commerce.

Before airing the dispute in public, however, Williams, Ames, Dilworth, McLaughlin of the AMA, and others tried to convince the Administration to endorse their urban approach to mass transportation. In meetings with White House aides and representatives of the involved agencies, the leaders of the urban-rail alliance emphasized that the Williams bill had wide backing and could readily be passed, while a Commerce-based transit program probably would die in the Smathers subcommittee. As for the merits of Hodges' claims, they contended that mass transportation was more of an urban than a transportation problem. Besides, they argued, the Department of Commerce was as devoid of transit experience as the HHFA. Particularly vehement objections to a Commerce program came from the big cities, which feared BPR involvement and, more important, distribution of transit aid through the states as in the federal highway program. Mayor Dilworth now emphasized the point that "It would be fatal if [mass transportation] went into the Commerce Department." Not only would the program be in the hands of "disinterested" highway engineers, but, "Even more serious from our point of view, [aid] would immediately be channeled to the States, and we would have to deal not with the Commerce Department, but . . . with the States." [10]

These negotiations convinced the White House that a decision to assign mass transportation to the Department of Commerce would be inopportune, but the discussions did not erase the Administration's objections to Williams' legislation nor settle the jurisdictional issue. Therefore, President Kennedy's housing message of March 9—which covered all aspects of the Administration's urban program—neither endorsed mass transportation assistance nor mentioned the organizational issue. Instead, the President emphasized that resolving the urban transportation problem would "put a heavy drain on our resources" and that "responsibility for working out . . . solutions rests primarily with local government and private enterprise." As for the federal role, Kennedy reported only that he had "asked the Administrator of the Housing and Home Finance Agency and the Secretary of Commerce to undertake an immediate and extensive study of urban transportation problems and the proper role of the Federal Government in their solution." [11]

Marshaling the Central-City Coalition

The disappointing treatment of mass transportation in the housing message strengthened the resolve of the urban-rail forces to press for the enactment of Williams' bill in 1961. Acceptance

of the President's proposal to await the outcome of the planned
study would mean at least a year's delay in getting a transit aid
bill passed. More important, acquiescence would lend credence
to the notion that the Commerce Department had a legitimate
claim to mass transportation responsibilities. Although Williams
and his urban allies were aware that the Administration's commitment to a study made their task more difficult, they believed
their chances of winning were good. Key elements of Kennedy's
domestic coalition were in the mass transportation camp. Williams had solid support for his bill in the Senate, including a
majority of the Housing Subcommittee.[12] The big cities wanted
action on mass transportation in 1961, and the AMA and the
U.S. Conference of Mayors were prepared to mobilize pressures
from cities large and small, as well as from various groups normally allied with the municipal lobbies on urban issues.

To display this support for the Williams bill, the urban-rail
leaders decided to muster their forces at another round of Senate
hearings. Upon learning that the President would avoid a decision on mass transportation in the housing message, Williams
persuaded Senator Sparkman to schedule three days of hearings
on the transit bill beginning March 20. In announcing the hearings, Williams fired the first salvo in the public battle for an
urban approach to mass transportation in 1961, emphasizing in
particular the central-city aspects of his proposals:

A really constructive program of Federal encouragement and assistance
in mass transportation can be a potent instrument in revitalizing our
great urban centers. We cannot renew our cities by just building new
buildings under the urban renewal program. We must also have a
mass transportation program, working hand in hand with other development programs, to help local leaders reshape 19th century cities
to meet 20th century needs.[13]

Williams opened the hearings with a detailed defense of his
bill and a point-by-point rebuttal of the Administration's position. His principal themes were the need for action and the urban
nature of the mass transportation problem. Singled out for criticism were the commuter railroad–commerce focus of the state

programs in New York and New Jersey, the Doyle Report, and
the ICC, which a few weeks before had recommended a federal
commuter railroad loan program.[14] Scorning the notion that "the
Federal Government should tailor its assistance to this particular
emergency," Williams insisted that

We must recognize that rail commuter service is only one of many
facets in the urban transportation complex. . . . Success or failure of
[commuter rail] improvement will depend largely upon the degree to
which we come to grips with the whole range of factors affecting public acceptance of mass transportation, from fringe area parking to
downtown transfer service.[15]

Williams proceeded to document his case with an impressive
parade of witnesses who, by and large, agreed that federal action
could be delayed no longer, that rail commutation and transit
were urban problems, and that the federal mass transportation
program belonged in the HHFA. Even William Saunders, a Commerce Department consultant, told the subcommittee that "It
makes more sense to give HHFA the basic responsibility for running this program." [16] Neither Secretary Hodges nor any other
representatives of the Kennedy Administration appeared to counter Williams' arguments and witnesses.

As in 1960, the star performers at the hearings came from the
great urban centers. Mayors Dilworth, Celebrezze, and William
Hartsfield of Atlanta were on hand, Deputy City Administrator
Maxwell Lehman represented Mayor Wagner and the MRC, and
Boston, Chicago, Pittsburgh, and San Francisco sent public transit
officials. Moreover, the range of urban interests—largely central
city in orientation—backing the Williams bill was broader than
in 1960. In addition to the AMA and the U.S. Conference of
Mayors, support came from the American Institute of Planners,
the American Transit Association, the National Association of
Homebuilders, the National Housing Conference, and New
York's RPA. The opposition of the U.S. Chamber of Commerce
—which found the proposal an unwise "Federal intervention"
into a problem "primarily local in nature" [17]—was offset by endorsements from local chambers and business leaders in Atlanta,
Boston, New York, Rochester, and San Francisco, as well as the
Pennsylvania State Chamber of Commerce.

Much of this new support from central-city civic and business groups was a result of efforts by the urban-rail leaders to add these more conservative elements to their coalition. Williams and his Philadelphia associates kept busy promoting their transit program throughout the winter. For example, on January 10, the day before the 1961 bill was introduced, a Dilworth aide discussed the proposals with a group of Newark civic and business leaders.[18] Two days later Williams secured an endorsement at the National Retail Merchants Association's convention in New York.[19] Williams' endeavors also won support for federal aid from a number of business leaders who attended a RPA conference on problems of the New York region in February.[20]

Support for federal aid in the New York region also was bolstered by a RPA report issued on the eve of the mass transportation hearings. An outgrowth of Senator Case's 1960 proposal for a "friendly" inquiry into the Port Authority and the regional rail problem, the study, financed by the Senate Commerce Committee, recommended a massive program of federal loans to underwrite an $800-million overhaul of the area's commuter rail system.[21] Once their research indicated that the region's commuter needs were beyond the area's resources, RPA officials decided to do everything possible to promote the federal aid concept. Their report endorsed Senator Williams' bill, terming it "pioneering legislation." More important, to enhance publicity for both their recommendations and the transit aid hearings, RPA arranged to release its findings on the day before Williams opened his Senate hearings.[22]

This maneuver proved quite effective. Federal aid received front-page treatment in newspapers throughout the region. Typical was the Newark *Evening News,* which had a four-column headline: "Two U.S. Moves on Transit Aid; Quiz Opens, Loan Plan Filed." [23] Many newspapers in the region, particularly in the older cities, greeted the recommendation for combined federal, state, and local action with enthusiasm. Radio station WCBS was particularly impressed, telling its listeners that "The Federal Government has been told the facts of New York City railroad life. If it didn't know before, Washington now knows it must come to the rescue of hundreds of thousands of commuters in the metropolitan area." [24] Another product of the report was an endorsement of federal commuter aid as absolutely essential to the region's survival as the nation's business, communications, and cultural center by the RPA's board of directors, which represented a broad cross section of central-city business, professional, and community leaders in the New York area.

Meanwhile, the original central-city business component of the federal aid coalition—the Eastern commuter railroads—held firm with their urban allies. Strong endorsements of the Williams bill from Symes and Alpert put to rest the worries of some urban leaders that the railroads would desert the urban approach for a direct federal commuter railroad aid program such as those recommended by the ICC and the Doyle Report. Instead, Symes joined Williams at the hearings in rejecting the suggestion of Washington transit operator O. Roy Chalk that federal loans be made directly available to private transit companies and commuter railroads. Symes pointed out that "if [the] loans were available to us, the Pennsylvania Railroad, and we took advantage of them and bought equipment, we still would not have the coordinated, integrated service that is so necessary in the overall picture." [25] A similar urban-oriented view came from Alpert, who applauded

the requirement that no assistance be given to any area after three years unless substantial progress has been made on a workable program [because] it compels a realistic and practical solution at the local level with Federal assistance which thus far has not been found.[26]

The States and the Suburbs in 1961

Metropolitan actors from outside the central city continued to form a small part of the mass transportation coalition in 1961. Unconditional support for the new Williams bill came from three governors, all from heavily urbanized states. Of these, only Lawrence of Pennsylvania, a federal aid booster since early 1960, was at the hearings, and he testified more as the former mayor of Pittsburgh than as the governor of Pennsylvania, strongly endorsing an HHFA program in the interest of close coordination of federal mass transportation and urban renewal activities. Governor Edmund Brown of California, whose administration was committed to the locally financed implementation of the mass transportation plans developed by the Los Angeles Metropolitan Transit Authority and the San Francisco Bay Area Rapid Transit District, submitted a statement urging Congress to broaden the Williams bill to include grants. Massachusetts' Governor John Volpe, a former state and federal highway official, called the legislation essential to the revitalization of Boston's deficit-ridden Metropolitan Transit Authority and a vital element in protecting highway investments from urban overcrowding.

Far less enthusiasm for the Williams proposals came from New York and New Jersey, the two states most heavily involved in the commuter problem. Both Albany and Trenton continued to view it in a commuter railroad–commerce frame of reference rather than from the mass transportation–urban point of view of the Williams bill partisans. This difference in outlook produced growing criticism of the state commuter rail programs by central-city-oriented federal aid proponents, which, in turn, increased state hostility toward the Williams approach. The RPA report had characterized the efforts of New York and New Jersey as "stop-gap programs [which] are keeping commuter service alive [but] do little to promote a future system which would be less costly to maintain and operate, which would provide better service and which could handle increased volume . . . if the need arose." [27] At the Senate hearings, former New York City Administrator Luther Gulick emphasized the point that "commuter rail problems . . . are urban problems," scored the "breathless approach to panic solutions [by] frightened legislative bodies and Governors," and concluded "that most of the money now being poured by the Federal Government, the States, and some localities into 'saving the railroads' is being thrown down the drain." [28]

Equally distressing to the states was the receptivity of the press to such attacks. The New York *Journal-American* concurred with Gulick that additional public help under the existing patchwork system would be futile. And the New York *Times,* although not yet prepared to endorse federal aid, found the state programs "piecemeal, a scattered fire instead of a unified multi-state attack." [29]

Opposition to direct federal-urban commuter aid, always strong in New York, was growing in New Jersey. Highway Commissioner Dwight Palmer, whose primary interest was "federal aid to the railroads," insisted that "The decisions on how to fit [federal] financial support into well-integrated transportation systems . . . must be made by agencies responsible to state government." [30] Palmer also thought that the federal government should emulate New Jersey and place mass transportation responsibilities in the same agency that handled highway programs. Palmer's views led Governor Meyner to reject the urban features of Senator Williams' bill in 1961. In a statement submitted to the Senate Housing Subcommittee, Meyner termed the HHFA inexperienced in the field of transportation and urged a program of "Federal assistance to the states . . . under the general jurisdiction and administration of the Department of Commerce." [31]

Only one suburbanite put in an appearance at the 1961 federal aid hearings. Although he endorsed the Williams bill, Elkins Wetherill, the chief elected official of suburban Montgomery County near Philadelphia, sounded the standard urban grass-roots theme of localism. He counseled the committee not to pay too much attention to the regionalism of the central-city interests, and urged Congress to recognize that "local self-government is a strong force in the suburbs" and suggested that federal assistance be made available to counties so that suburban communities could determine their own mass transportations needs.[32] The Bergen County Chamber of Commerce sent Senator Williams a brief endorsement, but otherwise suburban interests from the New York area were not heard from at the Senate hearings. Although a few suburban newspapers gave editorial backing to federal aid, far more representative of suburban opinion, at least in New Jersey, was the Ridgewood *Herald News,* which considered the Port Authority's agreement to contribute $7 million a year for New Jersey commuter rail projects—announced on the day the 1961 Senate mass transportation hearings began—far more important than "federal aid, low-cost loans, further studies, and all that." [33]

Maneuvering for Position

The impressive support exhibited by Senator Williams at the hearings did not persuade the Kennedy Administration, its internal conflicts unresolved, to reopen the transit issue. As a consequence, the Administration's omnibus housing bill went to Congress at the end of March with no mass transportation provisions. However, the hearings and other pressures mounted by the mass transportation coalition had convinced HHFA Administrator Weaver that he could remain neutral in the jurisdictional struggle only at the risk of alienating an influential and growing segment of his agency's clientele. But, because of his desire to avoid a battle with Secretary Hodges in the congressional arena, Weaver preferred to contest the jurisdictional issue within the joint Commerce-HHFA study of urban transportation ordered by the President in his housing message. Since this course of action meant postponing action on transit until 1962, it was unacceptable to the urban-rail forces.

The manifestation of urban support for an HHFA program at the Williams bill hearings also produced a response in the Department of Commerce. Four days after the hearings closed, in an attempt to bolster the meager urban support for a Commerce transit program, Secretary Hodges named a group of prominent planning and urban transportation experts to an advisory committee which was to have responsibility for his department's end of the joint study. Two members were chosen from Mayor Dilworth's bailiwick: University of Pennsylvania planner Robert Mitchell, a key figure in the development of Philadelphia's UTTB program, and Henry Fagin, director of the Philadelphia area Penn-Jersey Transportation Study.[34]

Both Commerce and the HHFA hoped to secure jurisdiction over mass transportation by controlling the joint study. Each proposed a course of action which promised a built-in advantage.

Commerce wanted to subcontract the major elements of the study with an interagency staff constructing the final report. Since Commerce's prospective subcontractors already were on Hodges' advisory committee, the HHFA argued for a single contractor, preferably New York City's Institute of Public Administration (IPA). However, the IPA's identification with an urban approach to transit distressed Hodges' aides. The IPA's retiring president, Luther Gulick, had endorsed the Williams bill in 1960 and 1961, stressing in each instance the need to coordinate mass transport with other aspects of urban policy. Gulick's successor at the IPA was Lyle Fitch, who as New York's City Administrator had been a colleague of HHFA chief Weaver, also a former member of the Wagner administration. Despite these misgivings, the Commerce Department, in the absence of viable alternatives and with the six months allotted for the joint study slipping away, reluctantly agreed to hire the IPA on the condition that close supervision would be maintained by both federal agencies over the study.

Senator Williams took little notice of the HHFA's victory in the study skirmish. Instead his mass transportation coalition continued to pressure the Administration for immediate action on the pending legislation. One hopeful sign was the Senator's success in mid-April in persuading the White House to assign the disputed open-spaces program to the HHFA. Another was an indication that the Administration was sufficiently concerned about the urban clamor on the mass transportation program to offer a compromise. Under a plan advanced a few days after the open-spaces settlement, the HHFA would get the planning and demonstration grants, while the loan program would go to Commerce.[35] But with urban pressures beginning to have an effect on the White House, Williams and his aides rejected the proposal, insisting that the entire mass transportation package go to the HHFA.

The omnibus housing bill was the Administration's Achilles' heel on the commuter issue. While President Kennedy was not eager to disappoint his advisers by reversing the decision to delay federal action pending the outcome of the joint study, even less did he want the transit dispute to frustrate urban supporters of his $6-billion housing bill. The importance to the Administration of the omnibus housing measure also offered the mass transportation forces a tactical opportunity, since the President could not continue to ignore the transit proposal if it were part of the housing bill. Accordingly, after scaling the authorization down to $150 million to increase the chances for success in the Senate, Williams offered his mass transportation proposals as an amendment to the Administration's housing bill. Enhancing the probable effectiveness of Williams' maneuver was the steadily increasing strength of the mass transportation coalition. Late in April, in response to urban pressures the ACIR gave "substantial endorsement [to] the objectives and major provisions" of the Williams bill.[36] Organized labor also threw its weight behind the mass transportation legislation, demanding immediate action on the Senator's proposals.[37]

Williams' gambit and the growing pressures had their intended effect. By early May the White House had been persuaded that some kind of positive federal commuter program would have to be enacted in 1961. Since the Administration's belated transit move was prompted by a desire to mollify those elements of its housing coalition demanding an urban-based commuter program, political logic dictated that the jurisdictional issue be resolved in favor of the HHFA. Commerce's failure to muster group support for its transit position left Secretary Hodges with no political rebuttal to this argument.[38]

Despite this important concession, the Administration was not prepared to capitulate completely. The President was publicly committed to a comprehensive study. Moreover, Budget Director Bell and HHFA Administrator Weaver remained unenthusiastic about Williams' loan proposal. Therefore, the White House proposed a bargain: in return for presidential blessings on an urban-based approach to the commuter problem and a token $10-million HHFA mass transportation planning and demonstration program to be considered apart from the housing measure, the urban-rail leadership was asked to forego Williams' proposed transit amendment to the omnibus housing bill.

Emboldened by their victory on the jurisdictional issue, Williams and his allies rejected the White House's offer and rallied the urban-rail coalition behind the transit amendment. Lacking a counterpart to Senator Williams in the House of Representatives and faced with the Administration's firm control of the House Banking and Currency Committee, the mass transportation forces wrote off the House. Their efforts were concentrated in the Senate, where Williams, in his role as the upper house's transit specialist, commanded widespread urban support. If Senate approval of the commuter amendment were secured, Williams and his central-city, railroad, and labor supporters could bargain for a favorable compromise in the conference committee.

The first target was the Senate Banking and Currency Committee, where the chief stumbling block was Senator Sparkman, floor manager of the Administration's housing measure. Although he had aided Williams in 1960, Sparkman now echoed the White House, arguing in committee that "It would be better and safer for us to go through with the study and get the thinking of the best experts in the country on all the many problems which are involved in mass transportation." [39] But Sparkman was unable to dissuade either Williams' urban supporters or his railroad-inspired conservative Republican allies, and the committee accepted the transit amendment by a nine-to-four margin.[40]

While the Senate Housing Subcommittee's recommendations were awaiting consideration on the floor, the Administration's housing bill emerged from committee in the House of Representatives. As expected, urban efforts to attach the mass transportation provisions were turned back by Representative Albert Rains of Alabama, the manager of the Administration measure.[41] The House subcommittee's action, however, aided Williams' cause by intensifying urban criticism of the Administration's negative attitude on mass transportation. In an attempt to offset these rumblings, the White House, in making public its $10-million pilot program, emphasized that President Kennedy favored a major federal commuter program in the future. More important for the fate of the Williams' amendment in the Senate, Administration spokesmen indicated that while the President preferred to await the outcome of the joint study, Kennedy would not "undercut" Senator Williams if Congress were to approve the pending legislation.[42] The Administration's new flexibility on the issue was reflected in the Senate, where Sparkman announced that he had "no disposition to object to the provision or to propose any amendment to remove . . . Senator [Williams'] proposal from the bill." [43]

As the crucial Senate vote neared, recruits continued to join the ranks of the federal aid supporters. Senator Clifford Case ended his long embargo on his colleague's proposals. With the characteristic fervor of a convert, he castigated the Kennedy Administration for its inaction on the mass transportation problem.[44] The New York *Times* also dropped its opposition to federal transit assistance. Chiding the Administration for dragging its feet, the *Times* warned that "Each new delay is costly. With each passing day there is further curtailment of rapid transit service and more glut on highways in city and suburb. The Williams program is modest but it represents a start. The proposal deserves Senate support." [45]

On the Senate floor, every iota of urban strength, as well as the Administration's benevolent neutrality, was required to get Williams' amendment through unscathed. The prime threat came from Ohio's conservative Democrat, Frank Lausche, who attempted to eliminate the $50 million for demonstration grants. Thirty-eight liberal Democrats, some of whom, like Sparkman, might have voted the other way if the White House had not eased its position, joined eight Eastern Republicans, half of them from the New York area, to defeat Lausche's motion by a 46–44 vote.[46] Four days later, on June 12, the Senate passed a $6.1-billion housing bill which included Williams' $150-million mass transportation loan, demonstration, and planning program.

"The First and Feeble Step"

Williams' victory in the Senate made it certain that some kind of urban-based mass transportation program would be enacted in 1961. But would it be the Administration's token $10-million pilot program, which House leaders favored, or the $150-million

Senate loan-demonstration grant package? The urban-rail alliance pressed hard for the latter. On the day after the Senate passed the omnibus housing bill, George Alpert urged the U.S. Conference of Mayors to "use every kind of persuasion at your disposal, both individually and jointly, to aid the passage" of the Senate bill.[47] Heeding Alpert's call, many of the big-city executives who were in Washington for the annual meeting of the mayors' conference put their influence to work to win further mass transportation concessions from the Administration.

In the face of these urban pressures, the White House yielded once again, this time paving the way for a compromise acceptable to the urban-rail coalition. On June 19, President Kennedy sent the Administration's $10-million pilot demonstration grant proposal to the House of Representatives. Along with the bill went a policy statement in which the President explained the decision to assign mass transportation to the HHFA, terming it a "distinctly urban problem." He also insisted that the "Final decision on the exact nature of a Federal program of loans, loan guarantees, or grants . . . must await the results of this executive branch study." But in the crucial section of his statement, Kennedy conceded that "Immediate emergency assistance to finance transportation equipment and facilities in a few metropolitan areas with especially urgent problems may be warranted to assure continuation of essential services." Accordingly, the President indicated his willingness to accept "a temporary one-year authority for emergency loans." [48]

Two questions remained to be settled. One dealt with the format of the federal mass transportation program. The Administration wanted the emergency loans to be considered in both Houses as part of its transit bill rather than as a section of the omnibus housing measure. The second concerned the size of the program: the $150-million Senate package was far in excess of what the Administration felt was needed for "emergency" assistance. Support for the Administration's position came from the House leadership, which turned back an attempt on the floor by New Jersey Republicans Florence Dwyer and William Cahill to add $150 million for mass transportation to the housing measure. This abortive effort was not supported by Senator Williams and his cohorts, who knew it would fail. Instead, the mass transportation forces were busy stiffening the resolve of the Senate conferees, who were pledged to retain the transit provisions of the Senate's housing bill in the conference committee.

Mass transportation was one of the knottier issues to be resolved during the two days of negotiation needed to produce an omnibus housing measure acceptable to both Houses. Sparkman and his colleagues argued for retention of the Senate's proposals, while the House delegation, led by Rains, supported the Administration's plan for a separate transit bill. A way out of the impasse was provided by the open-spaces measure, desired both by the Administration and by Senator Williams. The House version of the housing measure contained a $100-million allocation for open spaces; a similar provision had been dropped in the Senate. With Williams and ArDee Ames playing leading roles, a compromise was arranged which retained both transit and open spaces. On Monday evening, June 26, after five months of vacillation under growing urban pressures, the White House agreed to accept half of each program: $75 million for mass transportation and $50 million for open spaces.

HHFA Administrator Weaver reported the settlement the following morning to a House subcommittee which was commencing hearings on the Administration's now obsolete $10-million transit bill.[49] Weaver admitted that the compromise agreement was "an interim stop-gap approach . . . the first and feeble step toward dealing with this problem." [50] But he emphasized that the concept of the federal government fostering a planned and coordinated approach was more important than the size of the authorization. For the first time in many months, Williams agreed with Weaver. Sounding a familiar New Frontier theme, he told the House subcommittee that "What we want is to get moving here. We certainly wouldn't think the difference of a dollar amount would stand in the way of a program." [51] On the next day, the conferees reported a $5.6-billion housing bill, and Williams hailed the mass transportation provisions as a "major accomplishment in the annals of urban legislation." [52]

Two days later, on June 30, 1961, the final seal was put on the central cities' mass transportation triumph when President Kennedy signed the Housing Act of 1961. The new law authorized $50 million in federal loans for the acquisition and improvement of mass transportation facilities in urban areas. Another $25 million was to be used for transit demonstration grants, but not for "major long-term capital improvements." Finally, federal urban planning assistance was made available for "comprehensive urban transportation surveys, studies, and plans to aid in solving problems of traffic congestion, facilitating the circulation of people and goods in metropolitan and other urban areas, and reducing transportation needs." [53]

Conceived in the great urban centers, nurtured by the commuter crisis, given political substance in the alliance of the mayors and railroad presidents, and maturing into a full-fledged central-city coalition under the skillful leadership of Senator Williams, the campaign for federal mass transportation assistance had borne fruit. Heralding the transit provisions of the housing bill as "particularly welcome, albeit rather pale, beginnings," the New York *Times* advocated that the program "receive added funds next year." [54]

Postscript

"Added funds next year" was the rallying cry of the mass transportation forces during the thirty months following the 1961 transit victory of Senator Williams and his central-city allies. As expected, after resolving its internal differences and receiving the findings of the joint Commerce-HHFA study, the Kennedy Administration embraced an expanded federal aid program. Otherwise, little was changed in the federal-metropolitan politics of mass transportation assistance during 1962 and 1963. Central-city interests from the large metropolitan areas continued to provide the bulk of the support for federal aid. The Senate remained more receptive to urban pleas for transit help than the House, where the inability of the mass transportation coalition to win suburban and rural support prevented the new proposal from even reaching the floor until the summer of 1964. As a result, the 1961 Housing Act's $75-million "emergency" program was all that urban interests had to show for five years of effort on the mass transit issue until the summer of 1964, when a $375-million urban transportation bill was squeezed through the House and signed by President Lyndon Johnson.

The mass transportation program developed in 1962 was built around federal grants, which had always been the ultimate objective of the urban-rail alliance. In its report to the Department of Commerce and the HHFA, the IPA estimated that $9.8 billion would be needed for mass transportation improvements in the coming decade and suggested federal grants "predicated on the development of comprehensive regional transportation plans." [55] From these recommendations, Secretary Hodges and Administrator Weaver developed a program calling for $500 million in federal grants covering two-thirds of the cost of "mass transportation projects which are parts of comprehensively planned urban transportation systems." As a sop to areas lacking regional transportation plans, they also asked for federal grants of half of the project costs "for an emergency three-year period . . . when there is an urgent need to preserve an existing facility or service." [56] President Kennedy endorsed these proposals in his transportation message of April 4, 1962, and Senator Williams introduced legislation incorporating them the following day.

During the next year, successful mass transit hearings again were staged in the Senate and the House. As one reporter observed in 1963, "The setting was the same, the cast of characters was familiar, and if the Senate Banking and Currency Committee went in for theatre marquee advertising, it could have hung out a sign reading 'Now in Its Fourth Year.' " [57] Central-city mayors or top public officials from the dozen largest metropolitan areas appeared at one or more of these hearings to endorse federal grants. Also on hand were the commuter railroads, the transit industry, and other central-city groups. Backing continued to come from business leaders in the major urban centers, although the U.S. Chamber of Commerce stirred up opposition in smaller cities such as Binghamton, New York; Evansville, Indiana; Wausau, Wisconsin; and Zanesville, Ohio.[58]

While Philadelphia, New York, Boston, Chicago, and the other large cities remained the mainstays of the coalition, suburban and state support for the mass transportation legislation increased after 1961. In part, this development was a product of the growing acceptance of the idea of federal transit aid in the larger metropolitan areas. Also stimulating interest outside the central city was the prospect that substantial assistance would become available following the Administration's strong stand in April, 1962. Suburban and state leaders might doubt the propriety of federal aid, but if a $500-million program were to be enacted, they wanted their share.

Suburban backing came primarily from the larger metropolitan areas with existing or projected urban rail systems. Best represented was the New York region. When the NACO—suburbia's principal voice in Washington—endorsed federal transit aid for the first time in 1962, its views were presented by Westchester County Executive Edwin Michaelian. NACO's testimonial at the House hearings the following year was given by Nassau County Executive Eugene Nickerson. Also making their debut at a federal aid conclave in 1962 were the New Jersey suburbs, but the delegation from Morris County led by Thomas Taber did not match the turnout at the train-service hearings three years before.

Among the states, the most notable development after 1961 was the endorsement of the Kennedy Administration's urban-oriented mass transportation proposals by both New York and New Jersey. Underlying this apparent reversal of form was the failure of the 1961 urban transit victory to alter state control of regional transportation in the New York area. At the insistence of Albany and Trenton, Washington agreed that federal mass transport aid for the New York region would be channeled through a state rather than through a locally controlled areawide body. Created in August, 1961, and composed of twelve state officials and only one local representative,[59] the Tri-State Transportation Committee was to receive all HHFA transit funds allocated to the New York region.[60] With the states in firm control, the past objections of Governor Rockefeller and Highway Commissioner Palmer to direct federal-local aid, HHFA control, and the other urban features of the Williams bill faded. As a result, both gave mild endorsements to the Administration's program in 1962.[61]

Despite this growth of suburban and state interest, mass transportation remained primarily a big-city issue at the federal level. To overcome this political handicap, determined efforts were made to broaden the base of congressional support for the transit legislation. Back in 1960, Senator Williams had changed the focus from commuter railroads to mass transportation and added West Coast and Southern metropolitan centers to the older Northeastern cities which had spawned the idea of federal commuter assistance. Two years later, Williams and the Kennedy Administration were emphasizing that all forms of public transportation in cities of any size were eligible for aid.[62] Moreover, to avoid alienating the powerful rubber interests, great stress was put on the noncompetitiveness of transit and highways, and the sharp criticisms of the urban highway program common to the earlier mass transportation hearings were less frequent after 1961.

These endeavors neither erased the central cities' identification with the mass transportation issue nor overcame the apathy and opposition of powerful groups in Congress. Transit's troubles began at the close of the 1961 session, when conservatives on the House Appropriations Committee cut the mass transit authorization from $75 million to $42.5 million. The Administration's substitution of grants for loans the following year only stiffened opposition from entrenched congressional elements hostile to "spending," "socialism," and federal intrusion into local affairs. Bolstering their position were two conservative bulwarks, the U.S. Chamber of Commerce and the American Farm Bureau Federation. In addition, with the Administration's endorsement in 1962, partisanship returned to the transit issue and cut into Republican support.

As a consequence of this political situation, the only victories won by the mass transportation coalition in 1962 were in the urban-controlled Banking and Currency Committees. The Rules

Committee killed the bill in the House, and the Senate adjourned without voting on the proposal.[63] In 1963, with Senator Williams and the White House marshaling the same coalition of liberal Democrats and Eastern Republicans that had turned back the Lausche amendment in 1961, the Senate passed a much amended $375-million mass transportation grant bill in April.[64] But with tax reform and civil rights getting first call on the Administration's political resources during the remainder of the year, the urban leaders were unable to round up sufficient votes to risk a test of the transit legislation on the House floor.

In 1964, the mass transportation forces unfurled their tattered banners for another try at passing the transit bill in the Eighty-eighth Congress. With an election-year eye on the pivotal urban states, President Johnson gave mass transit a prominent place in his legislative program. More important than the President's support, however, were the persistent lobbying efforts of the big cities and their allies in the transportation industry. By late June, the central-city coalition, aided by the quadrennial enhancement of Republican concern for urban sentiments, rounded up sufficient support to convince the Democratic leadership in the House to risk a vote on the $375-million transit package.[65] With 39 Republicans, most of whom represented metropolitan constituencies, providing the margin of victory, the Urban Mass Transportation Act of 1964 was approved by the House of Representatives by a 212–189 vote on June 25, 1964.

For the group of urban leaders who crowded around President Johnson's desk a few days later, when he signed the mass transportation bill, success in 1964 produced a rather small pot of gold at the end of the mass-transit rainbow. The three-year $375-million program will about equal New York City's transit subsidies over the same period of time and is considerably less than half the estimated cost of the regional transit system being constructed in the San Francisco metropolitan area. Nor will federal commuter aid alter significantly the basic transportation and growth patterns of metropolitan America that are being forged by the massive interstate highway program. Nevertheless, like federal funds for urban renewal and public housing, mass transportation assistance offers the central cities another weapon in their desperate struggle to maintain the urban core in the face of irresistible pressures for decentralization. And its importance to the great cities is manifest in their persistence in promoting federal transit aid in the years since the Transportation Act of 1958 triggered the commuter crisis.

PART FOUR

Conclusion

CHAPTER X

The Pattern of Federal-Metropolitan Politics

Area-wide problems tend also to be nationwide problems, at least national urban ones. Their solution, therefore, demands not merely a higher degree of metropolitan integration, but also the most intimate linkage of metropolitan areas with other levels of government.

EDWARD BANFIELD AND MORTON GRODZINS [1]

"Case studies," writes a perceptive analyst of the political process, "never 'prove' anything; their purpose is to illustrate generalizations which are established elsewhere, or to direct attention toward such generalizations." [2] This final chapter sets forth some generalizations about federal-metropolitan politics. While these propositions are derived largely from the study of mass transportation, they are offered in the belief that they illuminate the relationships of the larger metropolitan areas with the national government.

A Diversity of Interests

Federal-metropolitan politics is a natural extension of the fragmented political system of the metropolis. Since the metropolitan area commonly lacks regional institutions, legal recognition, and public officials with areawide constituencies, the focus for political activity is submetropolitan or supermetropolitan. Regional issues are contested in terms of the interests of the central city, the suburbs, the authorities, and the states. From a welter of conflicting constituency interests comes a metropolitan political process in which the participants "are committed . . . to particular solutions of particular problems. What results is a competitive scramble for available resources and power. The notion that there might be common goals and resources becomes lost in the struggle." [3]

The mass transportation issue provides ample evidence of the pervasive influence of particularism on federal-metropolitan politics. When the commuter crisis first stimulated efforts to influence Washington, metropolitan actors from the New York area sought to save northern New Jersey's commuter service, safeguard New York State's tax relief program, secure federal aid for the New Haven Railroad, pacify constituents in Bergen or Morris County, shield New York City from new mass transportation financial burdens, or achieve some other limited goal. Enlisting federal help for the improvement of public transportation on a comprehensive regional basis tended to be ignored, particularly by state and suburban interests, until much later.

Regional interests are represented at the federal level by various metropolitan actors, each of whom perceives regional problems in the perspective of its particular institutional base and none of whom possesses a regional mandate. Each participant brings to federal-metropolitan politics a set of values and resources which differ little from those governing its behavior in the internal politics of the metropolis. Thus, suburbia seeks federal help preoccupied with local problems, inadequately equipped for effective action beyond its borders, and fearful of proposals which threaten autonomy or unequal costs and benefits. As for the regional congressman, his position in the larger metropolitan areas resembles that of the local politician. Since his district embraces only a portion of the metropolis and his constituents rarely perceive their problems as regional, the congressman is reluctant to devote his limited resources to complex metropolitan problems. State relations with the national government on regional problems are conditioned by the pressure of mushrooming urban demands on limited state fiscal resources and the necessity of the urban governor to function in a supermetropolitan constituency in which the rural sector traditionally has been overrepresented.

Dedicated to preserving the urban core, the central city comes to Washington with an areawide frame of reference and a willingness to use the region's most potent aggregate of political resources for revisionist purposes, particularly with respect to public finance.

The mass transportation issue illustrates how these differences in regional perspective and in influence at the national level interact with the traditional positions of the states, cities, and suburbs in intergovernmental relations to produce characteristic attitudes toward the involvement of the federal government in metropolitan affairs. All these factors—outlook on regional matters, capabilities in the federal arena, and orientation toward federal-metropolitan relations—combine to provide each metropolitan actor with a distinctive set of interests and goals in his Washington ventures. Different goals, such as the crisis-inspired endeavor of the New Jersey suburbanites to amend the Transportation Act, the states' efforts to save commuter service on the New Haven, or the central-city coalition's campaign to secure support for mass transportation, require distinct kinds of resources, investments, and influence. Activities in pursuit of these goals, in turn, shape the patterns of participation by the suburb, by the state, by the central city, and by the urban congressman in federal-metropolitan politics.

Since the federal government is not an important factor in suburban politics, participation in federal-metropolitan relations at the suburban grass roots tends to be sporadic, crisis-stimulated, and concerned primarily with the short-run local aspects of a problem. As the Transportation Act amendment episode indicates, even the commuter, often cited as the most cosmopolitan of the suburbanites by virtue of his daily journey across the metropolitan landscape, usually views his transportation dilemma in a localistic and remedial perspective. In pursuing their limited objectives in Washington, suburbanites are hampered by the meager political resources afforded by their fragmented institutional base, the absence of national suburban pressure groups, and their heavy dependence on the local congressman.

Like the suburbs, most urban states have a limited and negative orientation toward federal involvement in urban affairs. The

mutual interest of state and suburb in federal-metropolitan politics springs from partisan ties, as well as from a common fear of
financial involvement in regional arrangements, a shared antip-
athy toward the city, and a mutual interest in resisting the extension of federal-city links. This last factor is particularly important
since the states are extremely sensitive to the threat that direct
federal aid programs pose to their role in local affairs. The behavior of New York and New Jersey illustrates clearly the typical
state posture in federal-metropolitan politics: little interest in the
development of long-term federal urban commitments, opposition
to direct federal-local relations, and insistence that federal aid be
channeled through the states.

The role of the central city in federal-metropolitan relations
contrasts sharply with that of the suburbs and the states. Money,
political realities, and the adverse impact of the decentralization
of the metropolis on the urban core have made the central city
the major force behind the involvement of the national government in urban problems. Onerous burdens have been placed on
the city by the need to build expensive highways, to maintain
sagging public transport systems, to replace spreading slums, to
revitalize deteriorating downtowns, and to meet the burgeoning
demands of an increasingly lower-class and nonwhite population
on the local treasury. Suburban dedication to the fragmented
political and fiscal system prevents the city from tapping much of
the wealth of the metropolis. Help from the statehouse, where
rural forces are commonly overrepresented and exchequers are
chronically overburdened, is rarely adequate. As a result, argue
the mayors, the cities are "the unwelcome step-children of the
counties and the state" and "have no other choice than to journey
to Washington." [4] Here the political process is more responsive
to urban needs, here assistance can be obtained on terms favorable to the cities, and here the suburbanite can be tapped indirectly through the federal income tax.

Superior capabilities, an ability to mobilize interests from all
parts of the nation, and a sustained interest in broadening the
federal government's urban responsibilities make the central city
the most influential participant in federal-metropolitan politics.
In their efforts to enhance their alliance with Washington, city

leaders can employ the many resources of the region's major unit of government, the influence of its most prominent political and economic figures, particularly the mayor, the help of the nation's great metropolitan dailies, and the efforts of the national urban lobbies. On the mass transportation issue, a combination of these assets first forged the urban-rail alliance. Then the geographical base of support was widened; as an official of the American Municipal Association noted in 1961, "Two years ago interest in federal help for commuter railroads was centered almost entirely on the eastern seaboard. But now we have west coast cities, like Los Angeles and San Francisco, and even southern cities behind us." [5] Next, the familiar central-city alliance of Democratic politicians, downtown economic interests, commuter railroad and transit operators, metropolitan newspapers, planners, professors, and regionally oriented civic groups was reproduced at the national level in support of the federal transit legislation.[6]

Suburban, state, and central-city perspectives, as well as those of the city's various districts, are reflected in the behavior of the congressional delegations from metropolitan areas. Since House districts encompass few metropolitan areas with more than half a million residents, the average urban congressman, like most other metropolitan actors, views the metropolis from a subregional institutional base and in the light of the particularist demands of his city or suburban constituents. For most congressmen, identifications with their district, party, faction, and committee far outweigh any nebulous obligations arising from the fact that they represent part of a metropolitan area. Another factor inhibiting congressional involvement in metropolitan issues is the limited capability of the average urban representative for effective action in an area of emerging federal legislative concern. Efforts in the House on the mass transportation issue highlight the restrictions imposed by committee assignments, seniority, the lower chamber's conservative leadership, party loyalties and rewards, personal interests and abilities, and limited staff resources. Whether in response to constituency pressures or for broader reasons, most forays on the part of the urban congressman are both nominal and ineffective.

Compared with his colleague in the House, the urban senator

is more likely to bring to federal-metropolitan politics a regional outlook and an opportunity to affect the consideration of urban issues. The statewide constituency and the six-year term foster a broader perspective on the metropolis than is afforded the House member. On the other hand, the senator's Washington sphere of operations liberates him in large part from the constraints that the state institutional base imposes on the urban activities of the governor. A good example of the difference between the gubernatorial and senatorial role in federal-metropolitan politics is provided by Abraham Ribicoff of Connecticut. While governor he followed Rockefeller's lead and largely ignored the movement to develop a federal-urban mass transportation program, but after his election to the Senate in 1962 he moved to the forefront of those in Congress advocating federal assistance for metropolitan transit systems.[7] Mass transportation politics also illustrate the senator's superior capabilities for action on urban issues. Senators Case and Williams were more successful than Representatives from the New York area because they served in a smaller, less hierarchical, more liberal chamber, in which individual members have greater prestige, more committee posts, adequate staff assistance, and far greater opportunities for influence and leadership.

All these factors help explain the characteristic behavior of the various urban participants in federal-metropolitan relationships. As the many facets of the mass transportation issue emphasize, however, national forces also play a crucial role in shaping the pattern of federal-metropolitan politics. The variables affecting the outcome of federal-metropolitan interaction are national rather than local, regional, or state. The need for widespread urban support and national alliances is clear in the failure of the Transportation Act amendments compared with the success of the mass transit legislation. And because national considerations are the key to victory, leadership on federal-metropolitan issues is exercised more successfully by those urban actors who can mobilize for effective action at the national level.

The complexity of the national government and the multiplicity and magnitude of its tasks also shape federal-metropolitan relations. The federal government is hardly the monolithic entity

that its critics decry. Rather it is "a government of separated institutions sharing powers." [8] Within and among these institutions
exists a dynamic pattern of conflict and consensus, competition
and cooperation. Based on a national constituency, the federal
executive is more responsive to urban needs than Congress is.
But, as the 1961 mass transit controversy indicates, interagency
conflict, budgetary constraints, and the inexorable pressures of
foreign policy and national defense limit the effectiveness of the
Presidency in defense of urban interests. Another critical national
influence on federal-metropolitan politics is the scattering of
responsibilities for parts of problems such as transportation and
urban development among a host of executive agencies, independent bodies, and congressional committees. This lack of focus
multiplies and entangles the channels of information and influence to federal decision-makers. While widening the choice of
urban claimants, this diffusion of responsibilities also invites
competition, delay, and stalemate.

The result is a system in which the many pathways to the national capital attract numerous metropolitan actors, each motivated by a different perspective of the urban landscape and none
representing the metropolis as a whole. From a constellation of
federal agencies, commissions, committees, and individuals, most
seek particular remedies for the maladies of their particular frag-
ments of the metropolis. Few of the federal participants can satisfy
urban demands independently, but most can block action unilaterally. In this scramble, capabilities and influence are un-
equally distributed; perceptions, attitudes, interests, constituency
concerns, and goals vary widely. From the interplay of these many
variables comes the characteristic pattern of federal-metropolitan
politics.

Washington and the Future Metropolis

Innovation, experimentation, adaptation, and "mild chaos"
are the touchstones of the American federal system.[9] Rising population, increased urbanization, and the continued dispersal of the

metropolis promise to keep federal-metropolitan relations in a
state of flux for decades. Symptomatic of this unsettled situation
is the variety of dissatisfactions with the present system of federal-
metropolitan politics. One influential segment of opinion, well-
represented in the statehouse, contends that "Problems which
arise locally are best solved locally [since] the finances required for
their solution will most certainly come from the local community,
no matter how circuitous the route." [10] Another view, frequently
advanced by such defenders of state interests as Governors Rockefeller and Scranton, insists that federal aid programs give "maximum authority for implementation to a strong, effective state government." [11] Past successes as well as political and fiscal realities,
on the other hand, lead the cities and their spokesmen to press
for the expansion of existing direct federal-local programs and
the development of new ones. A recent list prepared by Senator
Clark called for more federal aid to the cities for "education,
urban renewal, public housing, housing for the elderly, housing
for middle income families, urban highways, urban and suburban
mass transit, water resources development, air and water pollution control, health and hospital services, [and] juvenile delinquency." [12] Also stressed by central-city interests is the need to
focus federal responsibilities for metropolitan problems. Finally,
troubled by the "lack of a unified metropolitan voice in Washington," some commentators urge the creation of "organized
[groups] concerned about the broad problems brought about by
the development of the metropolis." [13]

Of the possible trends suggested by these diverse views, the
least probable is a successful assault on the basic concept of federal
involvement in metropolitan problems. Instructive in this respect
was the experience of President Eisenhower's Joint Federal-State
Action Committee, which was supposed to check the growth of
the federal octopus by designating "functions which the States
are ready and willing to assume and finance that are now performed or financed wholly or in part by the Federal Government." [14] After more than two years of toil, the committee could
locate only two grant programs—vocational education and sewage
treatment—which together accounted for only $80 million, or

2 percent of all grants in 1957, for return to the states. Moreover, the Administration's attempt to implement this modest decentralization was killed by an alliance of mayors, the national urban lobbies, professional and other groups interested either in vocational education or in cleaner water, and governors.[15] In practically every urban program area, the forces dedicated to continuation and augmentation appear almost impregnable. Even when metropolitan interests are only partially mobilized, as was the case with mass transportation, the strength of those energized suggests that expansion of the federal government's metropolitan role will be the dominant trend.

While granting that political and fiscal considerations will entrench and expand federal urban responsibilities, some argue that the linkage between the metropolis and Washington need not be direct. This issue can be expected to foster sharp conflict between state and city in the federal-metropolitan politics of the future. Too much is at stake for the cities to forsake their ties with the national government without a struggle. The 1961 mass transit jurisdictional battle indicates the cities' strong distaste for the expansion of state-controlled federal assistance. The most crucial factor in this dispute is the cities' conviction that the states are reluctant to commit themselves to the revitalization of the city. As a result, the mayors feel that federal aid channeled through the states is likely to involve attrition of funds and negotiations with unsympathetic officials. On the other hand, the cities' federal partner, as President Johnson recently pledged, is committed to "restoring the hope and renewing the vitality of older cities and worn-out neighborhoods." [16]

Thus, the catalog of urban demands for direct federal assistance programs is constantly enlarged. So are the capabilities of the cities to secure action on their requests. An example is the increase in the number of cities employing lobbyists in Washington. Although familiar figures for decades at the statehouse, city agents only recently have appeared on the banks of the Potomac. Mayor Dilworth's effectiveness on the commuter issue unquestionably was enhanced because Philadelphia, unlike the other big cities in the transit coalition, had a man in Washington—Patrick Mc-

Laughlin, who also served on the staff of the AMA.[17] As late as 1958, Mayor Wagner indicated satisfaction with the traditional congressional channel, but within four years the proliferation of city interests in the Capital led him to dispatch a full-time lobbyist to Washington to promote legislation, deal with federal agencies, and provide counsel and guidance for New York's congressional delegation.[18]

While granting the central city's key role in federal-metropolitan politics, some observers question whether the city's representatives speak for the region's interests. Connery and Leach reach a negative conclusion because the "mayor . . . owes nothing, politically speaking, to residents of the outlying communities, and is in Washington on the city treasury only to advance the cause of his constituents." [19] Certainly there is nothing altruistic about the central city's efforts to secure federal action on metropolitan problems. Self-interest was a strong force in the development and support of the mass transportation aid program by the central-city cluster led by the mayors and railroads. None the less, in their dealings with the federal government, the cities demonstrated considerably more awareness of the regional aspects of the commuter problem than did the suburbs or the states. And because the city is the metropolitan actor with the biggest stake in regional development, an areawide outlook is likely to be a feature of their future involvement with Washington.

The chances that urban state leaders will check the cities' drive for direct aid are slim. It is almost certain, however, that Congress will continue to leave the door open for state participation in federal programs in metropolitan areas. Underlying this prospect is the state and local political base of the party system and the continuing influence of states' rights dogma on Congress. Morton Grodzins has emphasized that "What is remarkable in recent history is how consistently Congress has insisted that the states share responsibility in programs that, from constitutional and administrative considerations, might easily have been all-national programs." [20] State influence in Washington will insure that federal legislation continues to authorize grants to both "States and local bodies" in the fashion of the 1964 mass transit legislation.[21] While most aid will go directly to the local unit, such provisions allow the states to employ their formidable array of legal and political powers over their subdivisions to channel federal assistance through the state capital they so desire. Certainly this has been the case in the New York area, where Governor Rockefeller and Highway Commissioner Palmer have secured BPR and HHFA acceptance of the state-dominated Tri-State Transportation Committee as the region's primary recipient of federal mass transit aid.

Federal-metropolitan politics also will be affected by the revolution in legislative apportionment begun by the U.S. Supreme Court in *Baker v. Carr* and culminated in the epochal 1964 ruling that both houses of the state legislature must be apportioned on the basis of population.[22] Most observers of the federal system agree with V. O. Key's contention that "The combination of party system and the structure of representation in most of the states incapacitates the states and diverts demands for political action to Washington." [23] If rural domination has spurred the growth of federal-urban programs, might not the enhancement of urban influence in the state capitals cause the cities to direct their attention away from Washington?

Unquestionably, reapportionment will stimulate urban leaders to step up their demands in Albany, Springfield, Sacramento, and other state capitals. The receptivity of legislative chambers that represent cities more fairly is bound to grow. A more equitably apportioned legislature also will reduce rural restraints on the governor's ability to serve his metropolitan constituency. None the less, fiscal and political considerations will continue to justify the investments that the cities make in their federal-metropolitan efforts. Reapportionment will not automatically put more money into habitually barren state treasuries, nor will it decrease the political perils inherent in raising state taxes. Urban legislators are as squeamish about tax hikes as their rural colleagues, and urban voters seem no more inclined than the rest of the electorate to pay increased state taxes to finance the programs they demand.[24] Moreover, the Supreme Court's reapportionment efforts have not been limited to state legislatures.[25] The requirement of substantial equality of population among congressional districts promises to increase urban influence in the House. This could be a more significant development for the cities than state reapportionment. As the mass transportation case indicates, the conservative and rurally dominated House of Representatives has been the major stumbling block of the urban alliance in Washington.

Suburbia's role also must be examined in an assessment of the future of federal-metropolitan politics. In most states, the suburbs will gain as much as or more than the cities from state legislative and congressional reapportionment. The prime impact of this alteration of influence among geographical blocs will be felt at the state level. With both city and suburb better represented, the clash of metropolitan interests at the state capital may well increase. State leaders, particularly among the Republicans, can be expected to side with the reinforced suburban delegations in the state legislature. And their common adversaries, it was recently suggested by the Republican candidate for governor in Illinois, are the "big-city politicians and the national executive branch," who are "rushing to complete [an] alliance for a power monopoly" to bypass state governments and "freeze" urban power against the threat of the expanding suburbs.[26] Such an approach can only serve to fortify the cities' resolve to maintain their profitable relations with Washington.

Reapportionment also will increase the number of congressmen concerned with suburban problems. Functioning in the national arena, regardless of their philosophical preferences, suburban congressmen will tackle their constituents' problems with the means at hand in Washington. Moreover, awareness of suburbia's rapidly growing political strength will cause national leaders of both parties to seek suburban votes with promises of increased federal help. Yet a significant heightening of interest in the national government at the suburban grass roots does not appear to be on the horizon. The suburban congressman who supports federal aid for the metropolis discovers, as did Representative Peter Frelinghuysen on the mass transit legislation, that a majority of his constituents are apathetic or opposed.[27] And President Johnson's election-year bid for suburban support in a 1964 housing message which called for a cluster of new and expanded federal programs to insure more orderly growth on the urban fringe did not shake suburbia's characteristic torpor toward Washington.[28]

Prospects for a substantial broadening of the political focus of the suburban grass roots must be judged to be slight. When problems overrun the local community's fiscal or political capabilities, the suburbanite's programmatic interests and his partisan and philosophical inclinations will continue to produce a preference for state help over federal involvement. A good example was the waxing and waning of suburban interest in Washington as New Jersey leaders groped for a solution to the commuter crisis. Increased representation in the state legislature will only tend to enhance suburbia's natural orientation toward the statehouse.

Yet federal involvement in suburban affairs should increase despite this lack of constituency interest. Although fostered by the cities and regional civic and planning interests, federal aid for urban renewal, for local and regional planning, for open spaces, and for mass transit will attract a growing number of suburbs. Suburbs will continue to be the passive beneficiaries of the two federal programs which have had the greatest impact on suburban development—highways and mortgage insurance. As in the past, suburbia's interests will be protected by powerful surrogates dedicated to dispersed urban development—the highway and the real estate lobbies. In other policy areas, the primary burden of defending the suburban grass roots in Washington will fall on the limited capabilities of the suburban congressmen. Unless there is a fundamental change in the suburbanite's orientation toward the federal government, the development of effective national pressure groups will be slow, and the voice of suburbia will be heard sporadically in Washington, usually in response to emergencies and probably preoccupied with the immediate local implications of a problem.

Any politically feasible restructuring of federal responsibilities is not likely to have appreciable impact on federal-metropolitan politics. Both the 1962 plan for a Department of Urban Affairs and Housing and President Johnson's scheme for a Department of Housing and Community Development primarily involve an upgrading of the HHFA. Urban highways would remain in the

BPR, air and water pollution in the Public Health Service, education in the Health, Education and Welfare Department, airports in the Federal Aviation Agency, juvenile delinquency in the Justice Department, depressed-area assistance in the Commerce Department, and civil defense in the Defense Department. However, a cabinet department would increase the prestige of the Administrator of the HHFA, the cities' chief voice in the federal executive. Departmental status would also increase the chances that new federal ventures in the metropolis would be located in the housing agency. But the mass transit and open spaces jurisdictional clashes of 1961 indicate that departmental rank is not essential for the broadening of HHFA's responsibilities as long as the influence of the powerful national urban alliance is employed effectively.

The proposal for an urban affairs department can be expected to produce characteristic responses on the part of metropolitan actors. In 1962 central-city interests and their congressional and liberal-labor supporters were allied with the federal executive in support of the proposal. Opposition came from a coalition of state leaders, suburban spokesmen, various conservative groups, and their Republican and Southern Democratic supporters in Congress.[29]

None of these factors external to the metropolitan system—the states' desire to reduce or redirect federal aid to the metropolis, city pressures for more federal assistance, congressional and state legislative reapportionment, or structural change in Washington —will alter significantly the pattern of federal-metropolitan politics. One source of possible change remains—the internal political system of the metropolis. As long as the metropolis is fragmented and its parts are devoted to particular values and goals, metropolitan actors will journey to Washington in defense of subregional and superregional interests. By the same token, since the external relations of the metropolis are a natural extension of its internal political system, the former would be fundamentally altered by the evolution of the latter toward what Wood has called "a modern democratic system" for the metropolitan area, "a system which uses parties, pressure groups, professional politicians and executives and legislators elected on a regional basis." [30]

Basic changes in the political system, however, are extremely unlikely in most of urban America. More than 100 attempts at major institutional overhaul have produced metropolitan governments in only two single-county areas—Miami and Nashville. The dismal record of the metropolitan political reformers is a product of the absence of a "groundswell of rebellion at the existing order of government." [31] Deprived of the support of the central-city mayor, who may have a regional outlook but rarely an interest in beginning a new political career in an expanded and untested constituency, and of most city ethnic and neighborhood elements, who fear a dilution of their political influence in an enlarged policy, and assured of the opposition of most suburbanites fearful of a loss of autonomy, the downtown business and newspaper proponents of metropolitan government and their "good government" allies are almost always overwhelmed at the polls.[32] All the available evidence confirms Wood's findings in his study of the New York region: "We simply record that we know of no other time when a revolution took place when the existing system was solidly established and its citizens, as they understood the goals of their domestic society, content." [33]

Can regionally oriented interests representative of the entire metropolis be mobilized from the existing institutional base? Connery and Leach argue that "civic consciousness on an area-wide basis" can provide the "unified" metropolitan voice necessary for "an orderly and coherent federal program for metropolitan growth and evolution." [34] However, the conclusion to be drawn from decades of metropolitan political experience is that exhortation alone causes few converts to a regional outlook. Something more tangible than goodwill is required to alter perceptions and goals rooted in the fragmented political system of the metropolis.

One force that might foster more centralized and coordinated decision-making in metropolitan areas, and which thus might alter the pattern of federal-metropolitan politics, is the feedback of the output of federal-urban relations on the metropolitan political system. Perhaps the most significant product of the campaign for federal mass transportation assistance was the proposal that aid for transit and urban highways be conditioned on the existence of "adequate, comprehensive development plans for the metropolitan area." [35] More and more, federal assistance is likely to be related to regional development strategies and cooperative mechanisms. For example, the ACIR recently recommended that the Water Pollution Control Act of 1956 "be amended to provide an additional matching incentive for the development of sewage disposal systems on a regional or major subregional basis." [36] Legislation introduced in Congress in 1963 sought to "encourage State and local governments to establish or improve facilities for coordinating metropolitan development" by requiring that applicants for federal grants for most urban programs be reviewed by a state or metropolitan planning agency.[37] Also symptomatic of the developing pressures in Washington for more coordinated metropolitan decision-making is a bill prepared by Senator Case of New Jersey which would empower the HHFA Administrator to certify that federal grants for urban renewal, public housing, open space, highway, mass transit, and airport projects are consistent with an official metropolitan land use plan.[38]

Inducements from Washington, however, are not likely to brighten the prospects of general institutional reform. Instead, federal aid conditioned on regional plans and programs (and state assistance with similar stipulations) will stimulate change "on the basis of step-by-step, incremental, *ad hoc* adjustments made to answer specific needs and forces and demands, and not on the basis of adherence to any general doctrine." [39] Thus, by their separate endeavors in Washington, the ambassadors of the fragmented metropolis have helped sow the seeds of metropolitan political change.

The resulting metropolitan political system will be one in which the component units maintain their corporate existence while collaborating increasingly on areawide problems. Many areas of public policy will remain outside the realm of the slowly evolving regional consensus. On these issues, federal-metropolitan politics will continue to reflect the diverse values, goals, and capabilities of the components of the metropolis. In federal-metropolitan relations, as in the internal politics of the region, "the central-city mayor [will be] the leading figure." [40] As the region's most powerful and best-known political leader, he will represent the metropolis in Washington when more inclusive metropolitan cooperative arrangements are forged. And on those federal-metropolitan issues on which there is no areawide consensus, the central city will come closest to representing the regional perspective.

Notes

INTRODUCTION

The quotation at the top of the page is from John W. Burgess, "The American Commonwealth: Changes in Its Relationship to the Nation," *Political Science Quarterly*, Vol. I (March, 1886).

1. See, in particular, Edward C. Banfield, *Political Influence* (New York, Free Press of Glencoe, 1961); Edward C. Banfield and Morton Grodzins, *Government and Housing in Metropolitan Areas* (New York, McGraw-Hill, 1958); Scott Greer, *Governing the Metropolis* (New York, Wiley, 1962); Norton E. Long, *The Polity* (Chicago, Rand McNally, 1962); Henry J. Schmandt, Paul G. Steinbicker, and George D. Wendel, *Metropolitan Reform in St. Louis* (New York, Holt, Rinehart and Winston, 1961); Robert C. Wood, *1400 Governments* (Cambridge, Mass., Harvard University Press, 1961), and *Metropolis Against Itself* (New York, Committee for Economic Development, 1959).

2. One of Banfield's six short cases in *Political Influence,* "The Chicago Transit Authority," deals with a regional issue. Wood in *1400 Governments* treats briefly the politics of transportation and water supply in the New York region. Both are suggestive on the nature of external metropolitan politics. In a companion study to this volume, Jameson W. Doig examines internal and state-metropolitan politics on transportation in the New York region, focusing on the events surrounding the abortive attempt to create a Metropolitan Transit District in the late 1950s.

3. The category "metropolitan actor" is rather broadly conceived in this study. Metropolitan actors are all those participants in metropolitan politics who have significant parts of their constituencies in a metropolitan area. In the New York region, for example, in addition to the local officials and groups normally considered to be metropolitan actors, the three governors, the six U.S. senators, Connecticut's U.S. representative at large, and the forty other congressmen with

constituencies in the region (as well as subordinates and administration substructures) are all metropolitan actors.

CHAPTER I. THE SETTING

1. A note on definitions: "Public transportation" and "transit" refer to common-carrier service in urban areas, including buses, trolleys, rapid transit, and commuter railways. "Mass transportation" generally includes only rapid transit and suburban rail service. "Rapid," or "mass," transit is characterized by an exclusive right of way and the absence of grade crossings. "Suburban," or "commuter," rail service is provided by "steam" railways, uses standard railroad operating and employment practices, and features a seated ride and station-to-station fares with multitrip tickets. While a "commuter" generally is anyone who journeys to work, this study reserves the term to denote the users of suburban rail service.

2. The experience of one New York area commuter railroad in serving peak-time demand is typical of uneconomical utilization of equipment. In 1958 the New York Central required 304 coaches for 25 hours of the week to serve rush-hour traffic. During the remainder of the week, only 20 percent of these cars were needed for off-peak and weekend service. See *Railroad Passenger Train Deficit* (1959), 306 ICC 466 (ICC Docket No. 31954, May 8, 1959).

3. Railroads often set commuter fares at a noncompensatory level when services were initiated because of a desire to attract residential development along the carrier's right of way. In 1911, the ICC sanctioned below-cost commuter rates, terming commutation a distinctive bulk passenger service, in which fares needed only to be reasonable; *The Commutation Rate Case,* 21 ICC 428 (ICC Investigation and Suspension Docket Nos. 1 and 8, June 21, 1911).

4. In one hour an expressway lane accommodates 2,250 automobile passengers or 6,720 bus riders, while a single track of rail can handle 48,000 commuters; New York *Times,* Feb. 22, 1959. For a summary of the advantages and disadvantages of the various urban transportation modes, see Port of New York Authority, Comprehensive Planning Office, *Metropolitan Transportation—1980* (New York, 1963), pp. 297–302.

5. The RPA twenty-two county designation is used throughout this study. The counties are Bronx, Kings (Brooklyn), New York (Manhattan), Queens, and Richmond (Staten Island) in New York City;

Dutchess, Nassau, Orange, Putnam, Rockland, Suffolk, and West-chester in New York State; Bergen, Essex, Hudson, Middlesex, Monmouth, Morris, Passaic, Somerset, and Union in New Jersey; and Fairfield in Connecticut. With the exception of the community of Princeton in Mercer County, New Jersey, on the southwestern edge of the region, the New York rail commutation zone lies within the confines of this area.

6. New York *Herald Tribune,* Jan. 17, 1955.

7. AMA, *The Collapse of Commuter Service* (Washington, D.C., 1959), pp. 21–22, 28.

8. Robert C. Wood, *1400 Governments* (Cambridge, Mass., Harvard University Press, 1961), p. 131.

9. *Hub-Bound Travel in the Tri-State Metropolitan Region,* RPA Bulletin No. 91 (New York, 1959), pp. 12–14. RPA's figures are for 1956 and included the Hudson and Manhattan Tubes, now called Port Authority Trans-Hudson (PATH), an operation more akin to rapid transit than to commuter rail service.

10. During the same period, automobile crossings increased fivefold and trans-Hudson bus journeys increased tenfold. See New Jersey State Highway Department, Division of Railroad Transportation, "New Jersey's Rail Transportation Problem" (Trenton, 1960), p. 20.

11. *Commuter Transportation: A Study of Passenger Transportation in the New Jersey–New York–Connecticut Metropolitan Region with Particular Reference to Railroad Commutation,* report prepared by the RPA for the Committee on Interstate and Foreign Commerce, U.S. Senate, 87th Cong., 1st Sess. (1961), p. 26.

12. See *Railroad Passenger Train Deficit* (1959), 306 ICC 461, and Robert W. Purcell, "Special Report to the Governor of New York on Problems of the Railroads and Bus Lines in New York State" (New York, 1959).

13. Statement of Windsor F. Cousins, general solicitor of the Pennsylvania Railroad; U.S. House of Representatives, Committee on Interstate and Foreign Commerce, *Railroad Problems,* Hearings, 85th Cong., 2d Sess., (1958), p. 226.

14. Statement of Earl T. Moore, president of the Central Railroad of New Jersey, New Jersey Legislature, General Assembly, Committee on Federal and Interstate Relations, "Second Public Hearing on Assembly Bills No. 16 and 115 and Senate Bill No. 50" (Trenton, 1958), p. 16A.

15. Wood, *1400 Governments,* p. 118

16. Newark, 405,220; Jersey City, 276,101; Yonkers, 190,634; Bridgeport, 156,748; Paterson, 143,663; Elizabeth, 107,698 (all populations for 1960).

17. RPA "The Handling of Metropolitan Problems in the Tri-State Metropolitan Region" (New York, 1958), pp. 10–11.

18. In January, 1958, the organization changed its name to the Metropolitan Regional Council (MRC).

19. Statement of Executive Director Austin J. Tobin, New Jersey Legislature, General Assembly, Committee on Federal and Interstate Relations, "Public Hearings on Assembly Bills No. 16 and 115 and Senate Bill No. 50" (Trenton, 1958), p. 18.

20. Statement of ICC Commissioner John L. Rogers, U.S. House of Representatives, Committee on Interstate and Foreign Commerce, *Transportation Problems, Hearings*, 81st Cong., 2d Sess. (1950), p. 153.

21. James M. Landis, *Report on Regulatory Agencies to the President-Elect* (New York, 1960), pp. 23–24.

22. U.S. Commission on Intergovernmental Relations, *A Report to the President for Transmittal to the Congress* (1955), p. 52.

23. U.S. Joint Federal-State Action Committee, *Report . . . to the President of the United States and to the Chairman of the Governor's Conference*, Progress Report No. 1 (1957).

24. See President Eisenhower's message to the 1959 American Municipal Congress, AMA, *Better Urban Transportation* (Washington, D.C., 1959), p. 1.

25. Daniel P. Moynihan, "New Roads and Urban Chaos," *Reporter*, XX (April 14, 1960), 13–20; Wilfred Owen, *Cities in the Motor Age* (New York, Viking Press, 1959), p. 11.

26. Paul Ylvisaker, "The Deserted City," *Journal of the American Institute of Planners*, XXV (February, 1959), 5.

27. Statement of U.S. Senator Joseph S. Clark, Jr., AMA, *City-Federal Relations* (Washington, D.C., 1958), p. 19.

28. Charles L. Dearing and Wilfred Owen, *National Transportation Policy* (Washington, D.C., Brookings, 1949), p. 134.

29. Victor Jones, "Making the Highway a Tool for the Future City," *Urban Land Institute Technical Bulletin*, No. 31 (November, 1957), p. 76.

30. Albert M. Cole, "Highways and Urban Renewal," address to symposium on "The New Highways; Challenge to the Metropolitan Region," Connecticut General Life Insurance Company, Hartford, Sept. 9, 1957.

CHAPTER II. THE TRANSPORTATION ACT OF 1958

1. These deficit estimates are based on the ICC's method of fully apportioned costs; see *Railroad Passenger Train Deficit* (1959) 306 ICC 486 (ICC Docket No. 31954, May 8, 1959). If only the solely related costs of providing passenger service are considered, deficit estimates are considerably less: $152 million in 1957 as compared with $724 million under the ICC's fully apportioned formula. However, as James C. Nelson points out, "Solely related passenger train service costs considerably understate the avoidable costs for roads whose passenger-carrying businesses comprise large proportions of the total operations" primarily because of the large fixed facilities used primarily or exclusively for passenger service; *Railroad Transportation and Public Policy* (Washington, D.C., Brookings, 1959), p. 294.

2. Ford, Bacon & Davis, "Measures for Reducing Out-of-Pocket Losses of New Jersey Commuter Railroads under a Public Agency" (New York, 1957).

3. Statement of W. C. Grubbs, Louisville and Nashville Railroad, representing the AAR, U.S. Senate, Committee on Interstate and Foreign Commerce, *Study of Domestic Land and Water Transportation,* Hearings, 81st Cong., 2d Sess. (1950), p. 277.

4. *Board of Public Utility Commissioners of N.J. v. United States,* 158 F.Supp. 98 (1957).

5. Data complied by the NARUC indicated that in 1,274 passenger-service cases decided between 1951 and 1956, state commissions permitted discontinuance in 1,102 instances; see U.S. Senate, Committee on Interstate and Foreign Commerce, *Problems of the Railroads,* Hearings, 85th Cong., 2d Sess. (1958), p. 2027.

6. New Jersey Legislature, General Assembly, Committee on Federal and Interstate Relations, "Appendix to Public Hearings on Assembly Bills No. 16 and 115 and Senate Bill No. 50" (Trenton, 1958), pp. 91–92.

7. U.S. Presidential Advisory Committee on Transport Policy and Organization, *Revision of Federal Transportation Policy* (1955), p. 18.

8. U.S. Senate, *Problems of the Railroads,* p. 2.

9. See AMA, *City-Federal Relations* (Washington, D.C., 1958), p. 19.

10. Statement of AAR President Daniel Loomis, U.S. Senate, *Problems of the Railroads,* p. 6.

11. *Ibid.,* pp. 232–33.

12. See ICC Commissioner Anthony Arpaia to Representative J. Percy Priest, Dec. 22, 1955, quoted in U.S. House of Representatives, Committee on Interstate and Foreign Commerce, *Transportation Policy*, Hearings, 84th Cong., 2d Sess. (1956), and statement of ICC Commissioner Howard Freas, U.S. House of Representatives, Committee on Interstate and Foreign Commerce, *Railroad Problems*, Hearings, 85th Cong., 2d Sess (1958), p. 110.

13. Secretary of Commerce Sinclair Weeks to Senator George Smathers, April 22, 1958, quoted in U.S. Senate, *Problems of the Railroads*, p. 2350.

14. U.S. Senate, *Problems of the Railroads*, pp. 722–26 and 2310–11.

15. *Ibid.*, pp. 1410–28.

16. *Ibid.*, pp. 55, 414–15.

17. U.S. Senate, *Transportation Act of 1958*, 85th Cong., 2d Sess., S. Rep. No. 1647 and S. 3778 (1958).

18. The Transportation Act of 1920 permitted the ICC to prescribe intrastate rates when necessary to remove discriminations against interstate commerce. The Supreme Court upheld the general principle that Congress could restrain undue limitations on the earning power of an interstate carrier imposed by a state; see *Wisconsin R.R. Comm. v. Chicago, B.&Q. R.R. Co.*, 257 U.S. 563 (1921). But in January, 1958, the federal courts cut the ICC's power over intrastate commuter rates with a ruling that a state commission was not unduly burdening interstate commerce by basing suburban fares on all a carrier's revenues within the state rather than on commuter costs alone; see *Chicago, Milwaukee, St. Paul and Pacific Railroad Co. v. Illinois*, 168 F.Supp. 706 (1958).

19. *Congressional Record*, CIV:12 (July 30, 1958), 15529, and U.S. Senate, *Transportation Act of 1958*, S. Rep. No. 1647, p. 29.

20. New York *Times*, May 30, 1958.

21. *Congressional Record*, CIV:8 (June 11, 1958), 10837–39, 10852–53.

22. *Ibid.*, pp. 10850–53; see also Robert Bendiner, "The Railroads: From Overlord to Underdog," *Reporter*, XIX (August 7, 1958), 23.

23. See U.S. House of Representatives, *Transportation Act of 1958*, 85th Cong., 2d Sess., H.R. Rep. No. 1922 (1958), pp. 21–24.

24. In mid-1957, during the uproar over the $400-million MRTC plan, Osmers proposed an alternative which he asserted would cost only $100 million; see Paterson (N.J.) *Evening News*, June 28, 1957.

25. Osmers later boasted: "Out of the 435 Members of the House of Representatives, I was one of two Members who voted against the bill. It was perfectly clear to me that the passage of that bill in the form it was signed was the end of commuter service in the United States. This was rather scoffed at in the House"; U.S. Senate, Committee on Interstate and Foreign Commerce, *Amendments to the Transportation Act of 1958*, Hearings, 86th Cong., 1st Sess. (1959), p. 75.

26. New York *Times*, July 3, 6, 11, 14, and 15, 1958.

27. In addition to the passenger-service provisions, the Transportation Act of 1958 made five major changes in the Interstate Commerce Act: (1) the ICC was directed to place greater emphasis in rate determinations on the development of competition between the various modes of transportation; (2) the definition to private motor carriers was tightened to reduce unregulated motor truck competition with the railroads; (3) the list of exempted agricultural products was curtailed; (4) $500 million in loans guaranteed by the ICC was made available to the railroads on an emergency basis through March 31, 1961; and (5) the ICC's authority in intrastate rate making was strengthened to ease burdens on interstate commerce.

28. U.S. Senate, *Transportation Act of 1958*, S. Rep. No. 1647, pp. 10–11.

29. *Congressional Record*, CIV:8 (June 11, 1958), 10852–53.

30. U.S. House of Representatives, *Transportation Act of 1958*, H.R. Rep. No. 1922, p. 11.

31. U.S. Department of Commerce, *Federal Transportation Policy and Program* (1960), p. 7.

32. See *Railroad Passenger Train Deficit* (1959), 306 ICC 469.

33. Nelson, *Railroad Transportation and Public Policy*, p. 326.

34. The AMA's efforts were limited to the statement which Mayor Dilworth inserted in the record of the Smathers hearings.

35. See New Jersey State Chamber of Commerce press release of June 11, 1958, entitled "What Are the 'Smathers Proposals'? How Would They Help New Jersey's Railroads? What Do They Mean to the Economy of New Jersey?"

36. U.S. House of Representatives, Committee on Interstate and Foreign Commerce, *Passenger Train Service*, Hearings, 86th Cong., 2d Sess. (1960), p. 48.

37. Statement of Forrest Van Horn, Northern Valley Commuters Organization, New Jersey Legislature, General Assembly, Committee

on Federal and Interstate Relations, "Public Hearing on Assembly Bills No. 16 and 115 and Senate Bill No. 50" (Trenton, 1958), p. 128A.

38. New York *Times*, June 9, 1958.

CHAPTER III. THE COMMUTER CRISIS

1. New York *Herald Tribune*, Aug. 16, 1958.

2. Statement of ICC Commissioner Kenneth H. Tuggle, U.S. Senate, Committee on Interstate and Foreign Commerce, *Proposed Passenger Train Act of 1960*, Hearings, 86th Cong., 2d Sess. (1960), p. 28.

3. Statement of ICC associate general counsel Charles Jones, quoted in the New York *Times*, Sept. 11, 1958.

4. *New Jersey v. United States*, 168 F. Supp. 324 (1958).

5. "Railroad Passenger Train Deficit," proposed report, September, 1958 (ICC Docket 31954).

6. New York *Times*, Sept. 4, 1958.

7. New York *Times*, Sept. 8, 1958.

8. New York *Herald Tribune*, Nov. 18, 1958.

9. New York *Times*, Nov. 26, 1958; Perry Shoemaker, "A Study of Inequity," address to the New Jersey Press Association, New Brunswick, N.J., Dec. 5, 1958; Newark *Evening News*, Dec. 7, 1958.

10. See a forthcoming book by Jameson W. Doig (New York, Columbia University Press), Chap. VI, for a more detailed discussion of the expiration of the MRTC proposals.

11. New Jersey Legislature, General Assembly, Committee on Federal and Interstate Relations, "Public Hearings on Assembly Bills No. 16 and 115 and Senate Bill No. 50" (Trenton, 1958), p. 65.

12. New York *Times*, Dec. 10, 1958.

13. New York *Herald Tribune*, Feb. 11, 1959.

14. *Ibid.*

15. New York *Times*, Feb. 11, 1959.

16. Port of New York Authority, Executive Director Austin J. Tobin to Governors Nelson A. Rockefeller, Robert B. Meyner, and Abraham Ribicoff and Mayor Robert F. Wagner, Feb. 10, 1959.

17. New York *Herald Tribune*, Feb. 11, 1959; New York *World-Telegram & Sun*, Feb. 14, 1959; New York *Journal-American*, Feb. 15, 1959.

18. Newark *Evening News*, Feb. 17, 1959.

19. *New Jersey v. United States*, 359 U.S. 27 (1958).

20. New York *Times*, March 24, 1959.

21. New York *Times*, April 5 and 10 and May 7, 1959.

22. New York *Times*, June 4, 1959.

23. See New Jersey State Highway Department, Division of Railroad Transportation, "A Proposal toward Solving New Jersey's Railroad Transportation Problem" (Trenton, 1959).

CHAPTER IV. SUBURBIA: REMEDIALISM AND LOCALISM

1. With a slight amendment, Scott Greer's definition, "Suburbs are urban areas outside the governmental boundaries of the central city," is used throughout this study; *Governing the Metropolis* (New York, Wiley, 1962), p. 84. The New York region's major subcentral (or satellite) cities—Newark, Jersey City, Yonkers, Bridgeport, Paterson, and Elizabeth—are not considered as part of suburbia in this study and are treated in conjunction with New York City.

2. Robert C. Wood, *Suburbia: Its People and Their Politics* (Boston, Houghton Mifflin, 1958), p. 83.

3. Andrew Hacker, *Congressional Districting: The Issue of Equal Representation* (Washington, Brookings, 1963), p. 111.

4. Jerome Beatty, *Show Me the Way to Go Home* (New York, Crowell, 1959), p. 3.

5. Robert C. Wood, "A Division of Power in Metropolitan Areas," in Arthur Maass, ed., *Area and Power* (New York, Free Press of Glencoe, 1959), p. 67.

6. Herbert Askwith, "Railroads on the Wrong Track," *Harper's Magazine*, CC (May, 1950), p. 79. Askwith was founder and chairman of the Westchester Commuters Group.

7. Statement of August W. Knauber, New Jersey Commuters Association, U.S. Senate, Committee on Interstate and Foreign Commerce, *Amendments to the Transportation Act of 1958*, Hearings, 86th Cong., 1st Sess. (1959), p. 99.

8. See statement of John F. Kraus in New York *Times*, Dec. 15, 1950, and his "Statement to the New Jersey Press Association Seminar," New Brunswick, N.J., Dec. 5, 1958.

9. New Jersey Legislature, Concurrent Resolution No. 20 (1954).

10. See New York *Times*, Oct. 20, 1956, for criticisms of the ICC made by Mayor Wagner during his unsuccessful campaign for the U.S. Senate.

11. Northern Valley Commuters Organization, "Bulletin," Sept. 16, 1957. The groups signing the letter were the NVCO, the Citizens

United Transit Committee, the Bergen County Transit Committee, and the IMGBRS.

12. New York *Times,* Aug. 21, 1958.

13. U.S. Senate, *A Bill to Amend the Interstate Commerce Act,* 86th Cong., 1st Sess., S. 1331 (1959).

14. U.S. Senate, *A Bill to Amend Section 13a(1) of the Interstate Commerce Act,* 86th Cong., 1st Sess., S. 1450 (1959).

15. *Trains,* XXI (September, 1961), 24.

16. Representatives of the following groups testified: New Jersey Commuters Association, Citizens United Transit Committee, Northern Valley Commuters Organization, Susquehanna Transit Commuters Association, Lehigh Valley Passenger and Shippers' Association, and the Morris County Railroad Transportation Association. The IMGBRS inserted a statement. See U.S. Senate, *Amendments to the Transportation Act of 1958.*

17. Statement of Walter E. Zullig, Jr., Susquehanna Transit Commuters Association, *ibid.,* p. 119.

18. U.S. House of Representatives, Committee on Interstate and Foreign Commerce, *Passenger Train Service,* Hearings, 86th Cong., 2d Sess. (1959), p. 310.

19. Statement of Thomas T. Taber, U.S. Senate, *Amendments to the Transportation Act of 1958,* p. 362; Forrest K. Van Horn, Northern Valley Commuters Association, *ibid.,* p. 113.

20. See Thomas T. Taber, "Our Railroads—A Post Mortem or a Renaissance?" (1959).

21. New York *Times,* Jan. 18, June 5 and 11, 1959.

22. Statement of RLEA chairman George Leighty, U.S. Senate, *Amendments to the Transportation Act of 1958,* p. 131.

23. *Interstate Commerce Commission v. Railway Labor Executive Association,* 315 U.S. 373 (1941).

24. Commuter lines represented were the New Haven, New York Central, Lackawanna, Lehigh Valley, Southern Pacific, and Chicago & North Western.

25. U.S. Senate, *Amendments to the Transportation Act of 1958,* pp. 87–92.

26. Undersecretary of Commerce F. H. Mueller to Senator Warren G. Magnuson, quoted in *ibid.,* p. 488.

27. George A. Smathers, "Blueprint to Save Our Railroads," *This Week,* July 26, 1959, pp. 10–12.

28. *Congressional Record,* CV:3 (March 9, 1959), 3587.

29. New York *Times,* Feb. 3, 1960.

30. New York *Times,* Oct. 1, 1959, and Jan. 2, 1960.

31. New York *Times,* Jan. 21, 1960.

32. New York *Times,* Feb. 6, 1960.

33. U.S. House of Representatives, *Passenger Train Service,* p. 307.

CHAPTER V.
THE STATES: A WARY EYE ON WASHINGTON

1. Wallace S. Sayre, " 'Urbanism and Government, 1955–1977': A Rejoinder," *Annals of the American Academy of Political and Social Science,* CCCXIV (November, 1957), 84.

2. Wallace S. Sayre and Herbert Kaufman, *Governing New York City: Politics in the Metropolis* (New York, Russell Sage Foundation, 1960), p. 591.

3. Robert C. Wood, *1400 Governments* (Cambridge, Mass., Harvard University Press, 1961), p. 154.

4. Nelson A. Rockefeller, *The Future of Federalism* (New York, Atheneum, 1962), pp. 42, 54.

5. Robert W. Purcell, "Special Report to the Governor of New York on Problems of the Railroads and Bus Lines in New York State" (New York, 1959).

6. Statement of Stanley Tankel, *Wall Street Journal,* May 2, 1961.

7. New York City, Department of City Planning, "The Need for Comprehensive Land and Transportation Planning" (New York, 1960), p. 15.

8. Rockefeller, *Future of Federalism,* pp. 42–43.

9. New York *Herald Tribune,* Feb. 3, 1959.

10. New York *Times,* Feb. 16 and 17, 1960; the activities of this delegation are discussed in greater detail in Chap. VI.

11. New York State, Department of Public Service, Public Service Commission, *Report of Investigation by the Public Service Commission of the Financial Condition of the Railroads Operating in the State of New York* (Albany, 1959), pp. 31–33.

12. Purcell, "Special Report," p. 3.

13. New York *Times,* June 5, 1959.

14. U.S. Senate, *Transportation Act of 1958,* 85th Cong., 2d Sess., S. Rep. 1647 (1958), p. 11.

15. Public Law No. 302, 86th Cong., 1st Sess. (Sept. 21, 1959).

16. Identical petitions of the Citizens United Transit Committee

and the Northern Valley Commuters Organization are reproduced in New Jersey Legislature, General Assembly, Committee on Federal and Interstate Relations, "Public Hearings on Assembly Bills No. 16 and 115 and Senate Bill No. 50" (Trenton, 1958), pp. 127A and 133A, respectively.

17. New York *Times*, Dec. 10, 1958.

18. New York *Times*, Sept. 18, Nov. 5, and Nov. 11, 1959, Jan. 13 and 25, 1960.

19. New York *Times*, Nov. 13, 1959.

20. Jean Gottmann, *Megalopolis: The Urbanized Northeastern Seaboard of the United States* (New York, Twentieth Century Fund, 1961), p. 671.

21. New York *Herald Tribune*, Feb. 3, 1959.

22. Connecticut Commission on Intergovernmental Cooperation, Special Railroad Study Subcommittee, "Progress Report" (Hartford, 1959), p. 8.

CHAPTER VI.
THE CITIES: THE QUEST FOR FEDERAL AID

1. Statement of Mayor Richardson Dilworth of Philadelphia, AMA, *City-Federal Relations* (Washington, D.C., 1958), p. 52.

2. Donoh W. Hanks, Jr., "Neglected Cities Turn to United States," *National Municipal Review*, XXXV (April, 1946), 173.

3. Lawrence J. R. Herson, "The Lost World of Municipal Government," *American Political Science Review*, LI (June, 1957), 339.

4. AMA, *Better Urban Transportation* (Washington, D.C., 1959), p. 24.

5. Wallace S. Sayre and Herbert Kaufman, *Governing New York City: Politics in the Metropolis* (New York, Russell Sage Foundation, 1960), p. 657.

6. Scott Greer, *Governing the Metropolis* (New York, Wiley, 1962), p. 75.

7. Edward C. Banfield, *Political Influence* (New York, Free Press of Glencoe, 1961), p. 247.

8. *Plan and Program for Transportation* (Philadelphia, 1955). The complete report and the staff reports are contained in UTTB, *Plan and Program 1955* (Philadelphia, 1956).

9. See Mayor Dilworth's statement, U.S. Senate, Committee on Banking and Currency, *Housing Legislation of 1960*, Hearings, 86th Cong., 2d Sess. (1960), p. 744.

10. AMA, "Draft of Proposed Amendment to National Municipal Policy on Mass Transit" (1955).

11. National Conference Coordinating Metropolitan Transportation, "Proceedings," Chicago, May 27–28, 1957, p. 168.

12. Quoted in Robert H. Connery and Richard H. Leach, *The Federal Government and Metropolitan Areas* (Cambridge, Mass., Harvard University Press, 1960).

13. Quoted in U.S. Senate, Committee on Interstate and Foreign Commerce, *Problems of the Railroads*, Hearings, 85th Cong., 2d Sess. (1958), p. 725.

14. U.S. House of Representatives, *A Bill to Establish a Body Corporate in the Department of Commerce*, 80th Cong., 2d Sess., H.R. 11816 (1958).

15. See statement of James M. Symes, U.S. House of Representatives, Committee on Banking and Currency, *Metropolitan Mass Transportation*, Hearings, 86th Cong., 2d Sess. (1960), p. 85.

16. Ernest W. Williams and David W. Bluestone, *Rationale for Federal Transportation Policy*, Appendix to *Federal Transportation Policy and Program*, U.S. Department of Commerce (April, 1960), p. 53.

17. New York *Times*, June 29 and 30, 1955.

18. George Alpert, "A Better Deal for Commuters," *Harper's Magazine*, CCXIV (April, 1957), 29.

19. The Transportation Act loan guarantee program is discussed in Chaps. VIII and IX.

20. New York *Times*, July 14, 1954.

21. U.S. House of Representatives, Committee on Government Operations, *Federal-State-Local Relations: State and Local Officials*, Hearings, 85th Cong., 1st Sess. (1957); see p. 353 for Dilworth's statement and pp. 218–33 for Wagner's.

22. The other members of the Preusse committee were Corporation Counsel Peter Brown, Transit Authority chairman Charles Patterson, City Planning Commission chairman James Felt, and Tax Commissioner William Boyland.

23. See Robert F. Wagner, "Commuter Transportation," address, Chicago, Jan. 13, 1959.

24. MRTC, "New York Public Hearings on the Plan and Recommendation of Arthur W. Page, Project Director of the Metropolitan Rapid Transit Commission" (New York, 1957), p. 14.

25. Represented at the meeting were Allentown, Pa., Baltimore,

Boston, Chicago, Cleveland, Detroit, Kansas City, Milwaukee, New York, Philadelphia, St. Louis, and Washington and the Baltimore & Ohio, the Boston & Maine, the Chicago, Burlington & Quincy, the Milwaukee Road, the Chicago & North Western, the Erie, the Jersey Central, the Lackawanna, the Long Island, the Missouri-Pacific, the New Haven, the New York Central, the Pennsylvania, the Reading, the Rock Island, and the Southern Pacific railroads.

26. Wagner, "Commuter Transportation," address, Chicago, Jan. 13, 1959.

27. New York *Herald Tribune,* Jan. 14, 1959.

28. AMA, *The Collapse of Commuter Service* (Washington, D.C., 1959), p. 2.

29. Mayor Wagner proposed loans or bond guarantees as alternatives to federal grants on the eve of the Feb. 10, 1959, meeting with the three governors; see New York *Times,* Feb. 9, 1959.

30. AMA, *Collapse of Commuter Service,* p. 2.

31. New York *Times,* Dec. 1, 1959; see also statement of Mayor Raymond Tucker, U.S. Senate, *Housing Legislation of 1960,* Hearings, p. 763.

32. "Joint Statement of Mayors and Railroad Presidents," Nov. 30, 1959. The statement is summarized in the New York *Times,* Dec. 1, 1959, and AMA, *Collapse of Commuter Service,* p. 1.

33. See AMA, *Better Urban Transportation,* pp. 40 ff.

34. New York *Times,* Jan. 30, 1960.

35. New York *World-Telegram & Sun,* Sept. 10, 1958; New York *Journal-American,* Sept. 5, 1958.

36. New York *Journal-American,* Jan. 15, 1959; New York *Daily News,* January 15, 1959; New York *Herald Tribune,* Jan. 15, 1959; New York *Times,* Jan. 15, 1959.

37. New York *Times,* May 29, 1959.

38. New York *World-Telegram & Sun,* Feb. 14, 1959.

39. New York *Times,* April 16, 1959.

40. Robert F. Wagner, "Help for Our Cities," address before the National Conference on Government of the National Municipal League, Springfield, Mass.; reprinted in the *National Civic Review,* XLIX (January, 1960), 8. In the same speech, Wagner mentioned the train-service issue for the first time, calling the Transportation Act of 1958 a "serious backward step" and scored the federal government for showing "little concern for what happens when commuter service goes bad." The city's belated response on train service was a result of

the lack of constituency pressures, doubt in City Hall that changes in the Transportation Act would help the urban cause, and a desire on the part of the large cities not to antagonize their new railroad allies.

41. *Time,* LXXIII (June 22, 1959), 19.

42. New York *Times,* June 22, 1959.

43. New York *Times,* Jan. 25, 1960. The Republicans were Westchester County Executive Edwin Michaelian and Westport (Conn.) First Selectman Herbert Baldwin.

44. New York *Times,* Feb. 16, 1960.

45. MRTC Traffic and Transportation Committee, "Report for February 23, 1960, Meeting" and "The Bulletin of the Metropolitan Regional Council" (March, 1960).

46. See U.S. House of Representatives, *Mass Transit Financing Corporation Act,* 86th Cong., 1st Sess., H.R. 10343 (1960).

47. New York *Times,* Feb. 17, 1963.

48. *Congressional Record,* 87th Cong., 1st Sess., daily edition, June 8, 1961, p. 9206.

49. U.S. House of Representatives, Committee on Interstate and Foreign Commerce, *Passenger Train Service,* Hearings, 86th Cong., 2d Sess. (1959), p. 320.

50. AMA, *Better Urban Transportation,* p. 24.

CHAPTER VII. THE CONGRESSMEN: DIRECT AND INDIRECT CONSTITUENCY PRESSURE

1. Bertram M. Gross, *The Legislative Struggle* (New York, McGraw-Hill, 1953), p. 97.

2. Donald R. Matthews, *U.S. Senators and Their World* (Chapel Hill, University of North Carolina Press, 1960), p. 216.

3. Gross, *Legislative Struggle,* p. 167.

4. For evidence substantiating this proposition derived from rollcall analysis, see Lewis A. Froman, Jr., *Congressmen and Their Constituencies* (Chicago, Rand McNally, 1963), pp. 80–83.

5. U.S. House of Representatives, *A Resolution to Create a Select Committee to Conduct an Investigation and Study of the Existing and Probable Future Mass Transportation Problems in Large Metropolitan Areas of the United States,* 85th Cong., 1st Sess., H.R. Res. 231 (1957).

6. National Conference Coordinating Metropolitan Transportation, Chicago, 1957, "Proceedings," p. 168.

7. *Ibid.*

8. U.S. Senate, Committee on Interstate and Foreign Commerce, *Amendments to the Transportation Act of 1958,* Hearings, 86th Cong., 1st Sess. (1959), pp. 34–35.

9. New York *Times,* Aug. 21, 1958. Congress' purpose in enacting the Transportation Act became a persistent theme of discussion by the region's congressmen. During consideration of the train-service issue in 1959, almost every congressman from the New York area echoed Senator Kenneth Keating, who had voted for the Transportation Act as a member of the House from an upstate New York district, in declaring, "I do not believe that it was the intent of Congress in passing the Transportation Act of 1958 to permit arbitrary discontinuance of commuter service by the railroads, before needed solutions are found and put into operation"; U.S. Senate, *Amendments to the Transportation Act of 1958,* p. 66. Congressional intent is always a sticky question. There is some evidence in this case that Smathers and other members of the Commerce Committees were surprised at the speed with which the railroads moved to take off the commuter trains. It is also true that many congressmen vote for legislation that they do not fully understand. But there is little question that the ICC and the federal courts correctly read the rather clear language of Sec. 13a(1) of the Transportation Act of 1958.

10. New York *Times,* Oct. 6, 1958.

11. New York *Times,* Feb. 22, 1959.

12. U.S. Senate, *Amendments to the Transportation Act of 1958,* pp. 9, 11. Wallhauser, who was attending the Atlantic Congress in London, submitted a statement endorsing the Case bill.

13. *Ibid.,* p. 39.

14. One attempt at innovation on the commuter issue did come from a New York City congressman. Early in 1960, Manhattan Democrat Herbert Zelenko introduced a bill providing for a federal tax credit which would freeze suburban fares at their Jan. 1, 1960, level by permitting the rail commuter to subtract all future fare increases from his federal income tax. Zelenko characterized his plan as "federal assistance . . . without federal appropriations" (press release, Feb. 8, 1960). Predictably, the plan, which provided for no public control over fares, perished in committee after having aroused no enthusiasm.

15. U.S. Senate, *Amendments to the Transportation Act of 1958,* p. 9.

16. New York *Times,* March 8, 1959.

17. U.S. Senate, *Amendments to the Transportation Act of 1958,* p. 452.

18. The phrase is Arthur Krock's; see his column in the New York *Times,* June 5, 1959.

19. See Joseph S. Clark, *The Senate Establishment* (New York, Hill and Wang, 1963).

20. Clifford Case, press release, Sept. 2, 1959.

21. Clifford Case, press release, Sept. 9, 1959.

22. New York *Times,* Sept. 20, 1959.

23. U.S. House of Representatives, Committee on Interstate and Foreign Commerce, *Passenger Train Service,* Hearings, 86th Cong., 2d Sess. (1959), p. 26. The Passenger Train Service Act of 1960 followed Case's bill of the previous year in most of its major provisions. However, RLEA attorneys added a section which required the ICC to evaluate the effect of a service termination on the military and civil defense needs of the nation and another commanding the ICC to make the railroads exert all reasonable efforts to maintain safe and adequate passenger service according to standards to be developed and enforced by the Commission; U.S. Senate, *Passenger Train Service Act of 1960,* 86th Cong., 2d Sess., S. 3020 (1960).

24. Clifford Case, press release, June 23, 1960.

25. *Congressional Record,* CVI:6 (March 30, 1960), A2837.

26. U.S. Senate, Committee on Interstate and Foreign Commerce, *Proposed Passenger Train Act of 1960,* Hearings, 86th Cong., 2d Sess. (1960), p. 86.

27. IMGBRS, "Resolution Adopted March 28, 1960."

28. A statement of endorsement was issued by Mayor Edward Tiller of Garwood, chairman of the mayor's committee of the IMGBRS; August W. Knauber, president of the Hunterdon Hills Commuter Association; Thomas T. Taber, chairman of the Morris County Railroad Transportation Association; Frank Tilley, chairman of the Susquehanna Transit Commuters Association; and Forrest K. Van Horn, chairman of the Northern Valley Commuters Organization. See New York *Times,* Oct. 16, 1960.

29. New York *Times,* Jan. 19, 1959.

30. Public Law No. 380, 86th Cong., 1st Sess. (Sept. 24, 1959).

31. The membership of the ACIR was fixed by statute at three executive officers, three citizen members, three senators, three repre-

sentatives, four governors, three state legislators, four mayors, and three county officials.

32. Florence Dwyer, "Memorandum to [the] Advisory Commission on Intergovernmental Relations," Dec. 14, 1959.

33. See the statement Irwin inserted in the record of the 1959 train-service hearings, U.S. Senate, *Amendments to the Transportation Act of 1958*, pp. 204–06.

34. See, for example, an account in the New York *Times,* Dec. 29, 1959, of an inspection tour Irwin made of the New Haven's commuter facilities.

35. New York *Times,* Oct. 8 and Dec. 29, 1959, and Jan. 14, 1960. See also a letter from Irwin in the Ridgefield (Conn.) *Press,* Jan. 21, 1960, in which he called for federal aid and a national transportation policy.

36. At first, Williams criticized Case's bill for going "too far, too fast"; *Congressional Record,* CV:4 (March 18, 1959), 4407. At the 1959 hearings, however, he declared that "the goal in my mind is more important than any particular approach to achieving it"; U.S. Senate, *Amendments to the Transportation Act of 1958,* p. 20.

38. The Special Study Group on Transportation Policies was a by-product of the Transportation Act of 1958. Its primary purpose was to make a comprehensive study of the railroad problem. Pressures from Case and other northeastern senators led to the inclusion of a section on metropolitan transportation problems. The impact of the final report on federal mass transportation assistance politics is considered briefly in Chap. IX.

39. Stephen K. Bailey, *Congress Makes a Law* (New York, Columbia University Press, 1950), p. 100.

40. *Ibid.,* p. 46.

41. U.S. Senate, *A Bill to Amend Section 701 of the Housing Act of 1954 . . . and Title II of the Housing Amendments of 1955,* 86th Cong., 2d Sess., S. 3278 (1960).

CHAPTER VIII.
FEDERAL AID IN THE CONGRESSIONAL ARENA

1. *Congressional Record,* CVI:5 (March 28, 1960), 6678.

2. Norton E. Long, *The Polity* (Chicago, Rand McNally, 1962) p. 160.

3. In the Eighty-sixth Congress, the Housing Subcommittee of the

Senate Banking and Currency Committee was composed of Democrats Sparkman (Alabama), Douglas (Illinois), Clark (Pennsylvania), and Williams (New Jersey) and Republicans Capehart (Indiana), Bush (Connecticut), and Beall (Maryland).

4. The planning of these hearings, with the various urban figures playing roles assigned to them by the senatorial strategists, is an excellent example of the two-way relationships between Congress and pressure groups which are common in Washington. Stephen K. Bailey underscores the importance of this relationship in *Congress Makes a Law* (New York, Columbia University Press, 1950), p. 98; see also Donald R. Matthews' excellent treatment of the relations between senators and lobbyists in *U.S. Senators and Their World* (Chapel Hill, University of North Carolina Press, 1960), pp. 176–96.

5. See testimony of Maxwell Lehman, U.S. Senate, *Housing Legislation of 1960*, Hearings, 86th Cong., 2d Sess. (1960), p. 795.

6. *Ibid.*, p. 756.

7. *Ibid.*, p. 766.

8. Commissioner John H. Winchell to Senator A. Willis Robertson, May 5, 1960, quoted in *ibid.*, pp. 59–60.

9. In his report to the MRTC, Miller noted that "the same national policies which justify a national interest in highway building within and without city limits . . . would fully justify national financial participation in a program of mass public transportation within the region," but on the basis of the negative reaction he had received in Washington advised the MRTC that "further action depends solely upon political values yet to be determined, [and] hardly is a reliable basis upon which to project the financial feasibility of current proposals"; William Miller, *Metropolitan Rapid Transit Financing* (Princeton, 1957), p. 26.

10. Acting Secretary of the Treasury Laurence B. Robbins to Senator A. Willis Robertson, May 9, 1960; Under Secretary of Commerce Phillip A. Ray to Senator A. Willis Robertson, May 31, 1960; and HHFA Administrator Norman P. Mason to Senator A. Willis Robertson, May 6, 1960; quoted in U.S. Senate, *Housing Legislation of 1960*, pp. 56–59 and 1038–39.

11. Bailey, *Congress Makes a Law*, p. 109.

12. U.S. House of Representatives, Committee on Banking and Currency, *Metropolitan Mass Transportation*, Hearing, 86th Cong., 2d Sess. (1960), p. 68.

13. U.S. Senate, *Housing Legislation of 1960*, p. 912.

14. However, the mass transportation bill reported by the committee retained some appeal for the smaller cities, since it authorized a doubling of the $100-million revolving fund for public facility loans.

15. U.S. Senate, *Mass Transportation Act of 1960*, S. Rep. 1591 (1960), p. 3.

16. In a speech made after Lyndon Johnson assumed the presidency, Senator Williams, in reassuring the cities and suburbs that they "need have no fear that their problems will be neglected under President Johnson's administration," recalled that "In 1960 the idea of helping ease traffic congestion by restoring our deteriorating rail and bus service was brand-new to Congress. Lyndon Johnson showed great concern and understanding of the problem involved and he gave a commitment to do all he could to obtain Senate passage. The bill did pass, but I can tell you it simply wouldn't have been possible without Johnson's help"; Newark *Sunday News,* Jan. 5, 1964.

17. *Congressional Record,* CVI:11 (June 27, 1960), 14462.

18. New York *Times,* June 28, 1960.

19. U.S. Senate, *Housing Legislation of 1960,* p. 730.

20. U.S. House of Representatives, *Metropolitan Mass Transportation,* p. 7.

21. The representatives who appeared were Hugh Addonizio (D–Newark, N.J.), William Barrett (D–Philadelphia), James Burke (D–Boston area), William Cahill (R–New Jersey portion of Philadelphia area), Jeffrey Cohelan (D–Berkeley, Calif.), Robert Corbett (R–Pittsburgh area), Florence Dwyer (R–Union County, N.J.), Paul Fino (R–Bronx, N.Y.), Cornelius Gallagher (D–Hudson County, N.J.), Kathryn Granahan (D–Philadelphia), William Green (D–Philadelphia), Seymour Halpern (R–Queens, N.Y.), Elmer Holland (D–Pittsburgh), Donald Irwin (D–Fairfield County, Conn.), William Moorhead (D–Pittsburgh), Frank Thompson (D–Trenton and New Jersey portion of Philadelphia area), and Charles Vanik (D–Cleveland).

22. U.S. House of Representatives, *Metropolitan Mass Transportation,* pp. 69–70.

23. Representatives Addonizio, Barrett, Burke, Dwyer, Fino, Halpern, Moorhead, and Vanik.

24. U.S. Conference of Mayors "Resolutions Adopted by the 1960 Annual Conference of the United States Conference of Mayors," May 13, 1960.

25. New York *Times,* June 29, 1960.

26. New York *Times,* Aug. 14, 1960.

27. Kirk H. Porter and Donald Bruce Johnson, *National Party Platforms: 1840–1960* (Urbana, University of Illinois Press, 1961), pp. 593, 617.

28. AMA, *Better Urban Transportation* (Washington, D.C., 1959), p. 26.

29. See New York *Times,* Aug. 7, 1960.

30. See Theodore H. White, *The Making of the President, 1960* (New York, Atheneum, 1961), p. 206.

31. New York *Times,* Oct. 11, 1960.

32. *Traffic World,* CVI (October 22, 1960), 42.

33. U.S. House of Representatives, Committee on Interstate and Foreign Commerce, *Passenger Train Service,* Hearings, 86th Cong., 2d Sess. (1959), pp. 30–31.

34. New York *Times,* March 25, 1960.

35. Florence Dwyer, "Report to the People," IV (May 12, 1960).

36. U.S. Senate, *Housing Legislation of 1960,* p. 914.

37. New Brunswick (N.J.) *Home News,* March 30, 1960; Bergen (N.J.) *Evening Record,* June 20, 1960.

38. Newark *Evening News,* July 16, 1960.

39. Clifford Case, "Urban Transportation . . . What Kind of Federal Aid Is Needed?" *Newark Commerce,* V (September, 1960), 21.

40. The official was Lewis Sillcox; he recommended federal operating subsidies for interstate rail commutation and federal grants for facilities and equipment, state subsidies for intrastate operations, and local subsidies for stations, parking lots, and the like; New York *Times,* March 31, 1960.

41. WCBS–TV, "Hell on Wheels," program transcript of the telecast of July 21, 1960.

42. U.S. Senate, *Housing Legislation of 1960,* p. 820. One other state official supported the Williams bill at the Senate hearings: Colonel C. K. Harding of Georgia, who was interested in possible federal help for a projected mass transit system in Atlanta; see *ibid.,* pp. 903–09.

43. New Jersey State Highway Department, "New Jersey's Rail Transportation Problem," p. 12.

44. New Jersey Legislature, Senate, Commission Created under Senate Resolution No. 7, "Public Hearings . . . to Study the Financial Structure and Operations of the Port of New York Authority" (Trenton, 1960), p. 18.

45. The New Haven loan was for general railroad purposes, not

for the improvement of commuter facilities. The commercial interest rate feature of the loan guarantee program prevented its use for commuter rail improvements, since, as New Jersey's 1960 rail report indicated, "Prospects for passenger service earnings all but preclude obtaining guaranteed loans for new equipment or other capital improvements associated with sububan service"; New Jersey State Highway Department, "New Jersey's Rail Transportation Problem," p. 25.

46. New York *Times*, Oct. 26, 1960.

CHAPTER IX. FEDERAL AID ON THE NEW FRONTIER

1. New York *Times*, Dec. 9, 1960.

2. *New Frontiers of the Kennedy Administration: The Texts of the Task Force Reports Prepared for the President* (Washington, D.C., Public Affairs Press, 1961), p. 167. Three New Yorkers were on the six-man housing task force: Joseph MacMurray, a former New York State Housing Administrator; Harry Held, senior vice-president of the Bowery Savings Bank; and Mary Lavery, a former deputy New York City Housing Commissioner. The other members were Robert Wood, a Massachusetts Institute of Technology political scientist; Charles Wellman, a California banker; and John Barrier, the staff director of the House of Representatives' Housing Subcommittee.

3. James M. Landis, *Report on Regulatory Agencies to the President-Elect* (New York, 1960), p. 78.

4. See U.S. Senate, Committee on Interstate and Foreign Commerce, *National Transportation Policy*, preliminary draft of a report prepared by the Special Study Group on Transportation Policies in the United States, 87th Cong., 1st Sess. (1961), pp. 552–635. The study, which covered all aspects of federal railroad policy, grew out of the Smathers subcommittee's 1958 investigation of railroad problems and took its name from staff director John Doyle, a retired military officer. The metropolitan transportation portion of the Doyle Report was a product of the commuter-crisis-stimulated demands of Eastern senators, led by Case, for a Senate study of the suburban rail problem.

5. U.S. Senate, *Urban Mass Transportation Act of 1961*, 87th Cong., 1st Sess., S. 345 (1961).

6. RPA, *The Race for Open Space*, RPA Bulletin No. 96 (New York, 1960).

7. Harrison Williams, "Annual Murray Seasongood Good Government Lecture," Amherst, Mass., Nov. 12, 1960.

8. See A. H. Raskin, "Washington Gets 'the Weaver Treatment,'" *New York Times Magazine,* May 14, 1961, p. 36.

9. Weaver was the first of his race to be appointed to such a lofty position in a national administration. A former official of the National Association for the Advancement of Colored People and vice-chairman of the New York City Housing and Redevelopment Board at the time of his appointment to the HHFA post by President Kennedy, Weaver came under fire from Southern senators, led by Banking and Currency chairman A. Willis Robertson of Virginia, for his past espousal of integated housing; see U.S. Senate, Committee on Banking and Currency, *Nomination of Robert C. Weaver,* Hearings, 87th Cong., 1st Sess. (1961).

10. U.S. Senate, Committee on Banking and Currency, *Urban Mass Transportation—1961,* Hearings, 87th Cong., 1st Sess. (1961), p. 68.

11. John F. Kennedy, "Our Nation's Housing," Message of the President, March 9, 1961.

12. Six of the nine members of the Housing Subcommittee sponsored the Urban Mass Transportation Act of 1961: Democrats Clark, Douglas, Long (Missouri), and Williams and Republicans Beall and Bush.

13. Harrison Williams, press release, March 3, 1961.

14. See statement of Commissioner Everett Hutchinson, U.S. House of Representatives, Committee on Foreign and Interstate Commerce, *Guaranteed Loans for Railroads,* Hearings, 87th Cong., 1st Sess. (1961), pp. 8–9. The ICC also reaffirmed its support for the general principles of the Williams bill in 1961. However, it made no comment on the specific provisions or the jurisdictional issue. See Commissoner Everett Hutchinson to Senator A. Willis Robertson, March 14, 1961, quoted in U.S. Senate, *Urban Mass Transportation—1961,* Hearings, pp. 18–20.

15. *Ibid.,* p. 20.

16. *Ibid.,* p. 234.

17. *Ibid.,* p. 435.

18. The official was Philadelphia's City Solicitor, David Berger; see Newark *Evening News,* Jan. 11, 1961.

19. Newark *Evening News,* Jan. 13, 1961.

20. See A. F. Parrott, Consolidated Edison Company of New York, to Senator Harrison Williams, March 17, 1961, and K. T. Dutschman, New York Telephone Company to Senator Harrison Williams, March

17, 1961, quoted in U.S. Senate, *Urban Mass Transportation—1961*, pp. 439–40.

21. RPA, *Commuter Transportation,* report prepared for the Committee on Interstate and Foreign Commerce, U.S. Senate, 87th Cong., 1st Sess. (1961).

22. RPA had received the contract for the Senate Commerce Committee study on the recommendation of Senator Williams, who had become acquainted with RPA officials as a result of his interest in urban open spaces. Partisan considerations interfered with the hopes of Senator Case, who had suggested the New York area commuter study, to play an active role in the selection of a contractor to undertake the study. With Case up for reelection, the Democrats did not want him to receive any publicity if the contract was awarded before the election. Commerce Committee chairman Magnuson named two Democrats, Connecticut's Governor Ribicoff and former ICC chairman Anthony Arpaia, as committee consultants to select a contractor. They proceeded to endorse Williams' suggestion, and late in September, Ribicoff, Arpaia, and Williams announced that the $40,000 study would be made by the RPA. Magnuson then asked Arpaia to continue as a committee consultant, responsible for the preparation of the final set of recommendations, which he did, giving substantial endorsement to RPA's findings; see *ibid.,* pp. 3–9.

23. Newark *Evening News,* March 20, 1961.

24. WCBS, Editorial No. 57, March 20, 1961.

25. U.S. Senate, *Urban Mass Transportation—1961,* p. 181.

26. *Ibid.,* p. 438.

27. RPA, *Commuter Transportation,* p. 35.

28. U.S. Senate, *Urban Mass Transportation—1961,* p. 255.

29. New York *Journal-American,* March 25, 1961; New York *Times,* March 27, 1961.

30. Dwight R. G. Palmer, "State Government and Transportation," *State Government,* XXXV (Summer, 1962), 146.

31. U.S. Senate, *Urban Mass Transportation—1961,* p. 38. As in 1960, Governor Rockefeller ignored the transit hearings in Washington. However, an official indirectly responsible to the governor—Alex Hart, executive director of the NY-NJTA—did appear at the hearings to emphasize that "It might be well to spell . . . out very clearly in the statute . . . that problems of urban transportation and land use are primarily a local responsibility and that federal assistance should have as one of its goals the furtherance of this local responsibility"; *ibid.,* p. 308.

32. *Ibid.*, pp. 365–66.

33. Ridgewood (N.J.) *Herald News*, March 23, 1961.

34. Other members included Wilfred Owen of The Brookings Institution, author of *The Metropolitan Transportation Problem* (Washington, D.C., Brookings, 1956), who was to serve as chairman of the advisory committee; Edward Chase, a New York transportation consultant and author of "How to Rescue New York from Its Port Authority," *Harper's Magazine*, CCXX (June, 1960); Carl Feiss, an urban renewal consultant; Hans Heyman, an economist with the RAND Corporation; Boyd Ladd of Johns Hopkins University; and Richard Lester, a former secretary of the Civil Aeronautics Board. See New York *Times*, March 27, 1961.

35. New York *Times*, April 17, 1961.

36. U.S. ACIR "Intergovernmental Responsibilities for Mass Transportation Facilities and Services in Metropolitan Areas" (Washington, D.C., 1961), p. 55. The study was the product of Representative Dwyer's effort to secure an ACIR investigation of the commuter problem in the New York area. When the study was planned in mid-1960, the ACIR hoped to focus on the intergovernmental aspects of the mass transportation problem and to avoid the controversial question of federal aid. Accordingly, the draft report prepared by New York's IPA did not deal with the federal government's financial role. However, by the time the final report was prepared for the Commission's consideration in early April of 1961, urban pressures for federal aid from within and without the ACIR had become irresistible.

37. For the views of the AFL-CIO on the mass transportation issue, see the statement of George Riley in U.S. House of Representatives, Committee on Banking and Currency, *Urban Mass Transportation—1961*, Hearings, 87th Cong., 1st Sess. (1961), pp. 177–81.

38. Moreover, many of the BPR's clientele groups were a definite embarrassment to the Secretary of Commerce. For example, on the day the Williams hearings opened, the Eastern Conference of American Automobile Association Officials assailed the concept of public aid to transit with a statement that compared "pouring money into obsolescent rail transport" with "giving a transfusion to a dead horse." The motorist, they claimed, would "have to pay for this largess while at the same time highway needs for which he has been paying will go begging"; Newark *Evening News*, March 21, 1961.

39. *Congressional Record*, 87th Cong., 1st Sess., daily edition, June 2, 1961, p. 8772.

40. As a matter of fact, the senior Republican on the Banking and

Currency Committee and its Housing Subcommittee, Homer Capehart of Indiana, rather than the senator from New Jersey presented
the Williams' amendment to the subcommittee; see *ibid.*, p. 8686.

41. New York *Times,* May 25, 1961.

42. For an account of the White House's announcement, see New
York *Times,* May 28, 1961.

43. *Congressional Record,* 87th Cong., 1st Sess., daily edition, June
2, 1961, p. 8773.

44. Case was the only senator from the New York region not to
cosponsor the Williams bill in 1961. Before boarding his colleague's
bandwagon, Case had sought to preserve his identity on the commuter issue with a federal aid approach more attuned to his constituency interests and committee assignment. In March, Case won committee approval for an amendment to the legislation extending the
ICC loan guarantee program, which authorized the commission to
guarantee railroad improvement loans floated by state and local
governments. However, the House bill did not contain the amendment, and it was dropped in the conference committee; Newark
Evening News, April 4, 1961.

45. New York *Times,* June 7, 1961.

46. *Congressional Record,* 87th Cong., 1st Sess., daily edition, June
8, 1961, pp. 9202–07.

47. George Alpert, "Rail Commuter Services in Metropolitan
Areas," address to the Annual Conference, U.S. Conference of Mayors,
Washington, D.C., June 13, 1961, p. 14.

48. President John F. Kennedy to Representative Sam Rayburn,
June 19, 1961, quoted in U.S. House of Representatives, *Urban Mass
Transportation—1961,* p. 20.

49. Representatives Rains and Abraham Multer, a Brooklyn Democrat who introduced the Administration's $10-million transit bill, had
won urban congressional support for separate consideration of mass
transportation by promising immediate hearings on the Administration bill. Since the hearings before Multer's Banking and Currency
Subcommittee had been scheduled before the conference committee
compromise was negotiated, the June 27 session was held so that the
Administration's supporters in the House could retire gracefully from
the field.

50. U.S. House of Representatives, *Urban Mass Transportation—
1961,* p. 20.

51. *Ibid.,* p. 38.

52. Washington *Star*, June 28, 1961.

53. Public Law No. 70, 87th Cong., 1st Sess. (June 30, 1961), "Housing Act of 1961."

54. New York *Times*, July 5, 1961.

55. IPA, *Urban Transportation and Public Policy*, report prepared for U.S. Department of Commerce and HHFA (New York, 1961), p. VII-2. See also testimony of IPA president Lyle Fitch, U.S. House of Representatives, Committee on Banking and Currency, *Urban Mass Transportation Act of 1962*, 87th Cong., 2d Sess. (1962), pp. 465–77.

56. U.S. Department of Commerce and HHFA, "Joint Report to the President by the Housing and Home Finance Administrator and the Secretary of Commerce," March 28, 1962, p. 4.

57. William May in the Newark *Sunday News*, March 10, 1963.

58. See statements in U.S. Senate, Committee on Banking and Currency, *Urban Mass Transportation—1963*, 88th Cong., 1st Sess. (1963), pp. 120–27.

59. New York City's Planning Commission chairman. Other local governments had no voice on the Tri-State Transportation Committee itself, although local advisory committees were established to provide liaison with the grass roots.

60. In 1962–63, the Tri-State Transportation Committee obtained federal transit demonstration grants covering two-thirds of the project cost of (1) a $256,185 station and parking lot in New Brunswick, N.J., designed to test the impact of free parking on commuter railroad ridership, and (2) a $148,160 experiment which established a bus-train commuting route between Rockland County, N.Y., and Grand Central Station. Other federally aided Tri-State Transportation Committee demonstration projects planned in 1964 included automatic fare collection on the Long Island Railroad, new parking lots along the New York Central, and a study of subway and commuter rail service in Nassau and Queens Counties.

61. Palmer appeared at the Senate hearings, while Rockefeller indicated his support in response to a solicitation by Representative Multer, chairman of the House subcommittee which held transit hearings in 1962 and 1963. However, Rockefeller continued to give far more vocal attention to his preferred approach of a federal department of transportation. See, for example, the Newark *Sunday News*, June 16, 1963.

62. Efforts to broaden the political appeal of the transit legislation also risked alienating commuter-rail-oriented supporters such as Con-

necticut's Republican Senator Prescott Bush. After backing Williams in 1960 and 1961, Bush voted against the 1962 bill in the Banking and Currency Committee, charging that "A desirable program of limited application has been perverted into a $500 million 'pork barrel.' " See U.S. Senate, *Urban Mass Transportation Act of 1962*, 87th Cong., 2d Sess., S. Rep. No. 1852 (1962), p. 33.

63. For a more detailed discussion of the legislative politics of mass transportation in 1962 and 1963, see Alan Altshuler, "The Politics of Urban Mass Transportation," paper presented at the 1963 Annual Meeting of the American Political Science Association, New York, September 4–7, 1963, pp. 39–51.

64. Amendments approved by the Senate cut the grant authorization from $500 million to $375 million; added $375 million in guaranteed bonds; directed the HHFA to encourage federal guarantees rather than grants; placed a 12½ percent limit on the funds available to a single state; and, at the insistence of organized labor, which was concerned over the possible loss of bargaining rights, restricted the use of federal funds for the public acquisition of private transit systems.

65. For an analysis of the successful 1964 campaign in the House, see Vincent J. Burke, "The Wandering Paths of a Transit Bill," *Reporter*, XXXI (July 16, 1964), 31–33.

CHAPTER X.

THE PATTERN OF FEDERAL-METROPOLITAN POLITICS

1. Banfield and Grodzins restrict the designation "area-wide" to only three problem areas—circulation, civil defense, and air pollution —in their 1958 analysis; see Edward C. Banfield and Morton Grodzins, *Government and Housing in Metropolitan Areas* (New York, McGraw-Hill, 1958), p. 41. However, the utility of their generalization transcends their rather narrow conception of regional problems. Grodzins recognized this in later statements when he expanded the list of "metropolitan area problems that can be effectively attacked only with the aid of federal resources" to include water supply and sewage treatment; see Morton Grodzins, "The Federal System," in U.S. President's Commission on National Goals, *Goals for Americans* (Englewood Cliffs, N.J., Prentice-Hall, 1960), p. 282, and "The American Federal System," in Robert A. Goldwin, ed., *A Nation of States* (Chicago, Rand McNally, 1963), p. 16.

2. Harry Eckstein, *Pressure Group Politics* (London, George Allen & Unwin, 1960), p. 15.

3. Robert C. Wood, *Metropolis Against Itself* (New York, Committee for Economic Development, 1961), p. 32.

4. Ben West, "Federal-City Relations from the Cities' Point of View," in George Washington University, *The Federal Government and the Cities* (Washington, 1961), p. 21.

5. Statement of Patrick McLaughlin, *Wall Street Journal*, May 2, 1961.

6. By 1964 the central-city forces supporting the mass transit bill had organized an Urban Passenger Transportation Association, composed of representatives of the AMA, the U.S. Conference of Mayors, the Institute of Rapid Transit, the Railway Progress Institute, and the American Transit Association; for an account of the activities of the association in attempting to steer the bill through the House of Representatives, see Newark *Sunday News*, May 24, 1964.

7. In fact, Ribicoff made his maiden speech in the Senate in defense of the Kennedy administration's mass transit bill.

8. Richard E. Neustadt, *Presidential Power* (New York, Wiley, 1960), p. 33.

9. For an analysis of the political consequences of these features of the American federal system, see Grodzins, "The Federal System," in *Goals for Americans*, pp. 265–82.

10. Statement of Governor John Connally of Texas, Newark *Sunday News*, June 14, 1964.

11. Statement of Governor William Scranton of Pennsylvania, *Time*, May 1, 1964.

12. Joseph S. Clark, "What Are the Economic, Social, and Political Choices?" in Elizabeth Geen, *et al.*, eds., *Man and the Modern City* (Pittsburgh, University of Pittsburgh Press, 1962), p. 84.

13. Robert H. Connery and Richard H. Leach, *The Federal Government and Metropolitan Areas* (Cambridge, Mass., Harvard University Press, 1960), p. 64.

14. President Eisenhower also asked the committee "to recommend the Federal and State revenue adjustments required to enable the States to assume such functions." See Joint Federal-State Action Committee, *Report . . . to the President of the United States and to the Chairman of the Governors' Conference,* Progress Report No. 1, p. 21.

15. See Grodzins, in Goldwin, ed., *A Nation of States,* pp. 1–23,

for a more extensive examination of the lessons of the Joint Federal-State Action Committee experience in the framework of an analysis of the political barriers to "decentralization by order."

16. Lyndon B. Johnson, "Housing and Community Development," Message of the President, Jan. 27, 1964.

17. Dilworth hired McLaughlin to represent the city because he found that he and his aides were unable to be in Washington as often as necessary and because Philadelphia's six congressmen, who owed their election to the regular Democratic organization rather than to reformer Dilworth, were too preoccupied with the constituency concerns of one-sixth of the city and their other congressional and political interests to represent adequately the city's growing interests in Washington. See Dilworth's testimony before the House Subcommittee on Intergovernmental Relations in U.S. House of Representatives, *Federal-State-Local Relations: State and Local Officials*, Hearings, 85th Cong., 1st Sess. (1957), pp. 361–362.

18. Wagner told of his intention to rely on the congressional delegation in an appearance before the House Intergovernmental Relations Subcommittee in 1958: "We have gone to them to present our case and they have been very helpful. Although the two Senators are of the opposite political party from myself, they have always been very cooperative and helpful"; *ibid.*, p. 223. Wagner's reasons for establishing a liaison office in Washington included his desire to insure that the city received its full share of all federal programs, his interest in having the city play a more effective role on pending federal legislation, and his growing involvement in national affairs arising from his increased political prominence; see New York *Times*, June 7, 1962.

19. Connery and Leach, *Federal Government and Metropolitan Areas*, p. 92.

20. Grodzins, in Goldwin, ed., *A Nation of States*, p. 8.

21. Public Law No. 365, 88th Cong., 2d Sess. (July 9, 1964), "Urban Mass Transportation Act of 1964."

22. *Baker v. Carr*, 369 U.S. 186 (1962), and *Reynolds v. Sims*, 377 U.S. 533 (1964).

23. V. O. Key, Jr., *American State Politics* (New York, Knopf, 1956), p. 267.

24. For an analysis of the fiscal difficulties and high political mortality rate of governors during the postwar period, see Malcolm Jewell, "State Decision-Making: The Governor Revisited," paper presented

at the 1963 annual meeting of the American Political Science Association, New York, Sept. 4–7, 1963, pp. 1–2.

25. *Wesberry v. Sanders,* 376 U.S. 1 (1963). The impact of the decision requiring equal House districts within a state will, in turn, be reinforced by the 1964 Supreme Court rulings obligating both houses of the state legislature to apportion on the basis of population. Deprived of their automatic majorities in chambers once apportioned completely or largely on the basis of area, rural forces will find it far more difficult to gerrymander "substantially equal" House districts to their advantage.

26. Statement of Charles Percy, New York *Times,* June 3, 1964.

27. Three years after the introduction of Senator Williams' first mass transit bill, Representative Frelinghuysen found that only 39 percent of his Morris County constituents favored federal aid for commuter railroads; Newark *Evening News,* March 28, 1963.

28. President Johnson recommended federal grants and loans for the planning and construction of public facilities in suburbia, loan insurance for private developers constructing such community facilities, public facility loans with deferred amortization to permit suburbs to plan and build ahead of growth and to make advance land purchase, and federal insurance of loans to private developers for land acquisition and improvement for planned subdivisions; Lyndon B. Johnson, "Housing and Community Development" Message of the President, Jan. 27, 1964.

29. In the House vote on the departmental proposal, however, party affiliation was the key variable. Of the urban Democrats 79 percent backed President Kennedy, as did all but one of 29 suburban Democrats. Among the Republicans from metropolitan areas, only 7 of 64 supported the scheme; *Congressional Quarterly Weekly Report,* Feb. 23, 1962, p. 276.

30. Wood, *Metropolis Against Itself,* p. 43.

31. Scott Greer, *The Emerging City* (New York, Free Press of Glencoe, 1962), p. 189.

32. For a comparative analysis of the politics of metropolitan reform in St. Louis, Cleveland, and Miami, see Scott Greer, *Metropolitics* (New York, Wiley, 1963).

33. Robert C. Wood, *1400 Governments* (Cambridge, Mass., Harvard University Press, 1961), p. 199.

34. Connery and Leach, *Federal Government and Metropolitan Areas,* pp. 93, 237.

35. U.S. Department of Commerce and HHFA, "Joint Report to the President by the Housing and Home Finance Administrator and the Secretary of Commerce," March 28, 1962, p. 5.

36. U.S. ACIR, *Intergovernmental Responsibilities for Water Supply and Sewage Disposal in Metropolitan Areas* (1962), p. 120.

37. U.S. Senate, *A Bill to Provide for More Effective Utilization of Certain Federal Grants* . . . , 88th Cong., 1st Sess., S. 855 (1963).

38. U.S. Senate, *A Bill to Encourage Planning and the Programming, on a Coordinated Basis, of Land-Use Projects in the Development of Metropolitan Areas* . . . , 88th Cong., 1st Sess., S. 915 (1963).

39. York Willbern, *The Withering Away of the City* (University, University of Alabama Press, 1964), p. 106.

40. Banfield and Grodzins, *Government and Housing in Metropolitan Areas*, p. 158.

Index